Trans-generational Trauma and the Other

Often, our trans-generational legacies are stories of 'us' and 'them' that never reach their terminus. We carry fixed narratives, and the ghosts of our perpetrators and of our victims. We long to be subjects in our own history, but keep reconstituting the *Other* as an object in their own history. *Trans-generational Trauma and the Other* argues that healing requires us to engage with the *Other* who carries a corresponding pre-history. Without this dialogue, alienated ghosts can become persecutory objects, in psyche, politics, and culture.

This volume examines the violent loyalties of the past, the barriers to dialogue with our *Other*, and complicates the inter-subjectivity of Big History. Identifying our inherited narratives and relinquishing splitting, these authors ask how we can re-cast our *Other*, and move beyond dysfunctional repetitions – in our individual lives and in society.

Featuring rich clinical material, *Trans-generational Trauma and the Other* provides an invaluable guide to expanding the application of trans-generational transmission in psychoanalysis. It will appeal to psychoanalysts, psychoanalytic psychotherapists, and trauma experts.

Sue Grand, PhD, is clinical adjunct associate professor of psychology, faculty member and clinical consultant/supervisor at the NYU Postdoctoral Program in Psychotherapy and Psychoanalysis including their couples and family specialization, faculty at the trauma program at the National Institute for the Psychotherapies, The Stephen Mitchell Relational Study Center, and a fellow at the Institute for the Psychology of the Other. She is the author of *The Reproduction of Evil: A Clinical and Cultural Perspective* and *The Hero in the Mirror: From Fear to Fortitude*. She is in private practice in NYC and Teaneck, NJ.

Jill Salberg, PhD, ABPP, is clinical adjunct associate professor of psychology, faculty member and clinical consultant/supervisor at the NYU Postdoctoral Program in Psychotherapy and Psychoanalysis, and faculty and supervisor at The Stephen Mitchell Relational Study Center and the Institute for Contemporary Psychotherapy. She has contributed to and is editor of *Good Enough Endings: Breaks, Interruptions and Terminations from Contemporary Relational Perspectives*. She co-edits a new Routledge book series, *Psyche and Soul: Psychoanalysis, Spirituality and Religion in Dialogue*. She is in private practice in Manhattan.

RELATIONAL PERSPECTIVES BOOK SERIES

LEWIS ARON & ADRIENNE HARRIS
Series Co-Editors
STEVEN KUCHUCK & EYAL ROZMARIN
Associate Editors

The Relational Perspectives Book Series (RPBS) publishes books that grow out of or contribute to the relational tradition in contemporary psychoanalysis. The term *relational psychoanalysis* was first used by Greenberg and Mitchell[1] to bridge the traditions of interpersonal relations, as developed within interpersonal psychoanalysis and object relations, as developed within contemporary British theory. But, under the seminal work of the late Stephen Mitchell, the term *relational psychoanalysis* grew and began to accrue to itself many other influences and developments. Various tributaries—interpersonal psychoanalysis, object relations theory, self psychology, empirical infancy research, and elements of contemporary Freudian and Kleinian thought—flow into this tradition, which understands relational configurations between self and others, both real and fantasied, as the primary subject of psychoanalytic investigation.

We refer to the relational tradition, rather than to a relational school, to highlight that we are identifying a trend, a tendency within contemporary psychoanalysis, not a more formally organized or coherent school or system of beliefs. Our use of the term *relational* signifies a dimension of theory and practice that has become salient across the wide spectrum of contemporary psychoanalysis. Now under the editorial supervision of Lewis Aron and Adrienne Harris with the assistance of Associate Editors Steven Kuchuck and Eyal Rozmarin, the Relational Perspectives Book

1 Greenberg, J. & Mitchell, S. (1983). *Object relations in psychoanalytic theory.* Cambridge, MA: Harvard University Press.

Series originated in 1990 under the editorial eye of the late Stephen A. Mitchell. Mitchell was the most prolific and influential of the originators of the relational tradition. He was committed to dialogue among psycho-analysts and he abhorred the authoritarianism that dictated adherence to a rigid set of beliefs or technical restrictions. He championed open discussion, comparative and integrative approaches, and he promoted new voices across the generations.

Included in the Relational Perspectives Book Series are authors and works that come from within the relational tradition, extend and develop the tradition, as well as works that critique relational approaches or compare and contrast it with alternative points of view. The series includes our most distinguished senior psychoanalysts, along with younger contributors who bring fresh vision.

Vol. 76
Demons in the Consulting Room:
Echoes of Genocide, Slavery and
Extreme Trauma in Psychoanalytic
Practice
Adrienne Harris, Margery Kalb and
Susan Klebanoff

Vol. 77
The Ethical Turn:
Otherness and Subjectivity in
Contemporary Psychoanalysis
David M. Goodman and
Eric R. Severson

Vol. 78
Talking About Evil:
Psychoanalytic, Social, and Cultural
Perspectives
Rina Lazar

Vol. 79
Two Languages of Love:
Contemporary Psychoanalysis and
Modern Jewish Philosophy
Michael Oppenheim

Vol. 80
Psychoanalysis, Trauma and
Community:
History and Contemporary
Reappraisals
Judith L. Alpert and
Elizabeth R. Goren

Vol. 81
Body–Mind Dissociation in
Psychoanalysis:
Development after Bion
Riccardo Lombardi

Vol. 82
Wounds of History:
Repair and Resilience in the Trans-
Generational Transmission of Trauma
Jill Salberg and Sue Grand

Vol. 83
Trans-generational Trauma and the
Other:
Dialogues Across History and
Difference
Sue Grand and Jill Salberg

Trans-generational Trauma and the Other

Dialogues Across History and Difference

Edited by Sue Grand and Jill Salberg

Routledge
Taylor & Francis Group

LONDON AND NEW YORK

First published 2017
by Routledge
2 Park Square, Milton Park, Abingdon, Oxon OX14 4RN

and by Routledge
711 Third Avenue, New York, NY 10017

Routledge is an imprint of the Taylor & Francis Group, an informa business

British Library Cataloguing in Publication Data
A catalogue record for this book is available from the British Library

Library of Congress Cataloging in Publication Data
Names: Grand, Sue, editor. | Salberg, Jill, editor.
Title: Trans-generational trauma and the other : dialogues across history and difference / edited by Sue Grand and Jill Salberg.
Description: Abingdon, Oxon ; New York, NY : Routledge, 2017.
| Includes bibliographical references and index.
Identifiers: LCCN 2016027108| ISBN 9781138205819 (hardback : alk. paper) | ISBN 9781138205826 (pbk. : alk. paper) | ISBN 9781315466293 (e-book)
Subjects: LCSH: Psychic trauma. | Intergenerational relations–Psychological aspects. | Psychoanlysis and history.Classification: LCC BF175.5.P75 T695 2017 | DDC 155.9/3–dc23
LC record available at https://lccn.loc.gov/2016027108

ISBN: 978-1-138-20581-9 (hbk)
ISBN: 978-1-138-20582-6 (pbk)
ISBN: 978-1-315-46629-3 (ebk)

Typeset in Times New Roman
by Wearset Ltd, Boldon, Tyne and Wear

This book is dedicated to our patients, who have trusted us with their stories, to our friends and families, whose stories we share, and to those stories from others, still yet to be told.

Contents

Contributors

C. Fred Alford is Professor of Government and Distinguished Scholar-Teacher at the University of Maryland, College Park. He is author of over fifteen books on moral psychology, including *Psychology and the Natural Law of Reparation* (2006), *After the Holocaust* (2009), and *Trauma and Forgiveness* (2013), all from Cambridge University Press, and *Trauma, Culture, and PTSD* (Palgrave University Press, 2016). Professor Alford is Executive Director of the Association for Psychoanalysis, Culture and Society, and Co-editor of the Psychoanalysis and Society Book Series with Cornell University Press. He has served as President of the Psychology and Politics section of the American Political Science Association, and sits on the editorial boards of half a dozen journals. He has published many dozens of journal articles, book chapters, and Encyclopedia articles on everything from whistleblowing to natural law. He has received three Fulbright research fellowships. In 2009 he received the Chancellor's Award as best undergraduate teacher on the College Park campus. He writes the blog, www.traumatheory.com.

Maurice Apprey, PhD, DM, FIPA, is a tenured full professor of psychiatry at the University of Virginia School of Medicine. He is a training and supervising psychoanalyst at the Contemporary Freudian Society, Washington, D.C. He is the English language translator from French of Georges Politzer's *Critique of the Foundations of Psychology: The Psychology of Psychoanalysis* (Duquesne University Press, 1994).

Ofra Bloch, LCSW, is a supervising and training analyst at the National Institute of the Psychotherapies and a documentary filmmaker. She is in private practice in New York City. She is currently in production of the documentary feature *Afterward*, which explores the themes and experiences of her chapter.

David M. Goodman, PhD, is the Associate Dean of Academic Affairs and Student Services at the Woods College of Advancing Studies at Boston College, the Director of *Psychology and the Other*, and a Teaching Associate at Harvard Medical School/Cambridge Hospital. Dr. Goodman has written over a dozen articles on continental philosophy, Jewish thought, social justice, and psychotherapy. His recent book *The Demanded Self: Levinasian Ethics and Identity in Psychology* (Duquesne University Press, 2012) considers the intersection of psychology, philosophy, and theology as it pertains to narcissism, ethical phenomenology, and selfhood. Additionally, Dr. Goodman co-edited a book (with Mark Freeman), *Psychology and the Other: A Dialogue at the Crossroad of an Emerging Field* (Oxford University Press, 2015), which features some of the conversations from the first *Psychology and the Other* conference in 2011. He is also a licensed clinical psychologist and has a private practice in Cambridge, MA.

Sue Grand, PhD, is faculty and supervisor at the NYU Postdoctoral Program in Psychotherapy and Psychoanalysis; faculty, the couples and family therapy program at the NYU Postdoctoral Program in Psychotherapy and Psychoanalysis; faculty, trauma program at the National Institute for the Psychotherapies; faculty, The Mitchell Center for Relational Psychoanalysis; visiting scholar at the Psychoanalytic Institute of Northern California; fellow, The Institute for Psychology and the Other. She is the author of *The Reproduction of Evil: A Clinical and Cultural Perspective* (Routledge, 2002) and *The Hero in the Mirror: From Fear to Fortitude* (Routledge, 2011). She is co-editor with Jill Salberg of the book *The Wounds of History: Repair and Resilience in the Trans-generational Transmission of Trauma* (Routledge, 2017). She is an Associate Editor of *Psychoanalytic Dialogues* and *Psychoanalysis, Culture and Society*. She is in private practice in New York City and in Teaneck, NJ.

Janice Gump, PhD, received the Bachelor of Arts Degree from the University of Chicago, and a PhD in Clinical Psychology from the University of Rochester. She has been a faculty member of the Howard University Medical School and Howard University Psychology Department, a staff member of the University Counseling Service, and a faculty member of the Washington School of Psychiatry. She has also been a Consulting Editor for the *Journal of Consulting and Clinical Psychology*, a

Reviewer for the Mental Health Small Grants Committee, NIMH, and a member of the *Professional Psychology* Editorial Board. Dr. Gump has authored papers on African American women, shame, and the enduring consequences of slavery's traumas. She maintains a private practice in Washington, D.C., and is a member of the Institute of Contemporary Psychotherapy & Psychoanalysis.

Adrienne Harris, PhD, is faculty and supervisor at New York University Postdoctoral Program in Psychotherapy and Psychoanalysis and at the Psychoanalytic Institute of Northern California. In 2009, she, Lewis Aron, and Jeremy Safron established the Sandor Ferenczi Center at the New School University. With Lewis Aron she edits the Relational Book Series which has published over sixty volumes. She published *Rocking the Ship of State: Toward a Feminist Peace Politics* (Westview Press, 1989) and *Gender as Soft Assembly* (Routledge, 2008). She co-edited: with Lewis Aron, *The Legacy of Sandor Ferenczi* (Analytic Press, 1993), with Muriel Dimen, *Storms in Her Head: On Women and Hysteria* (Other Press, 1999), with Steven Botticelli, *First Do No Harm: The Paradoxical Encounters of Psychoanalysis, Warmaking, and Resistance* (Routledge, 2010), and with Steven Kuchuck, *The Legacy of Sandor Ferenczi: From Ghost to Ancestor* (Routledge, 2015). She writes about gender and development, about analytic subjectivity, about ghosts, and about the analysts developing and writing around the period of World War I.

Lynne Layton, PhD, is a psychoanalyst and Assistant Clinical Professor of Psychology, Part-time, Harvard Medical School. Holding a PhD in psychology as well as comparative literature, she has taught courses on gender, popular culture, and on culture and psychoanalysis at Harvard College. Currently, she teaches and supervises at the Massachusetts Institute for Psychoanalysis and is adjunct faculty at Pacifica Graduate Institute. She is the author of *Who's That Girl? Who's That Boy? Clinical Practice Meets Postmodern Gender Theory* (Routledge, 2004), co-editor, with Barbara Schapiro, of *Narcissism and the Text: Studies in Literature and the Psychology of Self* (NYU Press, 1986); co-editor, with Susan Fairfield and Carolyn Stack, of *Bringing the Plague: Toward a Postmodern Psychoanalysis* (Other Press, 2002), and co-editor, with Nancy Caro Hollander and Susan Gutwill, of *Psychoanalysis, Class and Politics: Encounters in the Clinical Setting* (Routledge, 2006). She is co-editor of the journal *Psychoanalysis, Culture & Society*, associate editor of *Studies in Gender and Sexuality*, and co-founder of the Boston Psychosocial Work Group.

Deborah Liner, PhD, is a graduate of the NYU Postdoctoral Program in Psychotherapy and Psychoanalysis. She is on the faculty of the Center for Psychotherapy and Psychoanalysis of New Jersey and serves on the executive board and the faculty of The Women's Therapy Centre Institute. She is a clinical supervisor at Rutgers University Graduate School of Applied and Professional Psychology. She has taught and presented on a variety of topics including trauma, intergenerational transmission of trauma, dissociation, and theory and technique in relational psychoanalysis. Dr. Liner is a psychoanalyst in private practice in Manhattan and Summit, NJ.

Donna Orange, PhD, PsyD, was educated in philosophy, clinical psychology, and psychoanalysis and teaches at the New York University Postdoctoral Program (New York); IPSS (Institute for the Psychoanalytic Study of Subjectivity, New York); ISIPSé (Roma and Milano); and in private study groups. She also offers clinical consultation supervision in these institutes and beyond. Recent books are *Thinking for Clinicians: Philosophical Resources for Contemporary Psychoanalysis and the Humanistic Psychotherapies* (Routledge, 2010), *The Suffering Stranger: Hermeneutics for Everyday Clinical Practice* (Routledge, 2011), *Nourishing the Inner Life of Clinicians and Humanitarians: The Ethical Turn in Psychoanalysis* (Taylor & Francis, 2016), and *Climate Justice, Psychoanalysis, and Radical Ethics* (Taylor & Francis, 2016).

Evelyn Rappoport, PsyD, is a licensed psychologist, psychoanalyst, and somatic experiencing practitioner with a full-time private practice in New York City where she treats individuals, couples, and families. Dr. Rappoport specializes in trauma resolution with somatic, psychobiological treatment approaches in the treatment of PTSD, adult onset trauma, and developmental trauma. She conducts ongoing private supervision groups, both in New York City and Jerusalem and is clinical supervisor at the National Institute of Psychotherapies as well as a number of analytic institutes in the tri-state area. Additionally, she is visiting faculty/clinical supervisor at the Hadassah Medical School in Jerusalem, Israel. Dr. Rappoport is on the board of the International Trauma Organization and is involved with a number of trauma organizations and NGOs in the US and Israel. She presents workshops and seminars on Trauma and Emotional First Aid to mental health practitioners, first responders, and community organizations.

Eyal Rozmarin, PhD, is co-editor of the journal *Studies in Gender and Sexuality* and Associate Editor of the Routledge book series *Relational Perspectives in Psychoanalysis*. He has published numerous articles in psychoanalytic journals, including *Psychoanalytic Dialogues*, *Contemporary Psychoanalysis*, and *Studies in Gender and Sexuality*, as well as book chapters, and presented in conferences around the world. His research takes place in the intersection of psychoanalysis and social theory, and explores the relations between subjectivity, collective forces, and history. He is in private practice in New York.

Jill Salberg, PhD, ABPP, is an adjunct associate professor of psychology, faculty, and clinical consultant/supervisor in the New York University Postdoctoral Program in Psychotherapy and Psychoanalysis, and faculty and supervisor at The Stephen Mitchell Center for Relational Studies and the Institute for Contemporary Psychotherapy. Her papers have been published in *Psychoanalytic Dialogues*, *Studies in Gender and Sexuality*, and *American Imago* and she has chapters in *The Jewish World of Sigmund Freud* (McFarland, 2010); *Relational Psychoanalysis Vol. 5: Evolution of Process* (Routledge, 2011); and *Answering a Question with a Question: Contemporary Psychoanalysis and Jewish Thought* (Academic Studies Press, 2013). She is a contributor to and the editor of the book *Good Enough Endings: Breaks, Interruptions and Terminations from Contemporary Relational Perspectives* (Routledge, 2010). She is co-editor with Sue Grand of the book *The Wounds of History: Repair and Resilience in the Trans-generational Transmission of Trauma* (Routledge, 2017). She has conceived of and co-edits the book series *Psyche and Soul: Psychoanalysis, Spirituality and Religion in Dialogue* at Routledge/Taylor & Francis Group. She is in private practice in Manhattan.

Sandra Silverman, LCSW, is a faculty member, supervisor, and co-chair of curriculum at The Institute for Contemporary Psychotherapy and a faculty member at The Stephen Mitchell Center for Relational Studies. She has written, published, and presented on the analyst's subjectivity and vulnerability as well as on gender and LGBTQ issues. She is in private practice in New York City.

Kirkland C. Vaughans, PhD, is a licensed clinical psychologist and a psychoanalyst with a private practice in New York City. He is the founding editor of the *Journal of Infant, Child, and Adolescent Psychotherapy* and first editor of the two-volume book, *The Psychology of Black Boys and Adolescents* (Praeger, 2013). He is a senior adjunct professor of psychology at the Derner Institute of Advanced Psychological Studies at Adelphi University and faculty member of their Postgraduate Program in Child and Adolescent Psychotherapy, a clinical supervisor at the National Institute for Psychotherapies, and visiting faculty member at IPTAR. He is a school psychologist at Hempstead High School and the former Regional Director of the defunct New Hope Guild Centers of Brooklyn. He has published articles on the intergenerational transmission of trauma among African Americans and presented widely on topics affecting Black male youth. He also serves on the Board of Directors for the Harlem Family Psychoanalytic Institute. He is also an Honorary Member of the Institute for Psychoanalytic Training and Research (IPTAR).

Editors' Introduction

Sue Grand and Jill Salberg

In psychoanalysis there is an evolving canon on the trans-generational transmission of trauma.[1] In focusing on the psychic shadows of Big History, this canon has largely emphasized *the haunting of our patient's psyche, the privacy of familial revelations*, and *the privacy of dyadic, clinical repair*. The trans-generational turn has been inspired by our increasing attention to massive trauma, to the way massive trauma can shape the familial unconscious. This familial unconscious is shaped through stories and relational patterning, by both resiliency *and* wounds (Salberg & Grand, 2017).

With this new look, the ghosts of our forebears have entered the analytic situation, producing a much-needed expansion in our vision of the human family. To heal human suffering, we often need to reclaim our elders, as well as the roots and branches of our family tree. Who were they? What political/cultural epoch were they living in? What was their position in that epoch? What cataclysms marked them? As the trans-generational turn takes hold in mainstream psychoanalysis, such inquiries have entered our clinical focus. Big History receives another layer of witnessing and recognition in this clinical process, as implicit knowing moves towards articulation. But, with the exception of work by Grand (2013), and Salberg and Grand (2017), this lens focuses on repairing the individualized wounds left by Big History. We have not yet imagined this lens as a method for repairing *the effects of history on itself*.

In this book, we want to imagine an intimate address to *history itself*. In our discipline, there have been recurrent splits between applied and clinical psychoanalysis. In the trans-generational turn, applied and clinical psychoanalysis finally begin to interpenetrate. Then, too, we are newly awakened to ethics and social justice and we have begun to incorporate these into clinical practice (Grand, 2000, 2010, 2014; Layton, 2009,

2015; Orange, 2016). To have an ethos of concern: we have begun to link this capacity to 'mental health.' We see empathic capacity as a necessary part of healthful functioning and the engagement with others as an outgrowth of this developed capacity. And so, as we parse the patient's genealogy of trauma, we are beginning to rewrite the psychoanalytic family. In this rewriting, the psychoanalytic family can become the more fully developed *human family.*

However, too often this trans-generational genealogy of trauma is still being mapped onto pre-Oedipal dyads and Oedipal triads. In our view, this mapping is a retreat from radical change in psychoanalysis. In this retreat, the psychoanalytic family remains mommy, daddy, baby,[2] and psychoanalytic theory remains intact, unaltered at its core. Not cracked open by genealogies of trauma, or by the violence of collective wounds. In this hesitation, we sustain the individualized insularity that has separated applied and clinical psychoanalysis. Certainly, in the trans-generational literature, analytic process moves individualized wounds towards reflective narrative. Psychic wounds are characterized as dissociated 'chronicles' (see Meares, 1998) about our pre-history. Healing is linked to a subjective narration of that inheritance (albeit mutually constructed), in the context of empathic witnessing. But, with rare exception (Frie, 2011; Grand, 2000; Guralnik, 2014) where is our *Other* in this healing trajectory? Is it really possible to create a liberating narrative of *our* history, while we retain a fixed, alienated chronicle of our *Other*?

In our view, the alienated, objectified *Other* will always correspond to some persecutory object inside of us, even if our efforts at splitting and projection are sanctioned by normative culture. Splitting and projection are never stable arrangements; they devolve into some form of destruction. Psychoanalytic work with trans-generational trauma certainly speaks to the internalized, alienated *Other* of our pre-history. But this turn has not yet spoken to another dimension of (personal and collective) healing: conversing with the alienated *Other who is actually outside of us.* As a social 'addendum' to traditional psychoanalytic models, transgenerational inquiry allows us to heal some patients, and some *parts* of our patients. But until psychoanalysis incorporates an address to the *Other* into the core of our theory and process, we believe that destruction will repeat, somewhere in the system. Most of us have an alienated *Other*, and most of us live in a world of alienated *Others*. The world is too much with us. Our family trees and their ghosts; our collectivities and our ethical position within our own epoch: now, *all* of this has pushed past our gates.

Psychoanalysis has always been concerned with social justice and cultural critique (see Altman, 1995; Aron & Starr, 2012; Hollander, 2010, etc.). It has always been permeated with both moralism and ethics. These themes have been potentiated, and illuminated, by the trans-generational turn. As editors, we sense a paradigm shift in psychoanalysis; this allows us to ask new questions. Can the psychoanalytic family expand into a wider I-We-Thou that is, and is not, a nuclear family? And if we expand into the wider I-We-Thou, what happens to the alienated *Other* of our own pre-histories? How do I speak to you: the 'enemy' descendent of my own ancestral persecution? How do we converse across dread, difference, and hatred? Can we recognize ourselves as *their* persecutory *Other*? What of our own shame and guilt? How and where do we locate our ethical responsibility? How do we share that responsibility, and make reparation? Is it possible to sustain our own historical subjectivity while knowing our *Other* as a historical subject? Can we enter into these *haunted dialogues*, and then, can we free ourselves from these repetitions?

As editors we are joining with other analysts who are considering these questions. Many of us are drawing on the work of Buber and Levinas – Jewish ethicists and philosophers who wrote after World War I and II. Centuries of Judeo-Christian ethical teachings were profoundly affected by the geo-political events of twentieth century Europe. As editors, we, ourselves, are inspired by these Jewish traditions, even as we hope to engage diverse religious/cultural/ethical traditions that can help us all speak to our Other. In this book, our tradition begins to meet some of these other worlds, and in the spirit of our mission, we would hope that this conversation keeps opening up within psychoanalysis. Meanwhile, Buber and Levinas are the lodestars of the ethical/social/historical turn in our discipline. Buber (1958, 1960), despite having broken with traditional Jewish religious life, drew upon both Jewish ethics and Hasidic ideals when writing his major philosophical thesis *I and Thou* (first written in 1923, translated into English in 1925). He was writing post WWI and during the upheavals in Europe and the revolutions in Russia. Big History demanded that questions be raised about the relevance of religious ideas, given man's inhumanity to man. In a parallel crisis, Levinas turned to the tradition of Talmud study, after the cataclysm of WWII and the Holocaust. He endeavored to imbue philosophy with the moral ethics he discovered it lacked, a vacuum he believed contributed to human capacity for destructiveness. His works, starting with *Totality and Infinity* (1969), paralleled Buber's ideas of *I and Thou* but Levinas expanded his work to be an ethics of the *other*. Levinas' work demands of us to be less God oriented and more responsible towards an-*other*, believing that holiness is in the face of the *other*.

As Goodman and Layton (2014) and Orange (2011, 2016) note, our turn towards ethics is embedded in historical-political analysis, it draws on Buber's I-Thou and Levinas' construct of the Other (Goodman, 2012; Orange, 2010).[3] Furthermore, this social-ethical turn recognizes what Grand (2013) calls the 'collectivized self,' a notion previously excluded from clinical theory. As these trends interpenetrate, we can now query our long tendency, in psychoanalysis, to conflate moralism and ethics, so that we have thrown the baby out with the bathwater. Once we were taught not to impose our morality on our patients, and then, we discovered that normative morality was still permeating our theory and practice. As we disentangle oppressive social edicts from the ethics of Buber and Levinas (Orange, 2011) we have gradually claimed the implicit *ethical* position that has always existed in psychoanalysis: a search for the I-Thou capacity. As we make this ethical position explicit, we radically alter the trans-generational perspective. We can recognize that we all live within haunted dialogues, we recreate and disrupt those dialogues. In the process, we hope to heal ourselves. And we can hope to heal *history itself*.

The authors in this book are trying, and failing, *and still trying* to have these conversations. As psychoanalysts, we sense that we cannot avoid the alienated *Other* of our pre-history. *And we cannot avoid being the alienated Other in someone else's pre-history.* As Layton notes (2015), we have multiple identity markers. Most of us hold multiple positions within multiple histories. For too many of us, there is a persecutory ghost that shape-shifts through the generations. As that ghost moves through time, it often moves between the imaginary and the real. In this volume, psychoanalysts try to cross the barrier to the Other, they query inherited narratives, discover the complicated inter-subjective truths of Big History, relinquish splitting, and try to rewrite the alienated loyalties of the past. They also consider the impediments to these trans-generational conversations; the nature of our resistance; the failure and collapse of that conversation. Throughout these chapters, the reader will find recurrent themes. What happens when life introduces us to the characters of our historic imagination? What happens when the Other does not conform to our imaginary Other? What happens to *our* wounds when our Other tries to discover *us*? Within our psyches, our lives, and in our global politics, we discover that we are fighting, or fleeing, our ancestors' war, as we carry out our trans-generational errands (Apprey, 1996, 2003). And many of us are still fighting over, or fleeing from, our ancestors' *culpability* for that war. For our authors, haunted dialogues address personal healing, but they also reckon with *history itself* – with the hope of forestalling the next war.

In the Jewish mystical tradition, God, before creating the world, needed to undergo a process known as *tzimtzum*, literally of contraction. God understood that for there to be room for a world, God would have to make room, contract God's being. In discussing this creative moment, Linzer (2016) writes, 'Ironically, though, if the creating is to build a space for the other, then such an act of personal expression must also be an act of personal contraction.' One does not need to believe in a divine being to understand the profound implications of this idea; that living a humane life involves an ethical responsibility to others. As in the creation myth/allegory, we will need to contract ourselves and our own needs creating and allowing space for an-*others* subjective world. This is our ethical goal, that in creating space for the wounds, histories, traumas, and triumphs of the *other* we will have created a better psychoanalysis and facilitated a more resilient world.

Notes

1 Apprey, 1996, 2003; Davoine & Gaudilliere, 2004; Faimberg, 1996, 1998, 2005; Frie, 2011, Grand, 2000; Gump, 2010; Guralnik, 2014; Reis, 2007; Richman, 2006; Salberg, 2015 and others.
2 Regardless of what sexed body is mommy or daddy.
3 It should be noted that these philosophical/theological roots differ in their formulation of the self-other relationship.

References

Altman, N. (1995). *Analyst in the inner city: race, class and culture through a psycho-analytic lens.* New York & London: Routledge/Taylor & Francis Group.
Apprey, M. (1996). *Phenomenology of transgenerational haunting: subjects in apposition, subjects on urgent/voluntary errands.* Ann Arbor, MI: UMI Research Collections.

Apprey, M. (2003). Repairing history: reworking transgenerational trauma. In D. Moss (Ed.), *Hating in the first person plural: psychoanalytic essays on racism, homophobia, misogyny, and terror*. New York: Other Press.

Aron, L., & Starr, K. (2012). *A psychotherapy for the people: toward a progressive psychoanalysis*. New York & London: Routledge/Taylor & Francis Group.

Buber, M. (1958). *I and thou* (2nd ed.). New York: Charles Scribner's Sons.

Buber, M. (1960). *The origin and meaning of Hasidism*. Atlantic Highlands, NJ: Humanities Press International Inc.

Davoine, F., & Gaudilliere, J. M. (2004). *History beyond trauma: whereof one cannot speak, thereof one cannot stay silent*. New York: Other Press.

Faimberg, H. (1996). Listening to listening. *Int. J. Psychoanal., 77*, 667–677.

Faimberg, H. (1998). The telescoping of generations: genealogy of certain identifications. *Contemp. Psychoanal., 24*, 99–117.

Faimberg, H. (2005). *The telescoping of generations: listening to the narcissistic links between generations*. London/New York: Routledge.

Frie, R. (2011). Irreducible cultural contexts: German-Jewish experience, identity and trauma in a bilingual analysis. *International Journal of Psychoanalytic Self Psychology, 6*, 136–158.

Goodman, D. (2012). *The demanded self: Levinasian ethics and identity in psychology*. Pittsburgh, PA: Duquesne University Press.

Goodman D., & Layton, L. (2014). Editors introduction to special issue on psychology and the other: the historical political in psychoanalysis' ethical turn. *Psychoanalysis, Culture and Society, 19*(3), 225–232.

Grand, S. (2000). *The reproduction of evil*. Hillsdale, NJ/London: Analytic Press.

Grand, S. (2010). *The hero in the mirror: from fear to fortitude*. New York & London: Routledge/Taylor & Francis Group.

Grand, S. (2013). God at an impasse: who is the psychoanalytic subject? *Psychoanalytic Dialogues, 23*(4), 449–464.

Grand, S. (2014). Skin memories: on race, love and loss. *Psychoanalysis, Culture and Society, 19*(3), 232–250.

Gump, J. (2010). Reality matters: the shadow of the trauma on African American subjectivity. *Psychoanal. Psychol., 27*, 42–54.

Guralnik, O. (2014). The dead baby. *Psychoanalytic Dialogues, 24*(2), 129–145.

Hollander, N. (2010). *Uprooted minds: surviving the politics of terror in the Americas*. London: Routledge.

Layton, L. (2009). Who's responsible? Our mutual implication in each other's suffering. *Psychoanalytic Dialogues, 19*(2), 105–120.

Layton, L. (2015). Beyond sameness and difference: normative unconscious process and our mutual implication in each other's suffering. In D. Goodman and M. Freeman (Eds.), *Psychology and the other* (pp. 168–188). Oxford: Oxford University Press.

Levinas, E. (1969). *Totality and infinity*. The Netherlands: Duquesne University Press.

Linzer, D. (2016). *What's the point*. Retrieved July 21, 2016, from http://rabbidovlinzer. blogspot.com/2016/03/a-thought-on-parasha.html.

Meares, R. (1998). The self in conversation: on narratives, chronicles, and scripts. *Psychoanalytic Dialogues, 8*, 875–891.

Orange, D. (2011). *Thinking for clinicians: philosophical resources for contemporary psychoanalysis and the humanistic psychotherapies*. New York: Routledge.

Orange, D. (2016). *Nourishing the inner life of clinicians and humanitarians: the ethical turn in psychoanalysis.* New York: Routledge.

Reis, B. (2007). Witness to history: introduction to symposium on transhistorical catastrophe. *Psychoanal. Dialogues, 17*, 621–626.

Richman, S. (2006). Finding one's voice: transforming trauma into autobiographical narrative. *Contemp. Psychoanal., 42*, 639–650.

Salberg, J. (2015). The texture of traumatic attachment: presence and ghostly absence in transgenerational transmission. *Psychoanalytic Quarterly, LXXXIV(1)*, 21–46.

Salberg, J., & Grand, S. (2017). *The wounds of history: repair and resilience in the transgenerational transmission of trauma.* New York & London: Routledge/Taylor & Francis Group.

Part I

When Our Histories Collide

Introduction

Haunted Dialogues: When Histories Collide

C. Fred Alford

Intergenerational Trauma is Always about Attachment

It is common today to write about intergenerational trauma in terms of phantoms, the past haunting the present. All three chapters in this section show the way in which children contain the unassimilated trauma of their parents, and often their grandparents and beyond. Each chapter includes an evocative case study. In one a daughter is almost sacrificed by her parents as an act of atonement to parents who had sacrificed themselves, or so it seemed to the girl's father, to save him from the Nazis (Apprey). The second is an account of a Jewish woman who would feel the historical oppression of black women in order to make a connection to her black analyst, so similar and so different from her beloved Russian Jewish grandmother (Grand). In the third the son of a Russian P.O.W. turned German soldier is treated by a therapist who is herself dealing with her aging mother, a Holocaust survivor (Liner).

Each paper is theoretical, Apprey's the most so. But it is the three authors' case studies, drawn from their own experience, that captivate me, even as I recognize that the goal is always to use practice to stimulate theory, and theory to inform practice. Rather than review the papers, which the reader can read for him or herself, I thought it more useful to think about the ghosts that we inherit from the past in terms of attachment theory.

All the papers either argue, or assume with Abraham and Torok (1994), that intergenerational trauma has the characteristics of a phantom. "The phantom is a formulation of the unconscious that has never been conscious—for good reason. It passes—in a way yet to be determined—from the parent's unconscious to the child" (p. 173). The key point is that the transmission is from one unconscious to another, a process Freud recognized (1914, p. 194) but like Abraham was unsure how to explain.

As Torok points out, Freud is not talking about some "mystical phenomena," but "most likely the beginnings of conscious communication" that never makes it past the unconscious (Abraham and Torok, 1994, p. 179). In other words, the phantom is a formation of the unconscious that is found there not because of the subject's own repression "but on account of a direct empathy with the unconscious or the rejected psychic matter of a parental object" (p. 181).

I have spent a number of years studying Holocaust survivors and their children. Most children seem to agree that they have suffered from an over-involvement in their parents' suffering at the price of their own development.

> I felt like I was the image of my mother's mother [who was murdered at Auschwitz]. I asked her today what she [grandmother] was like and I was told that I look like her, that I act like her. I was named after her. And I felt I don't want any part of this. I felt I don't even want to talk to my mother. I want me.
>
> (Mason and Fogelman, 1984)

In fact, it's not so simple. Most want to know more than they are able to bear, and some are able to elaborate their parent(s)' experience in creative terms, and so make it their own. Consider the artist David Gev.

> "I did not witness the most important events of my life," says artist David Gev. "They happened before I was born, yet their memory persists. How does one take on the memories of another individual, let alone the collective memory of millions?"
>
> Artist David Gev's work is meant to evoke the European landscape as seen from inside a train car on its way to a concentration camp. Gev did not directly experience this suffering, nor did he himself look out from the trains, or feel the pains of hunger and cold, but still he witnessed these things through pieces of stories told to him by his father. Without knowing all that occurred, he was forced to formulate images in his mind of what his father might have seen.
>
> (Berman, 2013)

As one looks at photographs of glass art by Gev, one is surprised by how pretty the abstract scenes are. If one did not know what they represent, one would be hard pressed to guess that they represent horror.

The general insight suggested by Gev's experience is that "we survive by forming relationships, and adapting to the minds of others" (Slade, 2013, p. 41). Gev, and second generation survivors like him, seem to have felt forced to imagine the horrors their parents went through in order to reach through a barrier of silence that was also a barrier against human connection, human attachment. Parents can love their children, but if they cannot share themselves with their children, if large portions of their minds are permanently closed to their children, then something will always be missing. It is this search for this missing piece, the lost connection with the mind of the parent, that also forms and frames the mind of the second generation survivor.

Gev seems to have found a particularly creative way of imaging the experiences of his father, melding the bits and pieces of what he was told into beautiful form. The usual cautions about art after Auschwitz (Adorno, 1967, p. 34) do not apply here, as Gev is not memorializing the Holocaust, but coming to terms with his own experience of the Holocaust, via his father.

Children want to know about their parents' emotional experience during the Holocaust, or other traumatic times. They want to be let in. To be denied this experience is the equivalent of being dropped by the mind of the mother, as D. W. Winnicott put it. This can happen at any age, and with either parent. For holding is not something that begins and ends in infancy and childhood. It continues throughout life, as we try to find a place in which we are secure enough to just be.

John Bowlby conceived of this place in spatial terms. "All of us, from the cradle to the grave, are happiest when life is organized as a series of excursions, long or short, from the secure base provided by our attachment figure" (Bowlby, 1988, p. 69). Winnicott conceived of this space not just in the arms of the mother, but in the mind of the parent and significant other, a mind shared with the child, but allowing the child enough space to be. For Winnicott (1989, p. 145), childhood trauma is a "failure relative to dependence." Often the child will do anything to restore this dependence, including attempting to share the parent(s)' trauma, which is experienced as a barrier between them.

Erik Hesse and Mary Main (1999), leading attachment theorists, explain the process slightly differently. During the normal course of child rearing, traumatized parents will reexperience their original trauma, leading to episodes of parental detachment and confusion. This is the case even with good, generally competent, parents. Incapable of understanding the source of the parents' distress, the child will either blame itself, or be drawn into compulsively trying to comfort the parent. Role reversal, the child comforting the parent, is a common attachment strategy undertaken by children of traumatized or disturbed parents. It is a leading marker of what is called ambivalent attachment, and is considered a response to unpredictably responsive care-giving.

The task of attachment is not just about feeling protected, having a secure base. The task includes being in emotional attunement with one's caregiver. We neglect the degree to which the child and adolescent needs to know and feel something of the parent(s)' horror in order to have access to the reality of the parent. Without this access, everything feels phony, unreal, including the child him or herself. If the child is securely attached, he or she can feel something of the parents' horror. This too is the attunement that supports attachment, preventing the horror from isolating the child from the parent, or encouraging the child to reenact the parents' horror in order to feel close.

How odd it is for the child to feel abandoned by the parent because the parent won't share his or her horror. But that seems to be the way it works. In this respect, the phantom that Abraham and Torok write about, an expression of the unconscious that stems from empathy with the unconscious or the rejected portions of the parents' psyche, arises naturally because the child wants to feel what the parent experienced but cannot know. To feel what the parent feels but does not know is a way to share the mind of the parent, the leading medium of attachment.

The problem of course is when the second generation wants what it cannot tolerate, at least not in unmediated form. The ideal would be if the child could help the parent articulate the phantom through his or her desire to know. It is difficult to identify how often this happens, for therapists seldom see happy children. One imagines that it is relatively rare. But therapy offers a second chance for the child to take what the parent could not tolerate and come to know it in him or herself.

Apprey refers to the ghosts of the pasts as *le revenant*, that which returns. Revenant is also another word for vampire. The undead yearn for young blood, and one might imagine that the task of the therapist and patient is to bring the darkness of the past into the light so that it can die a natural death through repression. Trouble is, the phantom is also a living link to the parent, and one suspects that the best one can do, and the best one should want to do, is to give substance to the past, so that it can embody the link between the generations.

References

Abraham, Nicolas and Torok, Maria (1994) *The Shell and the Kernel*, vol. 1. Translated by Nicolas Rand. Chicago, IL: University of Chicago Press.

Adorno, Theodor (1967) *Prisms*. Translated by Samuel Weber and Shierry Weber. Cambridge, MA: MIT Press.

Berman, Marisa (2013, Sept. 12) A legacy of survival. *Narratively*. http://narrative.ly/survivors/a-legacy-of-survival. Accessed April 26, 2015.

Bowlby, John (1988) *A Secure Base*. New York: Routledge.

Freud, Sigmund (1914) The unconscious. *Standard Edition* 12: 255–266.

Hesse, Erik and Main, Mary (1999) Second generation effects of unresolved trauma in non-maltreating parents: dissociated, frightened and threatening parental behavior. *Psychoanalytic Inquiry* 19: 481–540.

Mason, Edward and Fogelman, Eva (1984) *Breaking the Silence: The Generation After the Holocaust* [a film]. Waltham, MA: National Center for Jewish Film, Brandeis University.

Slade, Arietta (2013) The place of fear in attachment theory and psychoanalysis: the fifteenth John Bowlby memorial lecture. In J. Yellin and O. Badouk-Epstein (eds.), *Terror Within and Without: Attachment and Disintegration*, pp. 39–58. London: Karnac Books.

Winnicott, D. W. (1989) The concept of trauma. In C. Winnicott, R. Shepard, and M. Davis (eds.), *Psycho-Analytic Explorations*, pp. 130–148. Cambridge, MA: Harvard University Press.

Chapter 1

Representing, Theorizing and Reconfiguring the Concept of Transgenerational Haunting in Order to Facilitate Healing

Maurice Apprey

Aiz Siem Vartiem Vaid

"Beyond these gates [at Salaspils] the ground is crying."

Introduction

Psychoanalytic practices are gradually coming to include the analysis of transgenerational transmission of destructive aggression in their theoretical and technical praxes. This chapter starts with ordinary and extraordinary stories of *returning to oneself* as part of the narrative on transgenerational transmission. With the return to oneself in mind, I will ask: What basic conceptual assumptions could facilitate how we theorize transgenerational transmission? What *impediments* present themselves when we use existing psychoanalytic theories in inflexible ways as points of entry into psycho-analytic exploration? What may we come to grasp if, for example, we treat some forms of resistance as opportunities rather than opposition to analytic understanding? What, consequently, would constitute analytic readiness to receive the phantoms of transgenerational haunting when they return? These are some of the questions with which we will have to come to grips in order to represent, theorize and reconfigure the idea of transgenerational haunting so that we may facilitate healing. A transgenerational object rela-tions theory could then be proposed at the end.

The Return of the Subject to Oneself; or, Foreshadowing the Concept of the *Advenant*

This chapter will serve as a bridge in two respects: a bridge between theory and practice; and second, a bridge between African-American and

Jewish American experiences. The ethical standpoint subserving this bridge is also two-fold. First, although African-American and Jewish experiences are not interchangeable, they are horizonal; they tell us what heinous things human beings are capable of doing to each other (see Apprey and Stein, 1998). Second, human beings are defined by their capacity to overturn and to reconfigure the received. The theory of technique for upending the transgenerational transmission of destructive aggression in this chapter rests on this ethical position. Before entering into that domain, let us feed our imagination with the following three stories.

I

First, it is 1996, five years after the fall of the Soviet Union and the restoration of independence for Estonia. I am in Estonia as part of an interdisciplinary team of American scholars and diplomats who have come to ease tensions between indigenous Estonians and Estonian Russians after Sovietization. There is a break in peace-making proceedings. I decide to take a taxi to visit Salaspils, a notorious extermination camp in Latvia. In the words of Trudy Ulmann Schloss (1991), Camp Salaspils "was *a horrible place* from which *only very few returned*" (p. 60). I have now arrived by taxi at Camp Salaspils. The taxi driver has his orders from a gatekeeper at the death camp and mass cemetery. He may not drive in. I have to walk all alone into the death camp. Unexpectedly, I am seized with terror. I am immobilized. From where I am standing I can see the "cars" in which hundreds were burned to death. From where I stand, an image of "*the door of no return*" in *Cape Coast Castle comes to me*. Cape Coast castle is a slave castle in Ghana, the country of my birth, and from where hundreds of thousands of kidnapped people were bound in chains and ferried in their fetters to the United States. With the condensation of what I am physically seeing and that which I have now conjured up in my head, these words come to mind: "*if anything happened to me here, and if I did not return, no one would ever know*." Upon the translation of my terror into a narrative, I wake up from my temporary simulation of death and I am able to walk into the death camp alone. When death leaves its traces none of us can remain unaffected. It was not until I *had returned home* in a phenomenal and experiential way that I could be free to walk and to walk in. When I returned to my physical home in the

United States, I looked up the translation of the words that greet visitors at the gate of the death camp at Salaspils: *AIZ SIEM VARTIEM VAID.* These words translate into English as*: BEYOND THESE GATES THE GROUND IS CRYING.* I had intuitively joined the crying dead when I felt immobilized at the gate.

II

Second, it is the year 2009. A third-year psychiatric resident comes to my office for supervision on a psychotherapy case. He is quite distraught. Why? He has just come out of a clinical seminar where he has finished presenting a first session of a case to his peers and the faculty of child and family psychiatry at the University of Virginia School of Medicine. His medical colleagues ask him to report the case to the local Social Services for suspicion of child abuse and he vehemently disagrees with what he considers to be a premature mandate. What is on the videotape that upsets the faculty and his peers so much? In that first videotaped session, the child opens the shirt of his young psychiatrist and rubs his hands against his chest.

I chose to take a history from the parents. I heard the following. On the father's side, the four-year-old boy's grandfather was so physically violent to the boy's father that the grandmother had to take custody of all four children across the street. On the boy's mother's side, the grandfather was so "evil and mean" that he physically attacked most of his six daughters when he was intoxicated. In addition, he sexually violated two of them. When he tried to sexually attack a third she fought him. He killed her.

For what then did the parents from two separate and violent families recruit each other when they met and chose to marry? When the four-year-old boy's parents married they consciously vowed to raise their child in a non-violent home. They would be gentle with their son when he was born. They were. Upon his birth he had such a severe case of colic that they put him in their marital bed and did not release him until the day they walked into my office four years later. It was at this interview that I discovered that he was *without words*, only babbling like an infant, and that at pre-school he was beginning to be violent; hence the referral. I insisted that they put him to bed in his own room and that he could sleep alone. They insisted he would not. I prepared them. They did as I had asked. He was able to do so. They came to see me the next day with their "stunning" news.

With my supervision, treatment by the psychiatric resident took a little less than a year to restore him to where he should developmentally be. I saw the parents concurrently. Together, we managed to overturn the return of the composite of the violent paternal grandfather and the twice as violent and incestuous maternal grandfather. The child was not being physically or sexually abused. The victims were one generation removed. The perpetrators were two generations removed. He was unconsciously being nurtured to become like his grandparents. *What gives itself* as the story to be understood is a transgenerational story with *the return of the grandparents in the body of a four-year-old boy.*

III

A final story, to which I will return throughout this chapter. A prominent academic physician, a surgeon, refers his sixteen-year-old daughter to me. She is oppositional in his eyes and in his wife's as well. She has just learned to drive and although she is a "very good driver," she stays out till late at night driving her drunken friends home. In the eyes of the sixteen-year-old she must ensure that her friends are safely returned home. The father, in his turn, is an elderly academic physician with a reputation for saving lives. I decide to see the daughter twice weekly with a view to starting analysis at some future date if it turned out to be needed. I plan to see the parents monthly throughout this treatment. The parents agree to her work in psychotherapy and look forward to her success in treatment. After two months of seeing no immediate change in his daughter he and his wife decide to ask me to assist them to send their daughter to "a wilderness camp" where she would be subject to a boot camp type of treatment. What is this well-read man asking me to do? He knows what psychoanalysis is. He was analyzed for some seven years during his education in London by one of Anna Freud's colleagues.

In a very poignant session with the parents he berates me for focusing on the understanding of developmental and behavioral issues and not enough on his request for the child to go to "a wilderness camp" to be "tamed." His anger gradually turns into sadness. With recalcitrant resignation, he utters these words: "I wish I could push her and the car onto the top of some mountain and leave her there." His very loyal wife adds:

"…and I would tip it over." I follow up with these words: "and she will die." Father adds: "At least there will be two left." I add: "in contrast to your family of origin where everyone but you perished." Mournful tears fall like I have never seen dropping from a man's eyes. His wife wraps her comforting arms around him.

What have the parents given us? A new version of their history. In the original story, the father's discerning parents, anticipating danger, sent him to London to get his medical education. On his way to London, his entire family was seized by the Nazis. They perished in Auschwitz. Not one survived. When he completed his medical education, he married a German woman. They bore three children.

The sedimentations of history were reactivated in my office. The reactivation entered into the transference and the work of mourning and the meaning of his unconscious recruitment of his German wife were understood. They became freer to parent their daughter differently. She was no longer subject to the mandate to ransom her so that the other two siblings would live. Now she is a prominent violinist *back in Germany* where she works for a major symphony orchestra.

What do these stories have in common? There is a return where the present unconscious coincides with the past unconscious in the fulfillment of an errand where that errand is as much one's own as it is an errand of an Other. Parenthetically, it is not by accident that the French word for "ghost" is "le revenant"; that which returns.

IV

I have used three stories where the ordinary and the extraordinary intersect to feed our imagination about returns in transgenerational haunting and transmission. I shall now describe *impediments to theorizing transgenerational haunting* in psychoanalysis. We shall then look at *prospects for unpacking and theorizing the return.* Then we shall turn to an alternative way to read *"resistance"* in order *to enable us to receive that phantom* (Abraham, 1975) *that returns.* Finally, the idea of the *advenant* is filled in to enable us to see what happens in the middle space between analyst and analysand and what a middle-voiced happening is so that we can represent, theorize, and reconfigure the received transgenerational transmission of destructive aggression in psychoanalysis in order to facilitate healing.

Baldly presented, the operational format of this chapter is as follows. In Part 1 something toxic is injected from an ancestral place and bids us to carry out an errand. In Part 2 I suggest that in order to listen to this invisible and inaudible errand our conventional understanding of resistance must change from a phenomenon that obstructs knowing and meaning-making to one that potentially offers us an opportunity to grasps portals of entry into consciousness. In Part 3 representation is depicted as one of the ways in which ancestral or repressed phenomena reappear. They manifest themselves in the public space between self and other in psychoanalysis. In Part 4 we discover that what once looked like a representation of an errand can appear as a concrete presentation if the analyst is able to foster an analytic space for the subject of the analysis to co-create with the analyst the phenomenal return of oneself to oneself in a primary or original "place" of conflict. Here, we revisit Auschwitz to concretely present *a return of the subject to oneself.* This quiet return of oneself to oneself allows us to reframe Freud's instinct theory in Part 5. In Part 6 we have the beginnings of a transgenerational object relations theory.

None of these observations would be fully realized without the radical change in the analytic handling of resistance as obstruction to a new understanding of resistance as a conduit or portal of entry into consciousness.

Part I

Impediments to Theorizing: Transgenerational Transmission of Destructive Aggression in Individual Psychoanalysis

What is the mode of transmission in transgenerational transmission of destructive aggression? At the outset something is *injected* from an anterior source; that something is *housed* in a hospitable place for storage for an indeterminate time; that same something is *suspended*; that something that is stored in this time warp carries *a mandate for an errand* to be carried out. Upon the mandate's urgent/voluntary reception, the subject awaits a suitable new object to reawaken the project so that that pro-ject *can return to a public space away from a haunt,* as it were. By this time the subject shall have lost sight of who sent whom. *Active and passive have by now become interchangeable. A middle voice speaks and yet it does so in an invisible and inaudible way* (Apprey, 1993). At the end of this chapter we add Claude Romano's (2009) contribution on the subject that returns (*advenant*) to our understanding of transgenerational transmission.

What is the nature of this early ego that receives the mandate to die? Now let us bring in Freud. The ego that receives the intrusive mandate is an early and deep ego that is "not a master in its own house" (Freud, 1917). Freud (1917) recognized in his paper, "A difficulty in the path of psycho-analysis"; that it is a narcissistic blow when the ego recognizes that it is not a master in its own house, as it were, and that the early ego is subject to the dictates of interior and external forces. This idea of the early and deep ego is a necessary starting point for psychoanalytic accounts of transgenerational transmission. It is pivotal because *the early and deep ego cannot process the world "correctly" and for that reason it is at the mercy of conscious and unconscious parental and ancestral infusions.*

What if the theoretical object of psychoanalysis were built on unpacking phenomenological accounts of *givenness* as well as *interpreted constructs*? Here, we must be careful not to make a dichotomy between *pure description* (Husserl, 1913/1983) and *interpretation* as in multiple psychoanalytic traditions. *What if disciplined description were to precede interpretation?* More precisely, *what if we were to treat "resistance" in psychoanalysis not solely as an opponent of meaning-making but as an opportunity that gives yet another story?*

For the theoretical basis of this last question, let us turn next to Georges Politzer (1928/1968) and his critique of the structural theory as a starting point. Politzer saw Freud's creation of the structural theory as an impediment and not as an advance beyond the topography of mind of the period 1897–1923. In short, *structural theory*, for Politzer, *resorted to realism, abstraction and formalism* and in so doing, *lost the rich psychology of the first person singular: "I."*

Part 2

Remembering and Givenness: Revisiting "Resistance" in Psychoanalysis: Georges Politzer's Critique of the Structural Theory

The psychoanalytic concept of transference was initially treated as though it were inseparable from resistance (Freud, 1905, 1912). Now transference is considered the most indispensable tool in psychoanalytic treatment. Similarly, countertransference was initially treated as though it were an obstacle to treatment. Today the transference-countertransference continuum is considered pivotal to psychoanalytic treatment. *Now it is time to extend the same courtesy to "resistance" so that what is traditionally seen as an opponent to progress in treatment can now be considered, with qualification, as an event that gives itself in treatment as access to a private narrative.*

We saw, in the wilderness camp story, a father asking an analyst to treat his sixteen-year-old adolescent child in psychotherapy. We know of his latent desire to take her back to the wilderness rather than make meaning with me in psychoanalytic treatment. We understood that in that story, the event of that story gave itself or, more specifically, *the presentation of that event before me and with me* created an opening to further understanding. We know now that *the opening turned a concrete presentation of a story into a representation of a life-changing event.* This representation opened the door to the meaning-making in treatment he had originally asked for. Typically, such a clinical story can be understood in psychoanalytic terms from at least three standpoints: resistance, in terms of the parents' opposition to the creation of meaning; transference, in terms of their asking me as a clinician to abandon my role and regress into a concrete, syncretic position as an assassin; countertransference, in terms of my helpless appropriation, albeit temporary, of the father's feelings of hopelessness about his daughter's failure to cooperate with him.

It must be emphasized that a clinical story can be understood from multiple conceptual standpoints. At the risk of stating the obvious or debating ideas that have more or less been resolved, let us refresh our clinical minds with some of these conceptualizations for accessing a clinical story. We must do so before we turn to *why it took us so long to treat the concept of resistance as an opening rather than an obstacle.*

In Freud's work, as construed by Politzer, when a subject resists certain thoughts during analysis, these resisted thoughts express themselves in a dream. These resisted thoughts express themselves in a dream because a force impedes their entry into perceptual consciousness. Because this process of resisting thoughts and impeding their entry into perceptual consciousness is already there and beyond the subject's awareness, it cannot be contrived. Freud's conclusion: the existence of the thoughts must be as real as the resistance. Freud's proof: analysis can overcome the resistance and disclose the hitherto impeded thoughts.

Politzer's rendition of Freud's proof is as follows: (1) real thoughts are present; (2) *real thoughts are blocked by resistance*; (3) real thoughts may not be experienced by the subject; (4) real thoughts can have conscious effects; and (5) real thoughts require a real cause or causes. Therefore, an unconscious location for a real cause that generates real effect(s) has to be posited. *To posit that such resisted thoughts preexisted the analysis resorts to realism. To posit that a general life force accounts for the resistance resorts to formalism.* For Politzer, then, *it takes such presuppositions of realism and formalism to require the positing of the unconscious as a receptacle for inadmissible ideas.*

What is *Politzer's own reinterpretation of Freud's account* of the unpacking of the dynamic unconscious process? Politzer would privilege (1) description and (2) *sticking very closely to the facts presented to the clinician in the room.* When a subject, then, describes a particular difficult situation that presents itself in a dream, the clarification of both sets of descriptive material would unconceal a subject's wishes, sense of threat, feelings and attitudes toward the difficult situation without having to depart from the level of meaning presented by the naïve data. Politzer's charge: "To say that a subject has difficulty in admitting incestuous thoughts and to say that he has resisted them is the difference between a 'human' finding based on [human] drama and a psychological description implying realism and formalism" (1994, p. xxxiv; my translation). Freud's failure to stick to description leads Politzer to call Freud's unconscious a place of *"invented descriptions." All we need, to avoid positing the unconscious, is the human limitation that a human being cannot be omniscient.*

Absent a theory of the unconscious, what would Politzer's description of dream interpretation look like? First, the manifest content of a dream is but a first level of description. Politzer wants us to think of *the manifest level of a dream as only a "scenic montage" and an unconventional presentation that only partially and incompletely expresses the subject's lived attitude. The latent content of the dream is the legitimate second level of description.* Politzer wants us to think of the latent level as that second level of description that can unconceal the meaning of a lived attitude for the subject. *The description at the latent level reveals an adequate description at the level of meaning for "the first-person being."* Consequently, *a subject cannot live more than can be thought. Politzer calls this notion that a subject cannot live more than can be thought "the hidden assumption of articulate thought."* When, however, psychological analysis insists on completing or exhaustively completing the analysis of a given object or phenomenon, representation will have become privileged over being. Let Giorgi (1985), a phenomenological psychological researcher, drive home Politzer's viewpoint as follows:

> Being exceeds knowledge. The human subject is not omniscient and not everything that escapes the subject is available to the analyst. The [concept of] unconscious is not necessary, from Politzer's viewpoint, and a [Politzerian descriptively given] concrete science recognizes this sort of limit.
>
> (p. xxxvi)

We can summarize Politzer's link between the manifest and latent content of a dream as follows. Whereas the manifest content is the unconventional scenic montage, the latent content is the more complete description at the level of meaning; essence without essentializing the meaning. Whereas the manifest content dramatizes a scenario, the latent content thematizes the patient's narrative of wishes or perceived threats.

It may seem by now that we have lost sight of the original project, that is, reconceptualizing "resistance" in terms of "an opening" (ouverture) rather than closure, obstacle or hindrance to meaning-making in treatment. On the contrary, we are in the more decidedly secure position to say that *"the wilderness" in our patient's story is a scenic montage,* à la Politzer, *whose unconventional presentation opens the door to the latent meaning of a father's wish to ransom his first-born so that "there would be two left."* No linguistic analysis of the latent meaning is required. We could almost make what Politzer would call *"a simultaneous translation"* *between the manifest content and the latent content.*

From psychoanalysis, then, we have resistance as a concept. From phenomenology we have the guiding principle of "givenness." Here we see that *what is "given" is the "wilderness" or the wilderness camp.* If we treat what is given we have *an opening to a rich, powerful and haunting story. If we treat the request for help to find a wilderness camp to replace psychotherapy and its meaning-making process we have resistance.* If we collapse the two, givenness and resistance, as both an invitation to see the narrative in front of us, one that is crying out loud to be told, we encounter the *evential as in Romano; where the evential is* the reconfiguration of the meanings and impact of an historical event. It is this *reconfiguration from event to evential* that promotes growth and even fosters our arrival at a place where some partial resolution of that historical grievance is possible. *Patients have different degrees of readiness for the latent story. It is our ability to ready ourselves to receive that story that takes us from the scenic montage to the meaningful narrative that the patient gives us in the clinical relationship.*

In a theoretical way what constitutes readiness to receive the new and given narrative? What attitudinal position is needed to receive the phantom that returns?

In order to situate ourselves in a position where we are ready to receive the latent and given story we need to know an ensemble of phenomenological attitudes between description and interpretation. Before then let us disclose some basic assumptions behind the way stations between description and interpretation. *Presuppositionless* basic assumptions subserve the attitudinal positioning of either a phenomenological investigator or a clinical psychoanalyst who readies oneself to observe a phenomenon's appearing. When one observes in a disciplined way and according to a praxis that is either based on Husserl's epoché or is a derivative of it, there is mutual *encroachment*, mutual *divergence* and *negotiations* between the subject that observes and the object of the observation. In reverse, the object of the observation causes the subject that observes to become aware of oneself as a subject whose agency is not always master of its house, as it were. A project of determining *intentionality* therefore includes (1) the essential ingredients of one's directedness upon/toward an object, consciousness of the *aspectual shape* and tilt of a phenomenon's appearing, as well as (2) what the observing of the object does to the subject that observes. When one investigates a phenomenon, there is *a necessary tension between pure description and interpretation* as one strives to unpack it in the public space between the observer and the observed.

Equipped with an attitudinal position of *presuppositionlessness*, a readiness to observe how subject and object *encroach* upon each other, *diverge* or *negotiate meaning* in the clinical situation, and most importantly, *what intentionality accompanies the subject's transference wishes*, we can give up Politzer's realist view of Freud's Unconscious with a capital "*U*" as a concrete and reified place and keep that which is unconscious in perceptual consciousness.

The second adjustment we have to make in Politzer is to modify his rejection of the structural theory by making use of Freud's account of the "ego" in his paper, "A difficulty in the path of psychoanalysis" (1917). This ego precedes the ego of 1923–1938 that is more organized and structured as an executive function, among others. This ego of 1917 is, according to Freud, "not a master in its own house" and subject to narcissistic attacks. Easily shattered, it is an early and deep ego that is subject to influences from outside; subject to parental influences. We are not in a position to reject wholesale Freud's structural theory either. If we were to do so how would we account for the unconscious sense of guilt and other considerations that require us to describe conflict between embedded structures of experience?

Representing and theorizing transgenerational transmission, however, requires us to privilege and elaborate Freud's account of the ego of 1917. Haydee Faimberg (2005), André Green (2004) and Claude Romano (2009) will begin that conversation. All three accounts explicitly or implicitly stand on Freud's early ego which is more plastic than the ego of the structural theory in later Freud.

Part 3

Representing, Theorizing and Reconfiguring the Concept of Transgenerational Haunting in Order to Facilitate Healing in Psychoanalysis

How do traumatic ancestral legacies shape our lives? *Where are the missing narratives that could potentially make the inaudible cries of turbulence audible and the invisible visible? What is the narrative of reactivation?* In the transference wishes of our patients, what demands, pleas and/or requests are made to us to render palpable that turbulence that is striving to enter our contemporary scene so that healing can take place? I will turn to André Green, Edmund Husserl, Martin Heidegger and Claude Romano to frame and reframe our questions and our answers to these questions. I shall reference our "*wilderness*" story along the way to feed our imagination. Finally, I shall rework a theory of transgenerational haunting by radicalizing Freud's concept of *source, pressure, aim and object of the sexual component instinct.* To that end, let us revisit Husserl.

Throughout Husserl's work we see an emphasis on the translation of sedimented or "forgotten" *events of history* to a reactivated *sense of history*. In a previous work (Apprey, 2006), I have extended Husserl's account of *sedimentation* and *reactivation* to a third sphere of the *intentional supplement* where in psychoanalysis we interrogate not the sedimented events of history, not the reactivation but chiefly the *intentionality behind the transference wishes*. These transference wishes have travelled from (1) the domain of sedimented events to (2) a domain of reactivated and appropriated sense of history and now to an intentional sphere where the analyst may be prodded to, invited to, even bullied to join the analysand to overturn the impact of that psychologically toxic sense of history.

I shall now juxtapose two corollary accounts: Romano's account of events and the world of the subject, and André Green's account of representation in the interstices between internal and external fields of reference to how the subject situates oneself in the world. I submit that we would advance our knowledge of the world of representation, in psychoanalysis in general and in Green specifically, if we were able to juxtapose the idea of *the subject that returns to itself* in the process of engagement with events as a corollary discourse.

(A) From French Reception of German Phenomenology to Psychoanalysis with André Green as a Representative Model

It was stated earlier that a theory of transgenerational transmission cannot overlook Freud's (1917) statement that the ego is not a master of its own house. Similarly, Freud's idea has consequences for Green (2004). The first consequence of Freud's idea for Green is that because the early ego cannot initially process the world correctly, there must be negotiation between unrepresentable bodily demands and the psychical representations of those bodily demands.

For André Green, then, inner objects have a double existence: an inner and external world. Between these two worlds it is *representation* that *brings about communication*. Second, *the representational world makes it possible for the analyst to interpret thought*. Third, the capacity for *thought begins with* a child's *attempt to bring together* the initially *unrepresentable bodily experiences a mother cannot meet* in the external world, on the one hand, *with a child's potentially and psychically representable demands* on the other. Between the *unrepresentable* bodily demands and the child's psychic *representations of its demands*, there lies *a gap that will never be filled* no matter how good a mother is. *The psyche is therefore a conversation in the gap* within that spatial relationship *between two bodies*: *unrepresentable bodily needs* and the potentially *representable demands of the child*.

Another consequence of the early ego's unreadiness to be its own master is that it must depend on an object outside the body to sustain and support its being because of its *premature condition at birth*. Following Heinz Hartmann (1958) and Bolk (1926), Green (2004) suggests that the result of this premature condition at birth will become the matrix of the mind; a matrix that, in turn, will become constituted by the meeting of the psychical representative by which being is realized into existence. This coming to being comes about through the demands of the body and its association to the demands. The association to the demands depends on "what the mind has kept as *traces of former experiences of satisfaction that bear some similarity to the sought-for situation*" (Green, 2004, p. 54, emphasis in original). This concept is in Chapter 7 of Freud (1900) as perceptual identity but Green (2004) will use the idea to launch another, his own idea of *the dynamic restlessness of the subject that seeks a co-existence with the object*. Before then, let us see what he does with Freud's notion of identity of perception.

Green sees the co-option between the tension between the child's bodily needs and their associations as a dynamic one because it modifies psychic representatives of the child's demands and the ideational representatives of the drives through a modification of internal and external world. In my view, *the drives and the associations to the demands of the drives reciprocally change the child's internal fields of reference to the external world and in reverse the external fields of reference change the input to the interior*.

Clinically, parents who unconsciously wished to speak the drives by taking their daughter back to the wilderness manifestly to be tamed but unconsciously to be sacrificed had cathected the "wilderness" as an external field of reference to their interior turbulence and perennial anguish. Reciprocally, their daughter who had stored her parents' deferred anguish unconsciously created a palpable disturbance in the external world in ways that preserved the restlessness of the inner world; *keeping it very much alive*. A *reciprocal connection between the parents' reactivation and the daughter's appropriation of the toxic history had to be grappled with and understood before me. A reciprocal correction had to be made through an analytic reconstruction of the hitherto heavily sedimented traumatic history.*

Given then, the immaturity of the early ego and its dependence on an outside object to maintain and sustain its being how would Green theorize the relationship of the psyche to the three internal agencies – id, ego, superego – of the mind?

He links them as follows: the *id is the paradise of the mother–baby relationship – flesh to flesh; the relationship of the mother to her mother builds up the ego; and the superego represents the father's role as that which ends the two-in-one relationship between the mother and her baby to which she is bodily linked.*

I would clarify *the mother's relationship to her own mother as a building up of the ego* in the following way: *the mother as auxiliary ego to her child whom she is initially physically linked must simultaneously work through the psychical connection to her own mother.* The representation of that psychical connection informs what she consciously or unconsciously proceeds to do with her child. She does so in identification with her mother. *By linking the mother to her mother, we have begun to introduce the idea of three generations to define a subject. Three generations are therefore needed to define the human subject.*

(B) From the French Reception of German Phenomenology to Continental Philosophy with Claude Romano as Representative Model

Turning now to Romano (2009) let us still bear in mind that our starting point is the early ego and the difficulties it has in processing the world "correctly." In the face of the ego's immaturity, how does the subject translate events into a sense of history (Husserl) or in Romano, how does the subject translate an event into the new configuration that he calls "evential"? In the face of the ego not being a master in its own house who owns whom and what forms of dispossession are there? In the course of the reconfiguration of the subject's sense of selfhood what happens to activity and passivity? What structural delay accompanies the reconfiguration?

Event and Evential

He distinguishes between two types of *event*. When *events* happen, they actualize a possibility that is already present in the world, like lightening. On the other hand, events as *evential* overturn existing possibilities and in so doing *reconfigure* the world. In Romano's own words, in the evential reconfiguration,

> *the one* who understands is strictly implicated in the very act of understanding: I can understand an event as being addressed to me only if I am myself in play in the possibilities it assigns to me [me destine] and through which it makes history by opening a destiny for me.
>
> (2009, p. 30; emphasis in original)

This means that we need a system of mutual implications between the event as fact and the one to whom the event happens. The subject in turn reshapes what that event does to him or her or what it means to oneself.

The evential says Romano, is not a fait accompli. It is not inscribed in time and therefore can open up to a movement of futurition. By not being inscribed in time the subject of the evential can exercise a structural delay and thereby making it accessible from its own posterity from an-archic welling up from nothing. Whereas in Green (2004) the timelessness of the Unconscious brings up the paternal function to provide order, generalization and continuity, Romano's *evential* is not inscribed in time and opens up a movement of futurition that exercises a structural delay that in turn brings about what I will now call "*a pluperfect latency.*"

Romano's phenomenology of the evential suggests that during the reconfiguration of a subject's world, *a metamorphosis that is impossible to date* takes place. Once an event is brought about, it is already too late. We are never contemporaries of its actualization. *We can experience it when it has already taken place* and this is why, says Romano, an event in its eventness happens only according to *the secret of its latency.* Accordingly, an encounter is not the datable fact of the meeting of two beings but rather that which *lies in reserve* in this meeting and which gives it its future loading. The subject, therefore, is *an advenant* that comes back to oneself. The subject that returns to a prior latency *shall have come back* to oneself after revealing *the secret that lies or has lain in reserve.*

Eventials are not datable. Their secrets lie in reserve. After exercising *a structural delay* the subject of eventials returns to a prior latency, or more correctly to a pluperfect latency after *the subject shall have come back to oneself* as *advenant.* In this back and forth, past and present, subject and object oscillate in a series of vicissitudes with progressive and retrogressive steps. In Romano's own account, Passibility is "being exposed beyond measure to events that cannot be expressed in terms of passivity but [passibility] *precedes the distinction between active and passive"* (Romano, 2009, p. 72; emphasis added).

The Eventiol and the Proneness to Mis-Representation

What, then, makes us so vulnerable to mis-representation? Romano gives us a handle on this with his account of *birth, naming and dispossession of self.* For Romano (2009), to be born is to be connected to history. I am not my own origin. Mine is a destiny all too laid out and pre-assigned to me. So, poignantly, for Romano (2009)

> if I cannot take over this past, if this pre-personal past, coming before all memory and forgetting, preceding birth and opening to it, is *a pluperfect I always "come after,"* it is also what makes possible always "go before" me and thus well up from the future.
>
> (p. 78; emphasis added)

To be born, then, is to have a history before having *one's own* history. There is a pre-personal history the subject-as-advenant cannot take over. The subject-as-advenant cannot take over the history of Auschwitz. She would, however, participate with degrees of ownership in a human adventure imbued with excessive meanings that is incommensurable with her projections; projections that are radically inexhaustible. Born into a human adventure imbued with excessive meaning, the subject now has to be named. In what Romano (2009) calls "the inaugural dissymmetry of naming,"

> to be named is to be anticipated by the verbal initiative of another, called by a word that overhangs me and that I cannot completely

appropriate, since my name, symbol of my *ownership*, [symbol] of my "identity" is at the same time, symbol of this initial *dispossession*.

(p. 80; emphasis added)

Through *the inaugural dissymmetry of naming*, then, my name is just as much a symbol of my ownership as it is a symbol of my dispossession. We are, however, a little ahead of ourselves here. There is a dispossession of birth that precedes naming as yet another symbol of dispossession. How may we separate these two types of dispossession? Phenomenologically, we may link the dispossession of birth to that which is *"originary"* [*sic*]. We may link the second dispossession of naming to that which is "original"; original because the subject is now capable of self-projecting and capable of participating in a human adventure that is saturated with multiple, excessive and radically inexhaustible meanings.

Part 4

Back to Auschwitz

The Nazis are preparing to execute Polish Jews. A discerning family saves a son by sending him to London to train to become a physician. He marries a German woman. They raise three children; the oldest of whom must now be *ransomed* so that *two would be left*. Psychotherapy allows the adolescent and her parents to both represent what had hitherto lain *in reserve* until it became *representable* and until we could *reconfigure the sedimentations of history that had been reactivated in treatment and extended to serve a new and contemporary purpose*. A father and mother brought me *a transference wish* that *I could not meet*: a wish to join them *to send their daughter to the wilderness*. This is *simultaneously a transference wish and a phenomenological event*. It is a transference wish to this effect: "please join us as we revisit the wilderness where grandparents perished." It is a phenomenological event to this effect: "The incineration is not datable; its secrets lie in reserve. Once we get past the wilderness story we may be able to represent and reconfigure anew a project that does not kill." An adolescent daughter *could not represent* or reconfigure on her own and by herself what unrepresentable project had been injected into her. Rather, she created an *errand*; a *mistake*, a *wandering, an unconscious errand that had already taken place*. It was her new project to independently and singlehandedly save her endangered friends from death.

In *a pro-ject of passibility*, she was an advenant, a sub-ject that had been chosen to be ransomed, as it were, to save the other two siblings, and simultaneously a sub-ject who must rescue others from danger. Thanks to the work of psychotherapy, the return of the daughter to the wilderness was aborted. Now a world-class cellist in her own right, *the parental pro-ject has been overturned and upended by the sub-ject.* Now she can become a *subject (without a dash) with greater agency* in her selfhood.

Our clinical story tells us that the subject-as-advenant is a vulnerable figure who can be returned to the wilderness, as it were, to be ransomed so that others may live. We are now in a position to say that *fettered to history* the *advenant is eminently the subject of* utter *misrepresentation.* More accurately, we may say that the subject is both represented and misrepresented; representable and misrepresentable according to the intentionality behind the reactivation and the translation from the events of history to a sense of history.

Part 5

Returning to Freud to Link Freud's Theory of Instinct to the Transgenerational Transmission of Destructive Aggression in Order to Propose a Transgenerational Object Relations Theory

In Freud's 'Instincts and their vicissitudes' (1915), an instinct has a *source*, it operates under *pressure*, it has active and passive *aims*, and it has an *object*. By the *source* of an instinct, Freud meant a process of excitation that occurs in an organ. This is essentially of a biological and/or chemical nature. By the *pressure of* an instinct, Freud meant the amount of force, peremptory urge or demand for work, which it represents. By *aim*, Freud meant the aspectual direction—passive or active—that effects the bodily change that is felt as fulfillment or satisfaction. The *object* is the thing or figure through which the instinct or instinctual trend achieves its aim. We can now radicalize the world of instincts and instinctual trends into a phenomenological world as follows: The *source of turbulence* is an ancestral world, an anterior (m)other, a prior autochthony that hides a secret desire and renders it latent. The *pressure accompanying the reactivation* need not invariably be urgent or peremptory; rather, it is potentially a slow and insidious one that is passed through the generations. In the process of reactivation, *subject and object oscillate*; subject becomes cast under cover, "thrown under a bus," as it were. Subject gathers itself, binds itself in protest or in recalcitrant resignation and/or chooses one's own poison if one is perceived to be mandated to die. Finally, the figure of an object through which or through whom the fulfillment is to be derived can store, suspend, defer or inject the toxic representation or aberrant mis-representation into yet another subject; a suitable figure that can provide an object home for the mediating subject.

Part 6

Provisional Transgenerational Object Relation Praxis

When we are able to acknowledge the source of the internal turbulence as ancestral, when we are able to appreciate the slow and insidious ways in which the phantoms emerge, when we can see that subject and object, passive and active do change places, and lastly, when we can treat the object as a figure that has been recruited to bring us back to ourselves, we would be ready to see both the mysterious and the everyday features of the uncanny. This discovery of the uncanny as both mysterious and ordinary shows itself through *historical events* that are *staged* inside the analysis in the form of *new events* in front of our very eyes and in very palpable ways. Our readiness to treat these events *as givenness to tell an untold story* rather than as opposition to meaning-making brings the subject of an analysis face to face with the phantom.

The analytic subject, then, in this transgenerational praxis, is the one who

  i *embodies the phantom that seeks to return* to a hostile or hospitable place,
 ii *gives intentionality to the errand to fulfill a mandate to die or seek ransom*, and
iii *returns to oneself (advenant)* in the *new and public space* of the analyst-analysand relationship.

This new space is saturated with *transference wishes, pleas* or *demands* made by the subject in order to entertain the possibility of *a reconfiguration that fosters healing under new and favorable conditions.*

Bibliography

Abraham, Nicolas (1975). Notes on a phantom. In *The Shell and the Kernel*. Chicago, IL: University of Chicago Press, 1994.

Apprey, M. (1993). Dreams of urgent voluntary errands and transgenerational haunting in transsexualism. In *Intersubjectivity, Projective Identification and Otherness*, edited by M. Apprey and H. Stein. Pittsburg, PA: Duquesne University Press.

Apprey, M. (2006). Difference and the awakening of wounds in intercultural analysis. *Psychoanalytic Quarterly*, Vol. LXXV, pp. 73–94.

Apprey, M. and Stein, H. (1998). Ruptures in time. In *Blacks and Jews on the Couch: Psychoanalytic Reflections on Black-Jewish Conflict*, edited by A. Helmreich and P. Marcus. Westport, CT: Praeger, pp. 102–120.

Bolk, L. (1926). *Das Problem der Menschwerdung*. Jena: Fischer.

Faimberg, Haydee (2005). *The Telescoping of Generations: Listening to the Narcissistic Links Between Generations*. London and New York: Routledge.

First, Elsa (1970). Fixation. In *Basic Psychoanalytic Concepts on Metapsychology, Conflicts, Anxiety, and Other Subjects*, edited by H. Nagera. London: George Allen and Unwin.

Freud, Anna (1936). *The Ego and the Mechanism of Defense*. London: Hogarth Press.

Freud, Sigmund (1900). Interpretation of dreams. *Standard Edition, 4/5*. London: Hogarth Press.

Freud, Sigmund (1905). Fragment of an analysis of a case of hysteria. *Standard Edition, 7*. London: Hogarth Press.

Freud, Sigmund (1912). The dynamics of transference. *Standard Edition, 12*. London: Hogarth Press.

Freud, Sigmund (1915). Instincts and their vicissitudes. *Standard Edition, 14*. London: Hogarth Press.

Freud, Sigmund (1917). A difficulty in the path of psychoanalysis, *Standard Edition, 15*. London: Hogarth Press.

Freud, Sigmund (1920). Beyond the pleasure principle. *Standard Edition, 18*. London: Hogarth Press.

Giorgi, Amedeo (1975). An application of phenomenological method in psychology. In *Duquesne Studies in Phenomenological Psychology* (Vol. 2). Pittsburgh, PA: Duquesne University Press.

Giorgi, Amedeo (1985). The phenomenological psychology of learning and the verbal learning tradition. In *Phenomenology and Psychological Research*, edited by A. Giorgi, Pittsburgh, PA: Duquesne University Press.

Giorgi, Amedeo (1985). Sketch of a psychological phenomenological method. In *Phenomenology and Psychological Research*, edited by A. Giorgi et al., Pittsburgh, PA: Duquesne University Press.

Giorgi, Amedeo (2009). *The Descriptive Phenomenological Method in Psychology: A Modified Husserlian Approach*. Pittsburgh, PA: Duquesne University Press.

Green, André (1969). *The Tragic Effect*. Cambridge, UK: Cambridge University Press, p. 87.

Green, André (2004). *André Green at the Squiggle Foundation*. Edited by Jan Abram. London, UK: Karnac Books.

Hartmann, Heinz (1927). Understanding and explanation. In *Essays on Ego Psychology*. New York: International Universities Press, pp. 369–403.

Hartmann, Heinz (1958). *The Ego and the Problem of Adaptation*. New York: International Universities Press.

Heiman, Paula (1950). On counter-transference. *International Journal of Psychoanalysis*, Volume 31, pp. 81–84.

Husserl, Edmund (1962). *Ideas I: General Introduction to Pure Phenomenology, Book 1*. Translated by W.R.B. Gibson. New York: Collier Books. (Orig. 1913).

Husserl, Edmund (1983). *Ideas Pertaining to a Pure Phenomenology and to a Phenomenological Philosophy, Book 1*. Translated by F. Kersten. The Hague: Martinus Nijhoff. (Orig. pub. German, 1913).

Husserl, Edmund (1989). *Ideas Pertaining to a Pure Phenomenology and to a Phenomenological Philosophy, Second Book*. Studies in the Phenomenological Constitution. Translated by Richard Rojcewicz and André Schuwer. Collected Works, Vol. 3. Dordrecht: Kluwer Academic Press. (Orig. 1952).

Politzer, Georges (1968). *Critique des Fondements de la Psychologie*. Paris: Presses Universitaires de France. (Orig. pub. French 1928).

Politzer, Georges (1994). *Critique of the Foundations of Psychology: The Psychology of Psychoanalysis*. Translated by Maurice Apprey. Pittsburgh, PA: Duquesne University Press. (Orig. 1928).

Romano, Claude (2009). *Event and World*. New York: Fordham University Press.

Sandler, Joseph with Anna Freud (1985). *The Analysis of Defense: The Ego and the Mechanisms of Defense Revisited*. New York: International Universities Press.

Schloss, T.D. (1991). A farm called Jungfernhof. In *The Unfinished Road: Jewish Survivors of Latvia Look Back*. Collected and edited by Gertrude Schneider. Westport, CT: Praeger, pp. 57–59.

Chapter 2

Skin Memories

On Race, Love and Loss[*]

Sue Grand

In every psychoanalysis, there is a prevailing motif and a transference dynamism in which that motif comes alive. In my first analysis, that theme was aborted grief. For me, this grief had collective meanings, which would be illuminated by a racialized transference. But like all analyses, this process would begin in my personal past. When I was seven I lost my Russian Jewish grandmother, who cared for me while my parents labored, seven days a week. Grandma died and I was lost: lost to my parents' attention, small at her funeral, invisible to the adult mourners, all of them larger, more vocal, more clamoring than myself. I was without tears, without comfort, without her enveloping body. She was five foot one, and sometimes she weighed two hundred and fifty pounds. She had pendulous arms and a vast bosom. To me, her body was bountiful. It had held me and nourished me, and now it was gone.

My parents were first-generation Americans. Grandma had come through Ellis Island with her parents, in flight from conscriptions and pogroms. Then there was World War I, the Great Depression, unemployment and starvation, and then World War II. My father witnessed atrocities in battle, and after the liberation he was stationed at Dachau. Life was full of catastrophic reversals and moral imperatives. What we had was humor, our wits, and our labor. Children's lives were rough-and-tumble; they worked, if they could get work, and when they weren't working they ran in the streets. After Grandma was gone, I knew I would raise myself, on city streets. Childhood had already passed on. Of course, there was still laughter. There were riotous family stories, but none were told about Grandma. Where Grandma had been, there were vague memories of

* Reprinted with kind permission: This chapter first appeared in *Psychoanalysis, Culture & Society*, September 2014, Volume 19, Issue 3, pp. 232–249. Reprinted by permission of Palgrave MacMillan.

Russia, and the disappearance of others. There were absolute good-byes, and impossible distances. There were always holes in our mourning, and, now, after my grandmother's death, there was another hole in our stories.

If we were silent about her absence, that absence would be felt in Brooklyn. In life, Grandma was a presence. There was nothing inert about her heft. No: her bulk seemed to make her a formidable force. In Brooklyn, she knew who ran things; they owed her favors; and she could make things happen. By day, she bustled about and kibitzed and cooked and cleaned. In the evenings, she took off her apron and stepped out. She had always lived from hand to mouth. But on Saturday nights, her flesh poured out of her strapless gowns. She put on lipstick and powder, long white gloves, costume jewelry. Glorious in her plentitude, the Queen of Canarsie, she sallied forth to some political event. She schmoozed, and deals were struck. For family and neighbors, there was rent reduction and free doctoring; immigration officials melted away. Grandma had a kind of nurturing insistence, and she wouldn't back down. She saw need, and she took care of it. *With* me, she was tender, but she was also fierce *for* me.

But what inspired her to take care of Brooklyn? Even in the absence of stories, I sensed that there were other bodies nesting inside her body. I often played with those Russian puzzle dolls, painted, rotund wooden figures that contained ever-smaller replicas of themselves. Grandma was Russian, and she had the same shape. I thought those dolls must be alive inside of her. This would explain her devotion and her bulk. But exactly *who* were these bodies sequestered inside Grandma? This mystery found commentary in my grandmother's hands. Broad and calloused, they were full of competence, grace, and intention. They never stopped moving. And yet, each hand had several mutilated fingers; there were just rough stumps ending at the knuckles. Gradually, I absorbed the discrepancy between her hands and my own. One day, I asked, "Grandma, what happened to your fingers?" "I was working in a factory. They were severed in an accident. We were poor. We didn't have enough to eat. I was lucky to be working. I had to feed your father."

She goes on kneading dough and I am riveted by those fingers. I slip into the folds of time, assembly lines, harrowing sounds and sharp, implacable machines. The Great Depression, and my grandmother, bleeding. No money for a hospital, or a doctor. No one else to feed the family. I see her being saved by other, hungry, working hands. Those times layer into present time: there are mountains of food emerging from her deft movements. Now she is feeding Brooklyn, defying poverty's implacable machine. She is corpulent; she eats in memory of hunger, and for those who had nothing to eat.

Years after my analysis, I find myself visualizing her hands. They were a miracle of post-traumatic resilience and provision; they were proud, and they moved without shame or fear. But all of this is reawakened memory, a luxurious, unfolding vision, loosened by my psychoanalysis. When I came to see my analyst, I was depressed. I knew Grandma mattered, and I knew that she had died. What followed was a remarkable analytic excavation, between an African-American analyst and a Russian-Jewish patient. Between us, there were complex transgenerational legacies, interleaved with racial/ethnic identities and inscribed on our woman bodies.

In an analysis between a white patient and an African-American therapist, issues about racism will surface. But in *this* treatment, race trouble became a direct conduit to the plantation. It was as if racism moved swiftly backwards in time: through the assassination of MLK, Jr; Medgar Evers; Emmett Till, the bridge at Selma, lynchings, Jim Crow, Reconstruction, the Civil War, until we arrived at the cotton fields and the slave block. I have always been vulnerable to dual vision: life, here, now; and the long tangled history of violence. And this is what I knew at the beginning of my analysis. In my first consultation, I met an analyst who appeared to be white. After the first few sessions, I had random encounters with two white people who knew her. Each of them told me that my analyst identified herself as African-American. One of them had known my analyst in college and described her as an African-American student who was a political activist in the sixties. And I knew this: her name didn't sound like Brooklyn. It sounded like the deep South.

So what, then, did I know? I knew we lived in racial categories and that I had shame and guilt for perpetuating those categories. I wanted to be colorblind (see K. Leary, 2002). But I also knew, as Cornel West (2001) would put it, that "race matters" – that an African-American identity references an objective history of oppression (K. Leary, 2002). And I knew that there was a gap, a tension, between her *apparent* whiteness, and her identification as black. I knew too that she could "pass" as white, but that she had refused to pass. This is what I understood: that she had important familial and community attachments. She had a political position and solidarity with those who *could not pass*. What to do with this in my analysis? I knew that she thought I thought she was white. I thought she thought that I was "passing" her. As Kim Leary (1997) puts it, "Passing always occurs in the context of a relationship: it requires, on the one side, a subject who does not tell, and on the other, an audience who fails to ask" (p. 85). But what my analyst didn't know is that I knew without asking. Discovering her racial identification from external sources, it was as if I had plundered Pandora's box. I had forbidden, extra-analytic knowledge. I had the puzzle of white skin, black identity. I had questions that had no place in classical psychoanalysis.

It was the 1970s. My analyst and I were ten years apart; we were both products of a radical era: anti-war protests, feminism, the Civil Rights movement. But we were also embedded in a white psychoanalysis, which did not inquire into trauma or the intersection of psyche and culture. She was a politically active African American who was also successful in the white world of psychoanalysis. Faimberg, Laub, and Bergmann and others had begun to recognize transgenerational transmission, but this new lens was trained on the Holocaust and excluded slavery (see Bass, 2003; Leary, 2005; Gump, 2010; Fletchman-Smith, 2011). Eventually, we would trust each other enough to talk race trouble. But, in the trans-generational area of what Akbar (1996) calls "plantation syndrome" or J. Leary (2005) calls post-traumatic slave syndrome,[2] there were no words yet for the phantasms that would appear in my transference. From the first, my analysis was haunted by the ghosts who were, as Reis (2007) puts it, carrying "their mute messages and their enigmatic demands, seeking witness to hidden catastrophe" (p. 622). As Davoine (2012) might suggest, history emerged through unexpected events, through symptoms and the interpenetration of our psyches.

My transference would be personal, plastic, healing and imaginary. But it would also be defined by a real, and terrible, history. My racial conundrum referred to what Laub and Podell (1995) call "trauma's empty circle": a residuum of mass atrocity that exceeds speech and narration, in which "we are implicated in each other's traumas" (Caruth, 1995, p. 24). I knew, or sensed, that my therapist's "white" skin was *not* due to genera-tions of mutual, and loving, intercourse. In the United States, interracial love was as rare as it was forbidden and dangerous. For much of our history, it was illegal "miscegenation." But the rape of black women by white men was ubiquitous. White skin, African-American identity: this insinuated the predicament of slave women, whose descendants could emerge with light skin. Lying on the couch, I glimpsed these slave women in the shadows. They cried out at the edge of my consciousness, and they are crying out still. Of all the things I shared with my analyst, of this I never spoke.

Missing Stories: Testimonies of the Skin

White skin, African-American identity. I was silent, in a country that has kept its own brutal secrets for almost five hundred years. Women and girls, kidnapped in Africa, sold into slavery. The violence of white incursions was written, and rewritten, on their bodies, and on the skin of succeeding generations. There are the euphemisms for rape that persist in histories of slavery, even those written in 2012 (Swarns, 2012): that white masters "fathered" children with their female slaves. That more enlightened white masters, like Thomas Jefferson, had slave "mistresses" or "wives." One could say that these terms capture the varieties of love and desire that *could* exist between slave and master (see Fox-Genovese, 1988; Scharfstein, 2011; Berlin, 2003; Deramus, 2005; Swarns, 2012). They may acknowledge the rare, courageous love relationships that did occur (Berlin, 2003; Deramus, 2005). There were complex erotic switchbacks in the relationship of master and slave and relative degrees of agency available to some slave women (Gorden-Reed, 2008). But as Hartman (1997) elaborates in her excellent critique of "seduction" during slavery, the terms "fathering" and "mistress" presume a woman's freedom to say yes, when it is impossible to say *no*. As a slave, she cannot refuse her master. Even the most brilliant and compassionate histories of slavery (see Berlin, 2003, for example) embrace these euphemisms, and fail adequately to narrate this sexual trespass. I am white, but I am a woman, and I have a vagina, and I know what rape is. I know about power and submission. I know permanent wariness and predatory menace. I am a "free" white woman. I can try to escape. I have always had some laws to protect me. Slave women were bred like cattle, assaulted by their masters, coerced into sex with threats and promises. With a husband, or parents, who would be brutalized or killed for trying to protect her. Then: she was pregnant with another slave, with lightening skin – a child scarred by this heritage, and yet perversely privileged by that scar.

In a universe of such racial madness, this incursion of whiteness into black vaginas yielded a transgenerational legacy of shame, rage, terror, and a tendency to blame the victim (see hooks, 2001). But it also yielded children *who had the potential for race change.* As Kim Leary (1997) notes, "the very ability to pass from black to white – unlike other cultural or ethnic masquerades – is dependent on antecedent traumas like the sexual exploitation of African women and girls during slavery" (p. 89) (see also hooks, 2001). These children bore the complex stigmata of slavery. A girl's lightened skin spoke of her forebears' abjection. That skin still speaks of this abjection in contemporary America, but this historical violence is obscured by our collective "malignant dissociative contagion" (Grand, 2000).

But such was the perversity of this atrocity: that sexual violation also conferred degrees of whiteness on succeeding generations of slaves. This yielded a complex "color caste" system (see hooks, 2001) in which light-skinned blacks were considered superior to dark-skinned blacks. The master's offspring might receive easier work, better care, even some affection or education. During slavery, these children were denied, and were often persecuted by their masters' shame and fear, and by the mistress's jealousy and vengeance (see Fox-Genovese, 1988; Fleishner, 1996). But these children could also be humanized by proximity, becoming the locus of white ambivalence. When the Spanish dominated the Louisiana territory,

> [m]anumission began inside the slave owners' household. Among the first to be freed were the *lovers* and children of the slave owners themselves. During the first decade of Spanish rule, numerous masters freed their *slave wives,* and the children they bore, for reasons of "love and affection."
>
> (Berlin, 2003, p. 93, italics mine)

What a strange legacy of oppression. Through sexual exploitation, a woman is degraded. Her child becomes the ambiguous sign of a new category between black and white, perhaps the first beneficiary of freedom. Indeed, as Berlin (2003) notes, it was not mysterious that "the free colored population grew physically lighter as the slave population – much of it just arrived from Africa – grew darker" (p. 152).

Thus, for slave girls, to be "mulatto" was to become something between the human and the subhuman. This child could become semihuman to her mother's rapist, by whom she was owned, and by whom she could be freed. But like all slave girls, she was also prey for her master/father. Whether she succumbed to threats and promises, or was the object of a more violent assault, a girl understood her fate. This fate continued to mingle familial links and DNA. The whiter these children became, the more they exposed the sexual predation of their white masters. They complicated the ideology of slave masters and threatened the racial categories that sustained white dominance. But if light-skinned blacks kept awakening white ambivalence and moving towards emancipation, it would pose an economic loss, requiring the master class to keep purchasing new slaves. And so, the "one drop rule" was established to define blackness (Sharfstein, 2011). New laws insured that these children would follow the condition of their mother. Now, the offspring of rape *increased* slave holdings, and multiplied wealth. Even as the color line blurred, official racial categories often became *more* rigid and *less* permeable. Destabilized by racial ambiguities, the brutality of whites often escalated (Berlin, 2003; Sharfstein, 2011).

Nonetheless, sexual predation kept threatening the power hierarchies that it was consolidating. Thus, historian Charles Beard (in King, 1963/2010) could comment, rather poetically, on the way resistance eventually triumphs over regimes of violence, because the "bee fertilizes the flower that it robs." Indeed, rape fertilized women's bodies with the racial ambiguities that could destabilize white dominance. These contradictions kept infecting succeeding generations. Race change became increasingly possible (Sharfstein, 2011), even as racism was perpetuated and internalized. Reenacting the "color caste system" imposed on them by sexual violence (and by the relative privileges "lightness" had conferred), blacks would also become divided against themselves. "Lighter" skin became a marker of possibility and worth; dark skin potentiated shame, hopelessness and self-hatred (hooks, 2001; J. Leary, 2005; Powell, 2012; Thompson, 2012). The "erotics of terror" (Hartman, 1997) continued to be bedrock to white privilege, as Baldwin (1972), Fanon (1952), Hernton (1965), Hine (1993), and others have noted. Whites continued to be paranoid and persecutory about black men raping white women (thereby polluting their imaginary, untainted, "virginal" whiteness), while white men continued raping black women. Beginning with slavery, "[w]hite culpability was displaced as black criminality" (Hartman, 1997, p. 83). As Young-Bruehl (1996) notes, throughout the generations, this perversity has been worked out on black bodies: through sexual projections and sexual transgressions; through "the rapacious 'whitening' of the darker race" (p. 491); and through centuries of white secrecy. The subterranean intercourse between "races" contradicted our mythologies of racial hierarchies and separation. The result was a passing mechanism which "depended upon its operating in silence. Passing was a conspiracy of silence not only for the individual but for a biracial society, which had drawn a rigid color line based on visibility. Unless a white man was a white man, the gates were open to endless slander and confusion" (Jordan, 1968, p. 174).

When I arrived on the couch, I was just beginning to know that the Atlantic and domestic slave trade lasted over three hundred years. Millions lived and died in chains (see Berlin, 2003; Hochschild, 2005). African-American slavery was one of the most sustained forms of mass violence perpetrated by humanity. And in every epoch of mass violence, women are violated and these wounds are embodied in their descendants. But in the 1970s, this traumatic legacy had not registered in psychoanalysis. As Gump (2000, 2010), and Bass (2003) note, slavery is still not adequately recognized in trauma studies. Although we now have an expanding literature on the influence of race within psychoanalysis (Altman, 2000; Leary, 2002; Suchet, 2007; Bonovitz, 2012; Holmes, 2012; etc.), with the notable exceptions of Apprey (2003), Bass (2003), Fletchman-Smith (2011), slavery has not found a place in the transgenerational turn in psychoanalysis. This very absence may be a transgenerational legacy, an inherited trace of the belief that slaves were incapable of deep feeling. As haunted as he was by slavery, Thomas Jefferson promoted this view:

"Their griefs are transient. Those numberless afflictions ... are *less felt and sooner forgotten with them*. In general their existence appears to participate more of sensation than reflection."

(Jefferson, as quoted in Williams, 2012, p. 90 italics mine)

This conviction neutralized the master's guilt. For post-traumatic slave syndrome to gain recognition in the transgenerational turn in psychoanalysis, another voice must be heard:

I was compelled to stand and see my wife shamefully scourged and abused by her master: and the manner in which this was done, was so violently and inhumanely committed upon the person of a female, that I despair ... My happiness or pleasure was then all blasted; for it was sometimes a pleasure to be with my family even in slavery. I loved them as my wife and child ... But oh! When I remember that my daughter, my only child, is still there, destined to share the fate of all these calamities, it is too much to bear ... If ever there was any one act of my life while a slave, that I have to lament over, it is that of being a father and a husband of slaves.

(Henry Bibb, 1849 (ex-slave) as quoted in Williams, 2012, p. 114)

Slave Women on the Couch: Ghosts in the Transference

In the 1970s, I had not heard this voice. But somehow, its claims had penetrated my existence. I felt guilt about my whiteness and I wanted to make reparation. In the wake of the Civil Rights movement, I wanted to be colorblind. So I tried to have a colorless analysis, in a psychic world divorced from politics and culture. But in the United States, colorblindness is a wishful phantasm; this phantasm can actually negate the other's historical subjectivity (see K. Leary, 2002). As a young, progressive white woman, I had no exit from this loop. But I was also a Jew whose father had witnessed Dachau. And so my analysis would proceed in two registers. There was a "black analysis" in which history was trying to break in. There was a "black analyst", with whom I was white and bad. There was a "white analysis", configured as a "pure" and "untainted" psychic excavation. In this register, I had a "white analyst" with whom I was also white, and with whom I could be good. Sometimes, these registers were split off and dissociated, but mostly they were interpenetrating in my transference. My analyst became two grandmothers. Sometimes, these grandmothers were both in *ambiguous* racial categories. The Jewish one was not really white (see Altman, 2000; Suchet, 2007) and the African-American one was not really black. Sometimes they were both messengers of history. One fled from Russian pogroms and left her relatives behind. In claiming her African-American identity and refusing to "pass," the other would *not* leave her people behind. These figures were in flux; they moved in and out of shadows and they morphed through time.

From the beginning of my analysis, I needed a reparative bond of identification. I needed my analyst to be an intact Bubbie from Brooklyn. I was suffering from attachment trauma. I wanted a sense of sameness with my analyst, a sameness that was both familiar and safe. *Not* our shared, female vulnerability in a sexist culture. *Not* our legacies of persecution. In the United States, race has been the foundational marker for difference, conflict, and alienation. Skin color has been a firewall between "us" and "them"; it has subverted bonding and identification. If my analyst was going to be "like me" she would have to be white. It wasn't difficult to erase racial difference, because she appeared to be white. Still, I have wondered. How did I create this Jewish Grandmother transposition, in a treatment infused with the "unthought known" (Bollas, 1986) of slavery? My analyst was young and slender and graceful, almond-eyed, olive-skinned, with long brown hair that flowed to her waist. Her posture was relaxed and erect, and she moved like a dancer. In both body and spirit, one would have said these women were opposites: my analyst didn't have Grandma's noise, or her heft or her moxy. She was quiet and gentle and receptive, and her words were chosen with care. Her empathic attunement seemed meditative and transcendent. Grandma wouldn't know from this kind of quiescence. Clearly, my analyst maintained herself on exercise and salad, not on blintzes and chicken fat. When she spoke, it was educated and articulate, without a trace of a Yiddish accent. There was no reason to think she was a Brooklyn Jew; there was every reason to think that she wasn't. Her first name was resonant with the Deep South. And yet, my seven-year-old self recognized my Bubbie. I sobbed unexpectedly the first time she went away. Every session, I watched for the changes that would presage her disappearance.

Over time, my love for my analyst became, in many ways, reciprocal, faithful and tender. But my "normative unconscious" (Layton, 2006) was also infused with cultural prejudice; it repeated hegemonic practices (Hollander, 2011), which disqualified her African-American identity. To have an *intact* maternal bond, I had to have a *white mother*. I was a white child; how could I have a black mother? Wasn't race the ultimate sign of the "not me" and the "not mine"? On the one hand, I kept reconstructing racist categories, and *excluding a black woman as a legitimate love object for a white child*. But I was also living in the switchbacks of my analyst's transgenerational past. In my analyst's name, there were echoes of the plantation: mothers in the cotton fields and on the slave blocks. They were howling, chained, beaten, reaching helplessly for their children. There were mothers searching for their children, and children searching for their mothers (Williams, 2012). There were privileged white sons and daughters of the slave masters, cared for by these slave mothers who were bereft of their own children. Then these white children grew up to enslave their nanny and her children, recycling cruelty and loss into the very heart of her attachments.

For over three hundred years, the protective maternal shield had been violated. If my analyst was black, I became white and bad. As a white child, how dared I ask her for enduring love? If I asked her to love me, would I be turning her into my "black mammy"? If I acknowledged racial difference, would I discover that her love for me was tainted with resentment and hatred? To claim her love must I become her black child? But if I were her black daughter, I would share her fate. And I could be sold to another master, howling, again, as I was separated from mother. To Fleishner (1996), the loss of the mother is the originating moment of psychic enslavement for girls born to slavery.

So it was dangerous to be my analyst's black child, and it was impossible to be her white child. Our histories were thick with transgression and loss. So, I passed my analyst, *but I never forgot* that she was African-American, and that she would not pass herself. In the folds of this paradox, I reenacted persecutory history; but I was also trying to resist, and repair, this history. By *knowing* my analyst as an African-American woman who I could *imagine* as my white Bubbie, I trespassed on my analyst's subjectivity. But in the mad thicket of race, I was also creative and insistent: I wanted an intact, and inviolable, maternal shield. In my "black" analysis, this search kept testifying to the memories of slave children:

> My mammy (recalled Fannie Moore of South Carolina) she work in de field all day and piece and quilt all night ... I never see how my mammy stand such hard work. She stand up for her chillen though. De old overseer he hate my mammy, 'cause she fought him for beatin' her chillen. Why she get more whippin' for dat dan anything else.
>
> (As quoted in Genovese, 1972, p. 499)

These memories bore witness to the ferocity of Mother, even as she was forcibly separated from her own children:

> John Randolph of Roanoke, a slaveholder himself, who had known Patrick Henry, Henry Clay, and all of the great orators of the day,

and who himself ranked at the top, was asked whom he thought to have pride of place. "The greatest orator I ever heard," he replied, "was a woman. She was a slave and a mother and her rostrum was an auction block."

(Quoted in Genovese, 1976, p. 456)

This mother is not the "dead mother" (Green, 1986) of massive trauma. This was the "Alive Mother" described by Silberg (2012) and Main (2000). Her maternal capacity was fierce and unbroken. My analyst signified those slave women who risked torture to find and protect their children (Williams, 2012), despite three hundred years of severed attachments. And my analyst signified those who sustained strong familial and communal bonds as they crossed into freedom (see Cross, 1998). In my treatment, this maternal figure is a condensation of history. She is Sojourner Truth, and Harriet Tubman, and Septima Clark, and Rosa Parks. But this mother is also a primal imago, a wish fulfillment, a fantasy of an indefatigable super-Mother, larger than persecution, abjection, sickness, separation, and death. She is a slave mother, who cannot be vanquished by the chains or by the whip. She is an obese, Russian Jewish grandmother from Brooklyn who can live forever on chicken fat without dying of a heart attack. For African-American women, this imago can repeat stereotypes. As Hine notes, it is problematic to "create myths of the super-heroic black woman who stoically met every obstacle, endured total debasement, only to rise above her tormentors and captors" (Hine, 1993, p. 340). Still, I would suggest that this phantasm lurks in the unconscious of children who have been separated from mother, by death or violence. This imago contains longing and hope; it is an exemplar of justice and human dignity. It is an archetype of what hooks and West (1991) call the "love ethic" in the Civil Rights movement and in African-American faith and resistance.

In my analyst's steadfast empathic attunement, in her refusal to pass: I felt my analyst keeping faith with this mother. And so my analyst became a "transformational object" (Bollas, 1986); she was gentle, but she had all of Grandma's strength, devotion, and moxy. If lost Russian relatives were fed inside my Grandma's body, persecuted generations were sheltered in my analyst's racial solidarity. Even as I imagined her ethnic *sameness* with Grandma, it was actually her racial *difference* that restored the maternal bond. The "unthought known" (Bollas, 1986) of slavery was actually *res-*

urrecting Grandma and repairing the wounds of history, even as part of me negated race. It was here, between knowing and not knowing massive psychic trauma (see Laub and Auerhahn, 1993) that I had the sense that,

> [w]hen the world within us is destroyed, when it is dead and loveless, when our loved ones are in fragments, and we ourselves in helpless despair – it is then that we must re-create our world anew, re-assemble the pieces, infuse life into dead fragments, re-create life.
>
> (Segal, 1952, p. 199)

My African-American analyst, my Russian Jewish grandmother: they were so different in size and temperament and history. But they *did* have an essential sameness: they had *maternal dignity and clarity and force.* They possessed a queenly grace and womanly assurance; they bore their wounds with resilience and their pain with compassion. They were fierce; I knew that *they would fight for their children.*

All of this was distilled in my transference. My analyst's gentle strength was ameliorating my depression, and restoring the "love ethic" to human connection. But for me, this love ethic was also infused with doubt. I, me, and mine: *white people* had befouled the very Mother that I longed for. This truth mirrored a more personal moment, prior to my Grandmother's death. *Grandma is in congestive heart failure. She is seated, ashen, and still, in her apartment. Grandma is never still; I can sense that she isn't well. My heart breaks for her suffering. Carefully, I approach her, my hand outstretched in tenderness. An adult voice stops me: "Don't touch. Grandma isn't well. You will hurt her." I freeze. I never touch her again, and, in fact, I never see her again. My love is forever conflated with Grandma's destruction. I am it: the bossman, the machine that severed her fingers; the Cossaks who murdered her relatives in Russia. I can make no reparation: Grandma is dead. I am caught in paranoid-schizoid splitting and in severe depressive anxiety.*

Analytic Love: Answering Shame and the Memory of Evil

In the second year of analysis, I am revisiting this memory. Once, I tried to touch Grandma's suffering. Now, I am approaching the wound of race. I know that I am experiencing transference, but I also know that, as

Holmes (2012) put it, "...there is always an external reality of race. The lived reality of race in Western culture is that it always asserts itself" (p. 268). My *personal* melancholia seems to refract Cheng's (2001) notion of "white racial melancholy." Here, I was

> ...teetering between the known and the unknown, the seen and the deliberately unseen, (where) the racial other constitutes an oversight that is consciously made unconscious – naturalized over time as absence, as complementary negative space.
>
> (p. 16)

To Cheng, this co-constructs the "legislated grief" (p. 8) and "ambulatory despair" (p. 23) that is the melancholic predicament of the racially oppressed. From her perspective, the past is not dead, it is not past, and it cannot be "gotten over." Instead, "social, political and subjective beings" must grieve (p. 7). Would this be possible in my analysis? Or would I be repudiated, struck down, again, for my destructiveness? For the "micro-aggressions" and the "micro-traumas" I may have inflicted? There was no psychoanalytic discourse in which to speak this. How could I talk about passing and not passing and the historical significance of her white skin? How could I talk without becoming the evil other of history?

Then, too, my treatment was already overflowing with *one* abandoned seven-year-old child in relation to *one* lost mother. In my family we had emigration memories: grown women, howling, as they were parted, forever, from their Russian mothers. We had Dachau memories – millions of mothers and children, separated, forever, by the gas. If race were to actually arrive on my analytic couch, Jewish cries would be amplified by the cries of African mothers, reverberating back to the Middle Passage. Such trauma is always too much to bear, and too terrible to speak (see Laub and Auerhahn, 1993; Grand, 2000; Howell, 2005, etc.). I was in a paralytic predicament, when life intervened.

My analyst is in a high-rise building; I have to take the elevator to the 26th floor. Today, in the lobby, the elevator door opens. And there, inside, is a black man, looking very "street." My heart starts to pound with terror, anticipating rape, before I can arrive at my analyst's floor. At the elevator, we stare at each other. I hesitate, and I know what he's seeing: another racist white woman, projecting violence onto an innocent black man. To reverse discrimination, I must override my panic, get in the elevator, risk what feels like certain assault. If I don't get in, what am I? He is my analyst's people. I mumble an excuse. As I turn away, I see the bitterness in his eyes. I want to cry out that I am sorry, but I just can't. I want to tell him: I was a girl, an adolescent, a young woman, on city streets. I grew up hard and fast in some rough neighborhoods; I didn't feel privileged. By 17, I was living alone. I worked in a factory, and I took college courses at night. I returned home through violent land-scapes. Men of every color have exposed themselves, chased me, threat-ened me, stolen my purse, called out obscenities, grabbed my breasts, put their hands up my skirt on crowded subways. Once, a man came to the door of my apartment, claiming to be a repairman. I knew I hadn't called a repairman. I wouldn't let him in. He went away, and raped a more trusting woman, on the next floor. I am wary, and I have eyes on the back of my head. I don't trust strange men in enclosed spaces. As the elevator closes, I want to cry out, really, it's not just because of your skin and your "hoodie."

But if he were white, and dressed in a suit, I would have taken the risk. I took the next elevator and arrived, shaken with anxiety and shame and guilt. How could I tell my analyst this? At this moment, our racial lega-cies seemed salient. I was not expecting any solidarity about women's rape-dread from a sister who also moved through city streets (see Grand, 2009). I was anticipating black rage. The man on the elevator was her brother, son, father. He represented generations of black men, falsely accused, brutalized, strung up: he was one of Billie Holiday's "strange fruit." I was trying to tell my analyst what just happened, and I told her I was having trouble telling it. She asked me about my discomfort. I squirmed and cringed, and revealed what I had always known: that she was African-American. That she looked white, and that she didn't pass. That she had been a political activist in college. I was sure she would be offended by my behavior at the elevator. She was quiet, and the moment lasted forever. Was this the end of our bond? Had I turned her into another dead mother? Then she said that I seemed very frightened, and she asked me about my fear. I said I knew it was wrong to be so terrified of his violence, just because he was black. But I just couldn't get on that elevator. She asked me about memories of sexual trespass and about my fears of black men. I told her. I couldn't believe what I was telling her: about poverty and urban violence and racial projections and all the molestations. Later, much later, I would wonder: why are regimes of power infused with the "erotics of terror" (Hartman, 1997)? How have we constructed these transgenerational "elevator moments," so that my white vagina now appears as the sacrificial site for racial repair and restitution?

But in that moment in the analysis, a miracle was occurring: I was making a racist confession, and I still felt her with me. Perhaps she wasn't gone. I was weeping, and I said as much as I could say at that time. I never spoke about the slave women crouching in the shadows of her office. I never spoke about black vaginas, held hostage to their masters. I never spoke about vaginas held hostage to white shame. I didn't link slave children's lightening skin to my analyst's ability to pass, centuries later. And I didn't talk about white children on plantations, mothered by slave mammies. I didn't talk about "miscegenation," the criminalization of interracial love, and the ubiquitous sexual predation by generations of white power. I could only talk about the racism that we had words for, at that time. It took everything I had to confess that I didn't think I could have a "black mother." I didn't think that a black mother could want me, as a white child. I confessed that I was looped into these racial categories and contradictions, when I should have been colorblind.

It seems to me now that this conversation could have unfolded over years. Inside me, this story has continued to unfold for the last 30 years. It has informed my reading, my writing, and my political consciousness. In the analysis, we could have deepened our awareness of our transgenerational ghosts: her legacy from slavery; my Russian ancestors, and the memory of Dachau. We could have talked about the condition of women that prevails during mass violence. We could have shared what it was like to be a girl on city streets – the menace and the appropriation of our bodies. But I only gave this a few, very painful, sessions. Nonetheless, I did find my courage. To love, we must be willing to know the other. I reached into my own "love ethic," as I had, long ago, as a child: *Grandma, what happened to your fingers?* I asked about her racial experience and her racial heritage. What was it like to be taken for white among whites, as they expressed racist attitudes towards blacks? What was it like to be taken as white among blacks who could not pass as white? Had I hurt her by treating her like she was white?

In those days, we didn't ask personal questions in analysis, and we didn't expect our analysts to answer. But the African-American activist broke through her more classical constraints. Her response was sensitive and reflective and cautious. She didn't reveal much, but for those times she said a lot. I was frightened to hear the truth, and awed by her trust. I kept bursting into tears. She was tender, as always, towards my fear of loss. She said, "You are afraid you can't belong to me." And: "You are afraid I see you as bad." My sobbing got deeper. And, then, I asked her about her anger at white people like me. How could she love me? Finally, she said that her life had allowed her to love lots of different kinds of people. I could hear the experience, the sadness and the compassion in her voice. She was human. Her people had been wounded, and still she was an unbroken mother. I was flawed; I was human, but I was not the agent of her destruction. She was someone real, with whom I could grieve, and with whom I could make amends.

In this moment, I recovered the truth that I had witnessed in my Grandma's hands: that abjection's memory is inscribed on women's bodies; that massive trauma forecloses mourning and keeps breaking up our bonds; that resilience can transform that history into compassion; that history's wound is not really eradicated by time; but that the maternal capacity does survive the lost generations, even though that original love has been lost. In speaking of race, this truth opened up other questions. Can healing *one* interracial bond help to heal 500 years of history? Will love ever soften my white shame, and turn my guilt into a generative force? So much was spoken between us, and yet there was still so much that would remain unspoken: the ancestral howls that haunted our relationship. African, Jewish, Russian. The recurrent breaks in the imago of Mother. The recurrent breaches of attachment, which had spanned 300 years. For that era, we had courage. But together, we returned to an intrapsychic psychoanalysis; we moved away from the ghosts of history. Like all ghosts, ours continued to speak through us.

One day, my analyst announced that she was relocating to another state with her family. After everything she knew about Grandma, and everything we had tried to repair, I found myself betrayed. Like Grandma, she had seemed to love me, and like Grandma, she was leaving me forever. She was taking her *real children, and leaving me behind.* I had six months to grieve, and for six months, I raged and wept and howled, while she kept her empathic center and weathered the storm. Once again I was standing at my Grandmother's funeral. This time I wasn't invisible. I kicked and fought. Raging, I regained cinematic memories: Grandma's hands, baking;

the texture of her house dresses, the faded wallpaper in her kitchen; her old-lady shoes and dentures; the hard candy with the soft fruity center that she always carried in her purse; her long white gloves and costume jewelry and her graceful, zaftig arms. There was her immaculate, threadbare parlor, her bedroom simple, but cascading with light. Outside that window, clothes were fluttering from clotheslines, reeled in by pulleys. Then: the tiny bungalow at Rockaway, its ancient linoleum and its paper-thin walls; the joy of sand beneath my feet, and Grandma, fanning herself on the beach. I could hear the Yiddish inflections in her speech, and I could taste her food in my mouth.

In the cinema of those memories, I retrieved another ghost: Elzora, Grandma's black maid/sister/soul mate. They were standing at the kitchen sink, moving in their fluid rhythms, cleaning dishes, one washing, the other drying, They were bustling, rotund, replicas of each other. Their heads tilted towards each other in their woman secrets; they crowed in private laughter. They were twins: bossy and nurturing, quarrelsome, formidable, generous and kind. What was Grandma doing with a black maid? She was working-class. She lived from hand to mouth. She cooked and cleaned her own apartment; she didn't have servants. If Grandma was the boss, you wouldn't know it. If Elzora got a paycheck, I don't know where it would come from. Knowing Grandma, their financial arrangement was one of urgency, interdependence, and which of them had which bill to pay when. Their intimacy was a peculiar artifact of racism and poverty and love and the strange solidarity of their widowhood and persecution. I last saw Elzora at the funeral, weeping, in a sea of white faces. Then Grandma's white sisters took up their official mourning posts and Elzora vanished. I was twice abandoned. No one could really tell me where they'd gone.

Now Elzora reappears: Grandma's truest sister, my black grandmother, whose vanishing is renewed in my analyst's departure. I am finding, and losing, both of my grandmothers. Their racial markers are becoming blurred and their racial markers are illuminated by our collective, historical truth. Before age 7, I think I was colorblind. But Elzora was a "black maid"; she couldn't be Grandma's "real" sister, and she didn't belong to our family. She resides in the deepest core of my silence, her existence occluded by Cheng's "legislated grief" and by what Patterson (1982) calls "social death." Six months later, I say goodbye to my analyst. I wail, to the very end. My termination echoes with the grief of generations and with the "sorrow songs" of slavery (W.E.B. DuBois as cited in Cheng, 2001, p. 20). Are we all fated to re-live the dislocations and disconnections of the past? Will we ever repair our legacies of violence and create a sacred register for children and their mothers?

In the end, my analyst answered my despair with hope: we could find ways to stay attached. Our attachment has morphed, and deepened, for over thirty years. The analysis has held, my depression lifted. My grandmother speaks to me, every day. Now her body is nested inside my own. Over the years, I have heard my analyst's stories about her own formidable grandmother. My analyst has continued to live by the "love ethic" of Martin Luther King, Jr. With her, I have learned that "[l]ove takes off the masks that we fear we cannot live without and know we cannot live within" (Baldwin, as quoted in hooks, 2001, p. xxv). She has never forgotten me, and she has never let go of my hand.

Notes

1 Cross (1998) has offered an interesting critique of this concept, with its implicit tendency to emphasize pathology. He makes a persuasive argument that African Americans exited slavery with considerable strengths and resilience, and that the subsequent disintegration of African-American families and communities was due to post-slavery racist conditions. See also Akbar (1996).

References

Akbar, N. (1996) *Breaking the Chains of Psychological Slavery*. Tallahassee, FL: Mind Productions and Associates.

Altman, N. (2000) Black and white thinking: A psychoanalyst reconsiders race. *Psychoanalytic Dialogues* 10: 589–603.

Apprey, M. (2003) Repairing history: Reworking transgenenerational trauma. In: D. Moss (ed.) *Hating in the First Person Plural*. New York: Other Press, pp. 3–29.

Baldwin, J. (1972) *No Name in the Street*. New York: Random House.

Bass, A. (2003) Historical and unconscious trauma: Racism and psychoanalysis. In: D. Moss (ed.) *Hating in the First Person Plural*. New York: Other Press, pp. 29–45.

Berlin, I. (2003) *Generations of Captivity: A History of African-American Slaves*. Cambridge, MA: Belknap Press.

Bollas, C. (1986) *The Transformational Object in the British School of Psychoanalysis: The Independent Tradition*. New York: Hogarth Press.

Bonovitz, J. (2012) White analysts seeing black patients. In: S. Akhtar (ed.) *The African-American Experience*. New York: Jason Aronson, pp. 377–403.

Caruth, C. (1995) *Trauma: Explorations in Memory*. Baltimore: Johns Hopkins University Press.

Cheng, A.A. (2001) *The Melancholy of Race: Psychoanalysis, Assimilation, and Hidden Grief*. London: Oxford University Press.

Cross, W.E. (1998) Black psychological functioning and the legacy of slavery. In: Y. Danieli (ed.) *International Handbook of Multigenerational Legacies of Trauma*. NY: Plenum Press, pp. 387–403.

Davoine, F. (2012) The psychotherapy of psychosis and trauma: A relentless battle against objectification. *Psychoanalysis, Culture and Society* 17(4): 339–348.

Deramus, B. (2005) *Forbidden Fruit: Love Stories from the Underground Railroad*. New York: Atria Books.

DuBois, W.E.B. (1903, 1989) *The Souls of Black Folks*. New York: Bantam Press.

Fanon, F. (1952) *Black Skin, White Masks*. New York: Grove Press.

Fleishner, J. (1996) *Mastering Slavery: Memory, Family, and Identity in Women's Slave Narratives*. New York: New York University Press.

Fletchman-Smith, B. (2011) *Transcending the Legacies of Slavery: A Psychoanalytic View*. London: Karnac Press.

Fox-Genovese, E. (1988) *Within the Plantation Household: Black and White Women of the Old South*. Chapel Hill, NC: The University of North Carolina Press.

Genovese, E.D. (1972) *Roll, Jordan, Roll: The World the Slaves Made*. New York: Vintage Books.

Genovese, E.D. (1976) *Roll, Jordan, Roll: The World the Slaves Made*. New York: Vintage Press.

Gorden-Reed, A. (2008) *The Hemingses of Monticello*. New York: W.W. Norton & Co.

Grand, S. (2000) *The Reproduction of Evil: A Clinical and Cultural Perspective*. Hillsdale, NJ: The Analytic Press.

Grand, S. (2009) Strange vaginas. *Psychoanalysis, Culture and Society* 14(1): 58–64.

Green, A. (1986) *On Private Madness*. London: Hogarth Press.

Gump, J. (2000) A white therapist, an African-American patient – shame in the therapeutic dyad. *Psychoanalytic Dialogues* 10: 619–632.

Gump, J. (2010) Reality matters: The shadow of trauma on African-American subjectivity. *Psychoanalytic Psychology* 27(1): 42–54.

Hartman, S.V. (1997) *Scenes of Subjection: Terror, Slavery, and Self-Making in Nineteenth Century America*. Oxford: Oxford University Press.

Hernton, C.C. (1965) *Sex and Racism in America*. New York: Grove Press.

Hine, D.C. (1993) In the kingdom of culture: Black women and the intersection of race, gender and class. In: G. Early (ed.) *Lure and Loathing: Essays on Race, Identity, and the Ambivalence of Assimilation*. New York: Penguin Press, pp. 35–47.

Hochschild, A. (2005) *Bury the Chains: Prophets and Rebels in the Fight to Free an Empire's Slaves*. New York: Houghton Mifflin Company.

Hollander, N. (2011) *Uprooted Minds: Surviving the Politics of Terror in the Americas*. New York: Routledge Press.

Holmes, D.E. (2012) Racial transference reactions in psychoanalytic treatment: An update. In: S. Akhtar (ed.) *The African-American Experience: Psychoanalytic Perspectives*. New York: Jason Aronson, pp. 363–377.

hooks, b. (2001) *Salvation: Black People and Love*. New York: Perennial Press.

hooks, b. and West, C. (1991) *Breaking Bread: Insurgent Black Intellectual Life*. Boston, MA: South End Press.

Howell, E.F. (2005) *The Dissociative Mind*. Hillsdale, NJ: The Analytic Press.

Jordan, W.D. (1968) *White Over Black: American Attitudes toward the Negro 1550–1812*. Chapel Hill, NC: University of North Carolina Press.

King, M.L. (1963/2010) *The Strength to Love*. Minneapolis, MN: Fortress Press.

Laub, D. and Auerhahn, N.C. (1993) Knowing and not knowing massive psychic trauma: Forms of traumatic memory. *International Journal of Psychoanalysis* 74: 287–301.

Laub, D. and Podell, D. (1995) Art and trauma. *International Journal of Psychoanalysis* 76: 991–1005.

Layton, L. (2006) Racial identities, racial enactments, and normative unconscious processes. *Psychoanalytic Quarterly* 75: 237–269.

Leary, J.D. (2005) *Post Traumatic Slave Syndrome: America's Legacy of Enduring Injury and Healing.* Milwaukee, OR: Uptone Press.

Leary, K. (1997) Passing, posing and "keeping it real". *Constellations* 6(1): 85–96.

Leary, K. (2002) Race in psychoanalytic space. In: M. Dimen and V. Goldner (eds.) *Gender in Psychoanalytic Space: Between Clinic and Culture.* New York: Other Press, pp. 313–331.

Main, M. (2000) The organized categories of infant, child and adult attachment: Flexible vs. inflexible attention under attachment-related stress. *Journal of the American Psychoanalytic Association* 48(4): 1055–1095.

Patterson, O. (1982) *Slavery and Social Death: A Comparative Study.* Cambridge, MA: Harvard University Press.

Powell, D.R. (2012) Psychoanalysis and African Americans: Past and present. In: S. Akhtar (ed.) *The African-American Experience: Psychoanalytic Perspectives.* New York: Jason Aronson, pp. 59–85.

Reis, B.E. (2007) Witness to history: Introduction to symposium on transhistorical catastrophe. *Psychoanalytic Dialogues* 17(5): 621–626.

Scharfstein, D.J. (2011) *The Invisible Line.* New York: The Penguin Press.

Segal, H. (1952) A psycho-analytical approach to aesthetics. *International Journal of Psychoanalysis* 33: 196–207.

Sharfstein, D.J. (2011) *The Invisible Line: Three American Families and the Secret Journey from Black to White.* New York: The Penguin Press.

Silberg, L.M. (2012) Ghostbusting transgenerational processes. *Psychoanalytic Dialogues* 22: 106–122.

Swarns, R.L. (2012) *American Tapestry: The Story of the Black, White and Multiracial Ancestors of Michelle Obama.* New York: Amistad.

Suchet, M. (2007) Unraveling whiteness. *Psychoanalytic Dialogues* 17: 867–886.

Thompson, C.L. (2012) The African American patient in psychodynamic treatment. In: S. Akhtar (ed.) *The African American Experience: Psychoanalytic Perspectives.* New York: Jason Aronson, pp. 337–363.

West, C. (2001) *Race Matters.* New York: Vintage Books.

Williams, H.A. (2012) *Help Me to Find My People: the African American Search for Family Lost in Slavery.* Chapel Hill: The University of North Carolina Press.

Young-Bruehl, E. (1996) *The Anatomy of Prejudices.* Cambridge, MA: Harvard University Press.

Chapter 3

When the Shadow of the Holocaust Falls upon the Analytic Dyad

Deborah Liner

One recent evening, I received a call from my 89-year-old mother, a survivor of Auschwitz. Her voice was shaking and she seemed upset, scattered, and perplexed. When I asked her what was wrong, she told me she was having flashbacks. Feeling a familiar knot in my stomach, I inquired what she was remembering this time.

"It is Mengele, his face. So frightening," she said. "And when they brought in all those people from Theresienstadt, they went through the Selection. I knew what was going to happen to them. Then we could see the fires flaming up into the sky from the crematorium."

Silence.

An image of Mengele came into focus within my mind. I felt an urge to rescue my mother and pull her out of that hell into the comforting arms of her daughter. At the same time, I felt a slight coldness in myself: the option to go numb. But these were just fleeting impulses. I reminded myself that all she really needed at that moment was a witness. So much of my professional life has centered upon the healing power of witnessing and, at that instant, it was quite easy to give her that.

With a sense of certainty, but not without feeling a pain in my heart, I said, "I know facing Mengele was absolutely terrifying. And all those people, good innocent people, they all died. It is a terrible thing. And you were able to live through it."

More silence.

Aware of my mooring in present time, I continued speaking to her: "You have been a good person and you have brought children into this world who are now doing good for others. That was all in the past. It is not happening now."

She quietly muttered "yes" and soon got off the phone. About 10 minutes later, I received another call from her. This time, speaking with vitality and strength in her voice, she announced why she had been having such a hard time. It was the 70th anniversary of the week in which she was taken from her home in Sighet, Hungary to Auschwitz.

"They took us the first week in May, 1944. Now I know why I was having flashbacks. I feel better now."

There was something triumphant about this moment for both of us. Once again, my mother had fought her way out of the iron gates of Auschwitz. I emerged from the conversation with gratitude for our ever-deepening connection, resilience, and growth so many decades following the Holocaust.

In this chapter, I will illustrate through a case presentation the complex relational dynamics emergent when both the psychoanalyst and the patient are impacted by transgenerational transmission of trauma. Specifically, the analyst was the daughter of a Holocaust survivor and the patient's father, traumatized as a Russian POW, became a Nazi collaborator. The above vignette provides a glimpse into the inner world and experiences that an analyst may bring to this type of therapy encounter. Even in this brief excerpt one can identify dynamics that may facilitate or impede the analyst's psychoanalytic functioning: a personal knowledge of trauma, desire to repair or heal, tolerance for intense affect, and also defensive mechanisms for avoiding or escaping pain. My purpose is also to demonstrate how these dynamics serve to enhance as well as challenge the analyst's empathic attunement, holding and containing functions, and ability to take interpretive action. Because a primary source of suffering for a patient affected by transmission of trauma is the unarticulated, intolerable, or dissociated affects and identifications stemming from historical atrocities (Abraham & Torok, 1994; Davoine & Gaudilliere, 2004; Faimberg, 1988), enactment may be an essential vehicle through which this material is accessed and then made available to the analytic process. To this point, I will examine an area of mutual resistance that developed between the patient and me and the process of working through, which enabled the patient to gain greater access to himself. It also provided an opportunity for further growth and healing in the analyst.

Transmission of Trauma and the Analytic Relationship

Within the psychoanalytic literature, theories have emerged to explain how traumatic experiences are transmitted from one generation to the next. These theories provide working models, or heuristic metaphors, for analysts to consider when helping patients separate from parental trauma and carve out lives of their own. Early work by American analysts in the 1980s noted that children of Holocaust survivors identified with their parents' experience of atrocity at a primitive, unconscious level (e.g., Bergmann and Jucovy, 1982; Kestenberg, 1980). These children seemed to perceive their lives in terms of their parents' histories rather than their own.

At about the same time, French psychoanalysts began to theorize about the transgenerational transmission of trauma based on notions of children's introjection of and identification with a parent's unarticulated traumas. Abraham and Torok (1994) described "encrypted phantoms" derived from parents' ungrieved losses, the ghosts or phantoms in their own minds that are subsequently entombed in the psyches of their children. In Faimberg's (1988) "telescoping of generations," the distinction between the parent's traumatic past and the child's present reality collapses through the parent's narcissistic usage of the child and consequent identificatory processes in that child. Finally, Davoine and Gaudilliere (2004) give compelling case examples linking patients' psychotic symptoms to the unspoken and secret traumas of their parents' pasts.

From the perspective of contemporary attachment theory, Fonagy (1999) suggests that traumatic ideas are transmitted across generations through the frightened or frightening caregiving responses of the traumatized parent to the infant. These unintegrated or dissociative states in the parent promote disorganized attachment patterns in the child as well as primitively organized object relations along dimensions of both exaggerated helplessness and threatening power. Halasz (2002, 2012) echoes Fonagy's viewpoint, locating the passing on of trauma in interactive moments in which the parent's alternating emotional impingements and dissociative detachment traumatize the child.

To several psychoanalytic authors, the legacy of massive trauma entails transmission of a space of psychic vacantness, void, or absence. The failure of empathic connection (Auerhahn and Laub, 1989) or lack of faith in a protective world (Gerson, 2009) occurring in the face of massive trauma leaves survivors with a breakdown in the ability to represent their experience and, thus, with a gap or sense of absence in their psyches. Laub (1998) finds that this sense of void is passed on to children of survivors, symbolized as an "empty circle," which impacts and potentially disrupts their integrative functioning in the course of psychological development. Grand (2000) identifies transmission of trauma in the "reproduction of evil," where a person may be driven to cause pain or suffering in another in an effort to make contact with a psychically absent parent who had been traumatized. The descendant's body can also become a receptacle for transmitted trauma, holding the survivor's psychic vacantness through somatic representations of bodily deadness, damage, or fragmentation (Grand, 2010). Finally, Gerson (2009) views the genocide survivor as suffering from an internalized absence or "dead third" which emerges from the absolute lack of societal concern for his or her well-being while the inhumane victimizations are perpetrated. The "dead third" is transmitted to children of survivors, engendering in them a similar sense of unremitting absence.

Problems in adjustment have been well documented in the second generation post-Holocaust (e.g., Barocas & Barocas, 1980; Grubrich-Simitis, 1984; Kogan, 2002, 2012; Levine, 1982), supporting the concept of transmission of trauma. However, there has been criticism of these formulations of transmission as being too narrowly focused on pathological sequelae in successive generations, perhaps because they were derived from clinical case studies (Mucci, 2013; Ullman, 2014). In fact, empirical studies of second and third generation effects of the Holocaust, drawn from nonclinical samples, have shown that offspring of survivors do *not* have greater psychological problems than matched comparison groups (e.g., Sagi-Schwartz et al., 2003; Sagi-Schwartz, van Ijzendoorn, & Bakermans-Kranenburg, 2008; Tytel, 1998 as cited in Ullman, 2014; Van Ijzendoorn et al., 2003). These studies find considerable resilience in this population and even evidence of better coping and adjustment in some samples (Ullman, 2014).

Ornstein (2003) argues for a more complex depiction of survivors' psychological functioning in the aftermath of the Holocaust; one that includes resiliency and capacities for agency, active resistance, and social cohesion. She sees these qualities as essential personality traits of survivors of mass persecutions and calls for future theorizing to include how parents pass on these survival attributes. Perhaps a more robust and complex understanding of the psychological legacy for the generations following massive trauma may be derived from acknowledging and integrating both the capacity for resiliency as well as the dangers to attachment, object relations, and identificatory processes that may be transmitted.

There is a limited body of literature addressing countertransference themes that emerge when descendants of survivors of massive trauma and genocide treat patients with similar backgrounds. Surveys show that therapists who are children of Holocaust survivors feel that they have greater empathy for and understanding of their patients who are also children of survivors, but also report the risks of defensive "me too" experiences (Danieli, 1984) and the blurring of boundaries with their patients (Tauber, 1998). Gampel (1998) warns of countertransference "blind spots" due to therapists' over-identification with patients in such treatment dyads.

On the other hand, recent case studies demonstrate a facilitative impact on the analyst's functioning. Davoine (2007) suggests that a dream pertaining to her own mother's internment by the Nazis for participating in the French resistance provided an essential link to family Holocaust secrets that had been plaguing her patient's psyche. Topalian (2013) reports having struggled with fears that her experiences might impinge upon the treatment, but concludes that reliving aspects of her own history as a child of an Armenian genocide survivor provided a pathway to helping her patient integrate the horrors of her family's persecution in that same genocide. While a blurring of boundaries may be inevitable when the analyst and patient have shared histories of genocide, bringing the potential for a confusion of not knowing "whose trauma are we talking about anyway," the analyst's willingness to enter this danger zone may be an aspect of the resiliency that is essential to the healing process.

Clinical Material

History: Patient's and Analyst's

Alex was a neatly dressed, fit, and attractive man in his mid-forties. His appearance gave no hint that he harbored a profound sense of inadequacy and humiliation. In our initial session, I learned that the long-sleeved shirt, with its collar buttoned high at the neck and cuffs tightly hugging his wrists, was purposely donned to conceal his severe psoriasis which, he told me, he had inherited from his father. His open wounds caused not only constant irritation and discomfort, but embarrassment and despair as well. Alex described fears that his well-appointed facade would give way to unendurable shame, exposing his psychological weaknesses and inse-curities, as represented by the red, oozing sores on his skin. As we embarked on the treatment, I wondered what stories these wounds on his skin had to tell; what identifications and unintegrated affects, and, perhaps, what secrets had to be so scrupulously hidden from view.

Alex grew up in the South, in a cottage on the estate of his parents' employer. His father was a handyman for the estate and his mother worked as the family's housekeeper. While they had been treated kindly, he regarded his parents as servants to the wealthy employer. Alex had the benefit of an excellent public school education and was admitted into a prestigious private university on scholarship. However, he dropped out after a year and eventually earned a degree while working and attending a local college part-time. I wondered again what complex identifications was Alex holding onto that kept him from taking full advantage of his academic talents and enjoying a position of privilege.

Alex's father had died several years before treatment began. Alex introduced his father to me as having been a Russian soldier turned Nazi collaborator during World War II. His father was born in Russia and orphaned at a young age. Conscripted into the Russian army during World War II, he was captured by the German forces and imprisoned in a German POW camp. With a disdainful tone, Alex told me that his father then "chose" to join up with the Germans and spent the rest of the war as a Nazi soldier. This was documented in a photo of him wearing a German army uniform, which he would occasionally pull out and display with pride. While other significant events in his father's life came out in bits and pieces, his Nazi collaboration was revealed at the very beginning of treatment, signaling how central it was to Alex's identity.

Alex described his father as extremely controlling and overbearing, insisting that his rules be strictly followed. Alex vividly recalled being harshly criticized by his father while performing required chores and he felt thwarted and vitiated by his father's incessant attacks. As Alex grew older, his interests in philosophy and the arts were not only unappreciated but often ridiculed by his father. Alex believed his father took sadistic pleasure in dominating him, making him feel inadequate "so that he could feel on top."

Stifled at home, Alex was also discouraged from venturing out. His father communicated a profound distrust of people, warning, "If they have a chance to hurt you, they will. If you are stuck in a cave with a friend, he will kill you in order to eat that worm." The message was, "Don't wander off – your only hope for safety is here at home." Alex had felt trapped in an unbearable situation. I wondered, did his father's warnings come from a man who felt like he was in hiding.

Alex's mother, a devout Catholic, was a second generation Hispanic American who had grown up in the Southwest. Described as passive and submissive to her husband and devoted to pleasing him, Alex felt that he and she were conjoined as victims of his father's aversive control. While a source of soothing and comfort for him, particularly following altercations with his father, she failed to create a barrier to his father's attacks and imposition of suffocating rules. Alex resented what he experienced as his mother's failure to protect him or to set limits on his father's aggressive and destructive behavior. He complained, "She just turned to prayer to solve our problems." While Alex looked to his mother for consolation, he ultimately felt tricked by her solace, concluding bitterly, "In the end, she always just threw me back to the wolves."

Early on, in a reverie, I pondered what this treatment would hold for me. On the one hand, the idea of contributing to the healing of a descendant of a Nazi collaborator felt like a fortuitous twist of fate that seemed to hold the promise of deeper healing for me as well. Thus, one countertransferential motive may have been the hope for repair and for affirmation of humanity in response to what my mother had endured during the Holocaust. On the other hand, I noticed hints of foreboding over what I might encounter in myself in this treatment. I recognized that my own inexpressible outrage and horror over the atrocities committed against my family would inevitably be stirred in this work. Perhaps I also sensed other conflictual affects that might be evoked from my multiple identifications with the aggressors and victims of my mother's experience in the Holocaust.

My mother survived a year in Auschwitz, knowing most of her family and community had perished there. She was not one of those silent survivors. She shared happy memories of more carefree moments before the threats of the Nazis dominated her existence. But she also told me of the

nightmare of her transport to Auschwitz, her struggles to survive the concentration camp, the suffering during the death march, and her painful three
years in a displaced person's camp before she was allowed to immigrate to
the U.S. These were the fairy tales with which I grew up, including all
requisite components: terrifying, evil villains; threats of death and annihilation; cunning and strength on the part of a young woman protagonist; and,
finally, a reunion of a few loved ones and renewal. Sometimes, in my fantasies, I would place myself in these stories: hike with her in the forests of
the Carpathian Mountains or stand with her, hungry and cold, outside her
barracks in Auschwitz for the many hours it would take the for the SS
guards to count the prisoners each day, making sure no one had escaped.
Was this my way to remain close to her, to protect her in fantasy, to be a
witness for her? Transmitted into me from these stories, aided by *Life* magazine's photographic essay on Auschwitz, were vivid images of Nazi perpetrators and concentration camp victims.

Given the overlap in Alex's and my family histories related to the
Holocaust, and how they were manifested in transference and countertransference, the issue of the analyst's self-disclosure in the case is
brought to the fore. During the treatment, as Alex explored the meaning
for him of his father's Nazi past, images and themes from my mother's
Holocaust experience would often come into my mind. There were
numerous occasions in which I considered disclosing my family's Holocaust history to him, for the purpose of exploring underlying transference-
countertransference dynamics. However, I took my cues largely from
Alex, who often experienced contact and difference as excruciating and
damaging. I had the sense that to self-disclose would have felt impinging
and would have interfered with Alex's access to aspects of himself and
what he could express in the therapeutic relationship. I, therefore, decided
against disclosing my family's Holocaust history.

A Painful, Porous Contact Boundary

At the beginning of treatment, Alex's focus was on the discomfort, dis-
figurement, and despair caused by his psoriasis. I sought to understand
the psychological meanings of this painful skin condition. The raw, open
wounds on Alex's skin were discussed as metaphors for his damaged
sense of self-cohesion and painful interpersonal relationships. He feared
people could "see through him," certain that his feelings of inadequacy,

emotional hunger, and rage would be exposed to others, like the redness of his skin. He imagined his emotions oozed out of him, like hideous pus from grotesque wounds. Emptied, he was passive and paralyzed, longing to be "fixed by someone else." Repeatedly, Alex expressed his wish that I repair what was broken inside.

The autoimmune aspect of Alex's physical condition was mirrored in his emotional world. As his immune system attacked his skin cells from within, rendering even gentle touch painful, so too his own internal attacks upon his character were so abrasive that most interpersonal contact caused him exquisite pain. Caring and constructive contact from friends felt like harsh reproaches. My interventions, even the mildest of queries or empathic reflections, were experienced as pokes, prods, and scrapings against his psychic skin. This message, that I was repeatedly wounding him with my therapeutic efforts, led me to tread very lightly with him. Undoubtedly, my countertransference need to protect a wounded mother also contributed to my caution with Alex.

The Complexities of History

Alex associated his persistent sense of woundedness in relationships with his connection to his father. Exploration into these dynamics revealed an extremely strong tie to an internal representation of his father as a brutal, punitive other, in relation to whom Alex represented himself as subjugated and victimized. The emotional linkage between the self and object representations was a sense of despair, powerlessness, and inadequacy.

During this early period, I obtained new information outside of treatment that provided some potential meaning behind Alex's belief that he "had no choice in life." This pertained to the terrible plight of the Russian POWs during WWII. Stemming from centuries-old rivalries between Germany and Russia, the Nazis considered the Slavs an inferior race to be eradicated, along with Jews and other designated ethnic groups. The lives of Russian POWs were therefore extremely harsh, and the likelihood of death from starvation, maltreatment, or outright murder was very high. Once captured, many Soviet soldiers were given the choice of either collaborating with the Nazis or facing death.

Learning this piece of World War II history, I wondered about Alex's narrative of his father's "decision" to collaborate with the Germans. Alex had portrayed his father as the sadistically cruel and imposing parent; a man, as Alex once remarked, capable of "joining the enemy in order to enjoy the momentary power of being part of the German war machine." He did not seem to be very interested in this new information. However, for me, an alternate view of his father now came into focus – that of a man who was victim to the inhumane conditions that the Nazis imposed, a man possibly forced to make horrific choices for the sake of survival. I could now understand his father's brutality at home as emanating, at least in part, from his identification with the aggressor, his defense against the overwhelming helplessness and fear of annihilation that he faced at the hands of the Germans.

In thinking of his father as both victim and collaborator, I sought to hold a more complex image of him than Alex had been able to entertain. Perhaps, though, I was a bit too eager to strip Alex's father of his Nazi uniform. Was it too overwhelming for me to contemplate that his father had genuinely valued his position in the German army with its efficiency, complete power, and control? Or even that he may have committed atrocities? It was not uncommon for former Soviet POWs to be stationed as guards at concentration camps. While I contained many complexities for Alex; in the countertransference, I may have needed to view his father as a victim in part to avoid my feelings of horror, outrage, and very deep sadness over my family's victimization. I could thereby protect my connection with Alex from being disrupted by these feelings.

Those Left Behind

Next, it was Alex who brought new information into the analytic space that would shed light on the strong hold his father's past had on him. In the context of expressing hopelessness over ever feeling better, Alex explained, "The big message from my father was that things can go wrong. You can try to control things but mistakes may haunt you for the rest of your life." I asked if he thought his father was haunted by mistakes. Alex reflected upon this idea and described the following experience from his father's life. His father had a wife and son whom he left behind in Russia. After the war, having collaborated with the Germans, he could not return to Russia because he could have been shot or imprisoned as a traitor. Thus, he never returned home, and never found out what happened to the family who remained there.

Alex learned this horrific piece of his father's history from his mother. His father never spoke to him about it. Alex lived oscillating between knowing and not knowing about his father's devastating loss, vacillating between recognizing and denying its impact on him. He first insisted, "This happened but it has nothing to do with me." However, in response to my further inquiry, Alex elaborated on what had been transmitted:

> "My father's actions don't fit into this world, I know, but you can't help but pick it up. It's hard to distinguish between his world and my world. The world gets transposed. The voice of my father says 'Life isn't nice. No one says you'll find good out there. You expect to get attached to something. It could be taken away.' The loss was looming and it was the threat of it that filtered through him. The terror is there in me. It's my father's worldview that bled into me but it doesn't make sense. It is shapeless and timeless.... I was told to be afraid, I was trained to be afraid."

Yet, in his next breath, Alex's denial resurfaced:

> "If I admit to having feelings about it, I'd have to find out about him. Didn't you care? Didn't you feel guilty? Feeling is not what it's about. You have somewhere to live and sleep. You know where to be every day. That's it."

The transmission of Alex's father's psychic void, his internalized "empty circle" or "dead third," is evident in Alex's narrative. It was clear that his father's loss was ever present. However, as an unassimilable psychic rupture and an unarticulated family secret, Alex had not been able to hold this tragedy in awareness and comprehend its impact on him.

Hearing about the choice that haunted Alex's father, my reveries took me to the story my mother told me of a choice she made during the Holocaust that had haunted her for decades. When my mother first arrived in Auschwitz, all the prisoners had to line up to face "Selection" by Dr. Mengele. Mengele decided who was fit to go to the labor camp and who would immediately be sent to death. In finding her position in line, my mother made the conscious decision to go first, in front of her own mother. She reasoned that as a healthy young woman she was more likely to be allowed to live than her mother, who was in her mid-forties, an old lady in Auschwitz terms. By going first, my mother believed her fate would be determined separately from that of her mother's and, further, she would not feel compelled to choose to accompany her mother to the gas chambers. Despite their both being allowed to live, my mother has felt guilty over this imagined abandonment of her mother, and her own assertion to survive, ever since. Yet, it seems that this act of survival had taken on the meaning for her of an identification with the aggressor, thereby generating a perpetual sense of survivor's guilt.

Perhaps there was something that Alex and I shared by having a parent who was haunted by choices made for the sake of survival. In taking such action, both parents may have used identification with the aggressor as a defense against overwhelming affects under the threat of death. Subsequently, each seemed to have held onto a sense of horror over their identification with the aggressor, unconsciously transmitting to the next generation, to Alex and me, a sense of horror at our own identification with the aggressor.

Facing the Persecutor – Intergenerational and Inner Self-Representation

Over time, Alex began to shift his focus more inward and to register the intolerable anxiety our work together had tapped. For him, lying on the couch was like "diving into a freezing dark pool. You can't soften the shock of what's going to be found out." Placing me in his mother's position, Alex wished that I would magically transport him out of this foreboding place. On the other hand, I was also represented as the hurtful, critical, and over-demanding father. From this object relational configuration, he experienced me as the one who was inflicting the pain through my inquiries. This dynamic came to a head when he likened me to a Nazi doctor who took pleasure in causing torturous suffering.

Alex's accusation fell quite heavily upon me. In my mind, he was essentially regarding me as "Mengele" (the Nazi doctor). After shaking off the intrusion of an image of my mother and grandmother facing Mengele upon entering Auschwitz, I searched for evidence of my contribution to Alex's transference. I identified some feelings of frustration and irritation at Alex's victim stance, which I understood as stemming from my difficulties with my mother's helplessness or my identification with this aspect of her. Further, I entertained the possibility of unconscious retaliatory feelings towards Alex related to the Holocaust.

As I reflect upon this moment in the treatment, a salient complex emerges. On the one hand, I was able to maintain a holding stance and to inquire further into Alex's perceptions of me and into the familiar associations that ensued pertaining to his father. On the other hand, I was aware of feeling constrained and inhibited from intervening in ways that would be more challenging for Alex, such as raising the idea of his projection of aggressive feelings or pursuing his fantasies regarding his impact on me. I believe that my inhibition at this time was part of an enactment that had developed from the convergence of my childhood response to my mother's traumatic victimization and Alex's sense of being victimized in therapy. I would have the opportunity to revisit the persecutor–victim dynamics between us in the not too distant future.

Despite this enactment, our analytic work continued to progress. Alex's tolerance of his affective states grew stronger, as evidenced by a series of dreams in which he did step into that "dark, freezing pool." In the first dream, he attacked and overpowered a Nazi who was holding him captive. In the second, his siblings killed his mother and dismembered her, and he helped them cover up the crime. Alex's associations focused on his aggression towards his father, represented as the Nazi, and towards his mother, who was cut into pieces and hidden away. In his associations, Alex elaborated on how the aggression depicted in both dreams reflected his efforts at separating from his parents.

The last dream in the series confronted Alex with the identification that he deemed most unacceptable. In this dream, he looked into a mirror and saw himself wearing a long black leather coat. His associations led him to the black leather trench coats that were typically worn by the SS, the armed wing of the Nazi party. He was horrified at seeing himself as a Nazi, exclaiming, "It's like I've put on my father's mantle!" I offered that perhaps he associated the anger that had been emerging for him in therapy with being a Nazi. Together, we explored the distinction between his father's destructiveness and his own feelings of anger, furthering his work of separation and individuation.

Having a Life of One's Own

Thus mobilized, Alex began to make concrete changes in his relationships. He invited his mother and siblings to participate in monthly family therapy sessions, wanting to engage in honest interchanges with them

about his father and his family life growing up. He insisted that his girlfriend at the time enter couples therapy with him, in an effort to get out
of the masochistic position he had taken with her. As his conflicts with
his girlfriend intensified, Alex contemplated ending the relationship and
used the analytic space to explore his fears of being on his own.

While I was away on August break, Alex broke up with his girlfriend.
He initially felt quite solid and accomplished in taking this action.
However, the old self-representations and object ties soon reasserted
themselves. He proclaimed that he was "damaged goods, with only the
possibility of joining up with someone else who was equally flawed."
Similarly, he complained, analysis was a failure. I had tricked him, set
him up, encouraged him to "knock the house down" and then left him
alone, with nothing. When asked to elaborate on why I would have
wanted to sabotage and undermine him, Alex associated me with his
father whom he saw as the ultimate model for sadism, taking pleasure in
his son's failings so that he could feel superior. According to Alex, I, too,
had taken sadistic pleasure in things not working out for him. This time,
when I searched inside, I failed to find resonances with his accusations. It
seemed clear that Alex had taken decisive action, and yet needed to
disown his assertion, experiencing it in the transference as aggression
coming from the outside turned against him.

This encounter with Alex was quite different from our previous
victim-persecutor episode. The narrative was constructed in terms of
Alex's personal past as opposed to a maniacal World War II figure. In
addition, despite his protests over having to cope with the aftermath of
the break-up, Alex seemed to be stronger and more resilient than he had
been earlier in the treatment. It was time for me to interpret Alex's victim
stance as a defense against his aggression.

Delivering such an interpretation, however, required that I revisit the
earlier session in which Alex had accused me of being like a Nazi doctor
and thus gain a deeper understanding of my inhibition and the enactment
that had ensued. Looking back, it was apparent that Alex's depiction of
me had reverberated with aspects of my own identifications that were
clearly unsettling for me. As a child, knowing that my mother had been
so traumatized by the Nazis, I defended against my aggressive feelings
towards her. I realized that Alex's likening me to a Nazi doctor had
bumped up against vestiges of my conflating my aggression with Nazi
persecution, my assertion with my horror at identification with the

aggressor. I now understood the enactment as having been constituted, at least in part, by a collision of Alex's and my own concerns about identification with the aggressor. With this awareness, I was able to lift the barrier I had constructed against posing a potentially valuable interpretation to Alex. Reassured that I would not harm Alex, not be a Nazi to him, by saying the very thing he did not want to hear, I could now give back some of what I had been containing for him.

Soon the opportunity arose to point out to Alex how his feelings of contempt and aggression may underlie his victim stance. Contrary to my expectations, he became curious: "Perhaps I don't really know the depth of my contempt." He described his father has having been steeped in contempt.

> "His parents died, he lived in an orphanage, goes to the army, they are fuckers in the army, teams up with the enemy, fuck they are the loser, so he goes with the Americans and then it is fuck this country."

And then he elaborated on how his own daily experiences are permeated with contempt, how he blames others rather than takes responsibility.

Alex got it. He neither crumbled nor experienced me as wounding him. In the sessions that followed, together we unraveled how the roles of torturer and victim were played out between us. He felt encouraged. "If being a victim is something I map onto relationships, it is something that I can change."

We had arrived at a turning point in the treatment. As the analysis moved forward, we continued the work of disentangling Alex's assertion from identifications with his father's aggression and his mother's submissiveness. Alex occasionally cycled through periods of wanting me to fix things for him, but more readily identified his anxiety with differentiating himself from his family and was able to explore his burgeoning sense of agency. Further, he began to relate to his psoriasis more as a condition to be managed by medicine and lifestyle, and less as a signifier of the need to retreat from interpersonal contact or a marker of his embodiment of his father's shame and suffering. He also seemed more comfortable with himself in my presence. Alex soon entered a relationship with a woman who genuinely desired him and, having been promoted at work, bought his own property upstate, symbolizing a further distancing from his parents' indentured means of living. Perhaps most poignant, his preoccupation with what his father had done during the war faded. This aspect of his father's history seemed to have lost its grip on him and upon me as well.

Conclusion

In this chapter, I presented a case illustration of the complex interplay of identifications and transference/countertransference dynamics that can operate in the context of a treatment in which both the analyst and patient are impacted by transgenerational transmission of trauma. In such a case, the overlapping of inner worlds of transmitted trauma facilitates understanding and attunement on the analyst's part, but also contributes to "disturbances in the field" (Cooper, 2010), which must be overcome in order for analytic progress to occur. During more than six years of psychoanalysis, the patient's treatment addressed assorted conflicts and concerns, including immobilizing identifications with his mother, thwarted ambitions, and inhibitions of sexuality and desire, among others. However, for the purposes of the present discussion, I have focused on aspects of his analysis related to conflicts integrating aggression associated with his father's traumatic legacy. This was approached through holding, containment, and interpretations geared at differentiating the patient's own affective experience from his father's destructive inclinations and his father's identification with the aggressors of Nazi Germany.

A pivotal point in the treatment occurred with the resolution of an enactment that had arisen out of the collision of transmitted persecutor and victim identifications within the analytic dyad. Harris (2009) calls attention to the contribution of the analyst's object ties, which may contain elements of transgenerational transmission of trauma, to analytic impasse. By identifying the transgenerational roots of my constriction in analytic functioning, I was able to help the patient overcome his own inhibitions stemming from similarly transmitted concerns over identification with the aggressor. The treatment proved to be transformative not only for the patient but for the analyst as well, furthering both of our efforts to heal from the Holocaust.

At this time political, religious, and sectarian wars continue worldwide. Further research is needed to understand demographic, sociopolitical, and cultural influences on the transmission of trauma, so that treatments may most effectively promote recovery and repair in varying geopolitical contexts. In addition, it is important that we gain more insight into the interplay between factors of resiliency and vulnerability in the aftermath of persecution and violence. As psychoanalysis and psychotherapy continue to be disseminated globally, descendants of people who have been exposed to massive trauma and atrocities and descendants of the perpetrators of violence may meet, in various combinations, in psychotherapeutic treatment encounters such as the one discussed in this chapter. Further investigation into the complexities of psychoanalytic treatments in which the patient and the analyst have similar and overlapping backgrounds of genocide or massive trauma is a crucial component of future psychotherapy research.

Postscript

Alex's Commentary on the Case

At the conclusion of this case study, the reader may be wondering what thoughts Alex may have privately entertained about my family background during the treatment. He was aware that I was Jewish because I consistently rearranged our scheduled appointments around the Jewish holidays. While Alex expressed curiosity about what I might have been thinking or feeling about him during our sessions, he was not one to probe for information about my personal life. Despite our frequent conversations about his father's life during World War II, he did not inquire into my Jewish identity and he never raised a question about whether or not I was connected to the Holocaust in any way. Had such a possibility ever occurred to him?

Meeting with Alex several years following termination to obtain informed consent for publishing this paper, I was afforded the opportunity to explore this question with him. However, the process of following professional guidelines for publishing case material (American Psychological Association, 2010) placed me in an ethical conundrum. My decision not to raise my family's Holocaust experience with Alex during the analysis emerged from the negotiation of conscious and unconscious processes between us, especially my clinical understanding and formulation of Alex's needs within our relationship. By giving Alex access to this paper, he would be exposed to the many countertransference issues I revealed as well as gain direct knowledge of my mother's

Holocaust experience and my identification as a "child of a survivor." I had concerns over what impact this personal information about me would have on him and questioned whether I should risk altering his consolidation and integration of our analytic work together by sharing such material with him.

My worries about exposing Alex to the contents of this paper were assuaged by offering him several sessions, without fee, to process his reactions afterwards. Somewhat flattered by my interest in writing a paper about his treatment, Alex was eager to make a contribution to the field of psychotherapy, as he similarly had done in medicine by participating in clinical trials for his psoriasis. He seemed confident and at ease sitting in my office with me and showed none of the trepidation that he had exhibited in the past upon approaching the couch.

Alex began by expressing appreciation for our work together and reported that he was satisfied with his life as it had evolved in the arenas of both love and work. Referencing the animosity he had felt towards his father during the analysis, Alex volunteered that he had come to acknowledge and accept that some of his more valued qualities had in fact been derived from his father. He had apparently continued to engage in fruitful integration of his image of his father in the years following termination.

Alex read the paper in my office while I sat quietly nearby. Emerging from reading the narrative, he was visibly moved by my description of therapeutic containment. "I never thought about you holding all this," he said. "When you are on the couch, you don't think that someone is holding on to all of this hideous stuff for you."

I asked Alex if he had ever thought about how the Nazi content of our sessions impacted me. He replied, "I did not let myself think about it and would not have asked you about it. I was there to get fixed."

Finally, Alex had a very clear idea of what his response would have been to learning of my mother's history during the treatment:

> "It would not have been good for you to have brought it up. I would have censored myself and it would have spoiled things. I needed to get all this shit out without any concern for you. I needed you to be the doctor who could help me."

Whether Alex actually could have constructively used knowledge of my background may be a matter for theoretical debate. However, his conviction that such knowledge would not have been helpful echoed what I felt he had implicitly communicated to me during the treatment.

As the present case illustrates, when both members of the analytic relationship are impacted by intergenerational transmission of trauma, the analytic field can become a complex holding ground, a treacherous meeting place, for the patient's and the analyst's identifications with lost family members, sadistic torturers, prisoners faced with horrific choices, and victims striving with every ounce of their psychic and physical energy to just survive. While posing countertransference challenges, the trauma-related identifications that are evoked in the analyst may also provide vital links to the patient's internal objects, and thereby become integral to the process of reconfiguring the patient's inner world.

Alluding to the almost alchemical quality in our unique analytic pairing, Alex observed during our last follow-up session:

"Taking this as a literary text, the fact that two people with this background, this terrible history, can meet and make something good happen, is incredible … I wonder whether it would have gone as deep with someone who did not have your history."

References

Abraham, N., & Torok, M. (1994). *The shell and the kernel: Volume 1*. Chicago: University of Chicago Press.

American Psychological Association. (2010). *American Psychological Association ethical principals of psychologists and code of conduct*. Retrieved from www.apa.org/ethics/code/principles.pdf.

Auerhahn, N., & Laub, D. (1989). Failed empathy – A central theme in the survivor's Holocaust experience. *Psychoanalytic Psychology*, 6, 377–400.

Barocas, H. A., & Barocas, C. B. (1980). Separation-individuation conflicts in children of Holocaust survivors. *Journal of Contemporary Psychotherapy*, 11, 6–18.

Bergmann, M., & Jucovy, M. (1982). *Generations of the Holocaust*. New York: Columbia University Press.

Cooper, S. (2010). *A disturbance in the field: Essays in transference-countertransference engagement*. New York: Routledge.

Danieli, Y. (1984). Psychotherapists' participation in the conspiracy of silence about the Holocaust. *Psychoanalytic Psychology*, 1, 23–42.

Davoine, F. (2007). The characters of madness in the talking cure. *Psychoanalytic Dialogues*, 17, 627–638.

Davoine, F., & Gaudilliere, J. (2004). *History beyond trauma: Whereof one cannot speak, thereof one cannot stay silent*. New York: Other Press.

Faimberg, H. (1988). The telescoping of generations: Genealogy of certain identifications. *Contemporary Psychoanalysis*, 24, 99–117.

Fonagy, P. (1999). The transgenerational transmission of holocaust trauma: Lessons learned from an adolescent with obsessive-compulsive disorder. *Attachment and Human Development*, 1, 92–114.

Gampel, Y. (1998). Reflections on countertransference in psychoanalytic work with child survivors of the Shoah. *Journal of American Academy of Psychoanalysis*, 26, 343–368.

Gerson, S. (2009). When the third is dead: Memory, mourning, and witnessing in the aftermath of the Holocaust. *International Journal of Psychoanalysis*, 90, 1341–1357.

Grand, S. (2000). Loneliness and the allure of bodily cruelty. In S. Grand, *The reproduction of evil: A clinical and cultural perspective* (pp. 21–39). Hillsdale, NJ: Analytic Press.

Grand, S. (2010). Intrepid subjects: Rescuing lost generations. In S. Grand, *The hero in the mirror: From fear to fortitude* (pp. 135–152). New York: Routledge.

Grubrich-Simitis, I. (1984). From concretisim to metaphor: Thoughts on some theoretical and technical aspects of the psychoanalytic work with children of Holocaust survivors. *Psychoanalytic Study of the Child*, 39, 301–319.

Halasz, G. (2002). Can trauma be transmitted across the generations? In Z. Mazor, F. Konig, A. Krammer, H. Brod, & W. Witzlisz (Eds.), *The legacy of the Holocaust: Children and the Holocaust* (pp. 210–219). Cracow: Jagiellonian University Press.

Halasz, G. (2012). Psychological witnessing of my mother's holocaust testimony. In N. Goodman & M. Meyers (Eds.), *The power of witnessing: Reflections, reverberations, and traces of the Holocaust* (pp. 145–158). New York: Routledge.

Harris, A. (2009). You must remember this. *Psychoanalytic Dialogues*, 19, 2–21.

Kestenberg, J. (1980). Psychoanalyses of children of survivors of the Holocaust: Case presentations and assessment. *Journal of the American Psychoanalytic Association*, 28, 775–804.

Kogan, I. (2002). "Enactment" in the lives and treatment of Holocaust survivors' offspring. *Psychoanalytic Quarterly*, 71, 251–272.

Kogan, I. (2012). The second generation in the shadow of terror. In M. G. Fromm (Ed.), *Lost in transmission: Studies of trauma across generations* (pp. 5–20). London: Karnac Books.

Laub, D. (1998). The empty circle: Children of survivors and the limits of reconstruction. *Journal of the American Psychoanalytic Association*, 46, 507–529.

Levine, H. (1982). Toward a psychoanalytic understanding of children of survivors of the Holocaust. *Psychoanalytic Quarterly*, 51, 70–92.

Mucci, C. (2013). *Beyond individual and collective trauma: Intergenerational transmission, psychoanalytic treatment, and the dynamics of forgiveness*. London: Karnac Books.

Ornstein, A. (2003). Survival and recovery: Psychoanalytic reflections. *Progress in Self Psychology*, 19, 85–105.

Sagi-Schwartz, A., van Ijzendoorn, M. H., & Bakermans-Kranenburg, M. J. (2008). Does intergenerational transmission of trauma skip a generation? No meta-analytic evidence for tertiary traumatization with third generation of Holocaust survivors. *Attachment and Human Development*, 10, 105–121.

Sagi-Schwartz, A., van Ijzendoorn, M. H., Grossman, K. E., Joels, T., Grossmann, K., Scharf, M., Koren-Karie, N., & Alakaly, S. (2003). Attachment and traumatic stress in female Holocaust survivors and their daughters. *American Journal of Psychiatry*, 160, 1086–1092.

Tauber, Y. (1998). *In the other chair: Holocaust survivors and the second generation as therapist and clients*. Jerusalem: Gefen.

Topalian, S. (2013). Ghosts to ancestors: Bearing witness to my experience of genocide. *International Journal of Psychoanalytic Self Psychology*, 8, 7–19.

Tytel, T. (1998). Trauma and its aftermath: A differential picture of aftereffects of trauma in daughters of Holocaust survivors. Ph.D. thesis, New School for Social Research, New York City.

Ullman, C. (2014). The personal is political, the political is personal: On the subjectivity of an Israeli psychoanalyst. In S. Kuchuck (Ed.), *Clinical implications of the psychoanalyst's life: When the personal becomes professional* (pp. 98–111). New York: Routledge.

Van Ijzendoorn, M. G., Bakermans-Kranenburg, M. J., & Sagi-Schwartz, A. (2003). Are children of Holocaust survivors less well-adapted? No meta-analytic evidence for secondary traumatization. *Journal of Traumatic Studies*, 16, 459–469.

Part II

Political Legacies, Encrypted Hauntings

Introduction

Confronting the Other Within

Kirkland C. Vaughans

It is with a sense of great appreciation to be asked to write the introduction to these four very moving, challenging, and informative papers on collective, historical, and state-sponsored traumatic oppression, as well as the resulting intergenerational transmission of that trauma. These authors represent a new wave of psychoanalytic thinking that challenge the criticism made by Bulhan (1985) that castigate psychoanalysts as: "Uninterested bystanders in the history and status quo of oppression. On the contrary, establishment psychologists have not only been active participants in social oppression, but also silent beneficiaries of many of its privileges" (p. vii).

Such a privileged status may also constitute a fundamental barrier to understanding the traumatic legacy of the other and serve as a motivation for our continuing to "other" them. This barrier also serves a containing function against knowing one's own collective traumatic past. It therefore seems to require that we reach beyond the immediate social milieu of our patients and that we must come to understand the present as well as the particular historical context from which both the analyst and the patient have come through. This stance then precludes any pretext of neutrality. The authors in general document the impact of horrific events across generations, the traumas are in the words of Seeley (2008): "Like phantom limbs that can still be felt even though they no longer exist" (p. 1).

It is also evident that none of these conceptual depictions of trauma are given any clinical credence in the *DSM-5*, however, by all historical indications perhaps they will be included in the *DSM-10*. All of the authors give recognition to having been in one way or another impacted by historical or collective trauma of their own era. These authors conspicuously avoid common sentiment and moralistic posturing that would eliminate the possibility of their personal reckoning, as well as that of a psychoanalytic understanding. These authors through their narratives take us on very personal and traumatically stressful journeys that require incredible courage, self-reflection that speak to opportunities of social liberation.

They all seem to echo Bettelheim's (1984) remark, "What cannot be talked about can also not be put to rest: and if it is not, the wounds continue to fester from generation to generation" (p. 166). Bettelheim's comment mirrors the analysis of Franz Fanon, the psychiatrist from Martinique who studied the effects of Black oppression, who argued that it was not simply the body that had been imprisoned but also the psyche had become colonized by the oppressor resulting in a non-articulated social melancholy (Oliver 2004).

Throughout these articles the powerful case is made on the clinical necessity of confronting the other within ourselves, as well as learning from those that we have Othered. In order to consider such an undertaking, one must be prepared for the fury with which such an undertaking will unbridle of one's own fragmented sense of self. This is no simple intellectual exercise or clinical feat and can result in painful dissociative and confusing states of mind. It is only through such interpersonal engagements that the unknowable and the unspeakable can become known. According to Kakar (2014) anything less invites the dangerous illusion of minimizing his personal cultural impingement into clinical scenario. What the clinician needs is not "cultural competence" in the patient's cultural background but an "awareness of the assumptions underlying his own, that is the culture he was born into and the culture in which he has been professionally socialized as a psychoanalyst" (p. 28).

One of the very unfortunate results of trauma is the sense that our lives are left without meaning or purpose. These chapters illustrate that broken ties can be mended in order to move from a sense of being socially disposable to that of being a member of the family of the community.

References

Bettlelheim, B. (1984). Afterword to C. Vegh, *I Didn't Say Goodbye*. New York: Dutton.

Bulhan, H. (1985). *Franz Fanon and the Psychology of Oppression*. New York: Plenum.

Kakar, S. (2014). *Culture and Psyche*. New Delhi: Oxford.

Oliver, K. (2004). *Colonization of Psychic Space*. Minneapolis: University of Minnesota Press.

Seeley, K. (2008). *Therapy After Terror: 9/11, Psychotherapists, and Mental Health*. New York: Cambridge University Press.

Chapter 4

The Demonization of Ethel Rosenberg

Adrienne Harris

Introduction

On Saturday June 20th, 1953, my father announced, without warning or explanation, that I was not to read the newspapers on that day. The Toronto *Globe and Mail*, the *Toronto Telegram*, and the *Toronto Star* for that Saturday, summarily disappeared from the house. As a 12-year-old avid reader and student, I had a vague idea that this unexplained but draconian prohibition had something to do with death. I remember hunting through later editions of the newspapers, my father's sanctions having made me actually now anxiously curious.

The material he sought to shield me from was the account of the death in the electric chair, of Julius and Ethel Rosenberg, an execution that took place in Sing Sing, a prison in the town of Ossining along the bucolic Hudson River. After a number of years of trials, appeals, protests, and passionate argument about spying, the Cold War, and the death penalty, and a final last ditch attempt to stay the execution, the Rosenbergs were executed early on a Friday evening (8 p.m.), designed in a stunningly insensitive but surely not unconscious move in relation to the Sabbath (which would begin at 11 p.m.). This occurred as the state pursued the death of this couple relentlessly and despite a massive international movement arguing for clemency and basic justice.

Now after half a century and a life both of activism, of protest, of feminism, and of psychoanalysis, I can see that this trial and execution was a sequence of events, unfolding with inexorable horror, that marked the generation of the Rosenbergs' peers but also my generation, the cohort of their children, Robert and Michael, who were 6 and 10 respectively at the time of their parents' deaths. The arrest, trial, and execution of the Rosenbergs is the dark center of the postwar Cold War and McCarthyism hysteria that swept America. Black lists, jobs and pensions lost, careers destroyed: these casualties are simply the most visible. The toll on the physical health, mental health, and on the psychic and political resilience of the wide spectrum of progressive persons who would have felt at risk is probably incalculable, certainly very far reaching.

The Cold War historian Ellen Schrecker (1999) describes the tactic of intimidation and hostile surveillance that dogged thousands of progressive and left wing Americans after the Second World War. At the heart of that activity was the execution for espionage of Julius and Ethel Rosenberg. Although others were suspected or even known to have passed information, no other arrests resulted in the death penalty or in execution. These deaths were the horrifying specter that caught the heart and mind of anyone on the left in that period, probably anyone even mildly progressive. This seems to have been, as many have argued, the government's intention.

At the time, these events were highly traumatic, marking the consciousness of progressive persons worldwide. In this chapter I want to pursue the idea that these events cast a long dark shadow, operating at both conscious and unconscious levels. I believe that for my generation, the 1950s, including these events and these executions, are much more determinative than we had imagined. I include in this generational roll call people engaged in anti war activism, civil rights work, second wave feminism, gay liberation, coming into political consciousness in the 1960s and 1970s, with the eruption of anti war protest and identity politics.

Even as the politics of the 1960s, cultural and more traditionally political, were seen as a break for freedom, as explosive change and cultural transformation, I think this tragic and difficult postwar and Cold War past followed us, haunted us, entered mind and heart, led us, and accompanied us. *Nachtraglichkeit* is the filter through which to see the impact of these events. Looking back at the context of the Cold War and postwar repressive environment and looking forward to the 1960s and the activism of civil rights, anti war work and feminism and gay liberation, the linked worlds of Old and New Left, I see the persistence, the reverberations, and the pervasive reach of this trial and these deaths. It might be better to think of the notion of caesura (Bion, 1962; Civitarese, 2008) to describe and frame the experience of continuity and discontinuity between the decades of the postwar and the years around and after 1968.

I am tracking intergenerational transmission of trauma at a social and cultural level, a pervasive climate of anxiety and surveillance and control that entered individual consciousnesses at deep and often unconscious levels. I think this period begins shortly after the end of the Second World War and continues into the 1960s. The degree to which these executions reached and entered the consciousness of many North American citizens, regardless of their political sensibilities, says something about the deep reach of the state, the capacity of the government to upend normalcy, family, decency, democracy, and the rule of law in the service of state power. This lesson was deep and sure and, given the anxiety-filled quality of life in the 1950s, particularly its anxious conformity, one sees how well this lesson worked.

There was one overwhelming message to progressives, to immigrants, to Jews, and to women, emergent from the relentless pursuit and murder of this couple, in particular, the wife in this couple, Ethel Rosenberg. It was a brutal and clear warning to shut down any political activism, to give up radicalism, progressive politics and, most crucially, the Communist Party. I think my personal story and the persistence of memory of these events is not at all unique, however it is personal. I am increasingly sure that the underground, less obvious anxieties of the postwar Cold War period are, to an important degree, bedrock for my cohort's consciousness as a feminist, and bedrock to progressive political activism generally.

Two other concepts might be helpful here. Apprey (2015) writes about the unique presence of errands in the unconscious experience of individuals who carry out tasks for which they were often unaware they were marked and bidden. Apprey, I think, is bringing together *nachtraglichkeit* and *interpellation* to describe an errand targeted in the future but also, however it appears to be found, it has already been undertaken.

Abraham and Torok (1994) call these 'encrypted identifications'. While these kinds of processes are primarily thought of as transmissions within families, it seems useful to imagine these errands as often social and collective in their effect, even while remaining often unconscious in their transmission. Andrea Ritter (2011) has written about the understanding of intergenerational transmission of trauma in Hungarian psychoanalysis since Ferenczi and notes that there, it was important to notice the effect of collective trauma in which individual traumatic transmissions were embedded. She cites the work of Veres who looked at the impact on very early archaic attachments, on the deep both paranoid and compensatory need to keep children safe, often at the expense of their individuation, when there was ongoing collective trauma. Each setting will have its own level of collective trauma, of course, and North American life has not been stained with the fascist and then totalitarian regimes that lasted half a century in Europe and in Russia. The Cold War period (and the postwar adjustment and reorganization) has its own character. In particular, I would say, this overriding frightening world of state control penetrated the consciousness of many political movements across many kinds of projects (anti war, racism, identity politics, women's rights, etc.). We might see the ongoing presence of collective trauma in contemporary crises around race and around the safety of women.

From the world of political science, Guralnik, Guralnik & Simeon (2010), and others have brought into psychoanalysis Althusser's concept of interpellation. The execution of the Rosenbergs and the demonization of Ethel Rosenberg are forms of interpellative claim, an address from the state to citizen subjects that instructs, dictates, and in that process makes a subject. The subjects thus constituted, may resist, but will also transform the warning into a command, sensing, accepting, and also refusing and ignoring the dangers both predicted and already taken place.

The Rosenbergs' Trial

The arrests and prosecution followed a usual course. A grand jury was called and in the aftermath of the testimony of about 40 persons, including Ethel, both Ethel and Julius were indicted on charges of espionage. The trial began on March 6th, 1951. Ethel's brother and his wife (David and Ruth Greenglass) gave testimony implicating Julius primarily and thus both the Greenglasses were immune from prosecution. They had a new baby.

Political appeals and strong pleas for mercy were mounted. The newsreels often pictured the young Rosenberg children going to and from Sing Sing. One photo clip from the period shows them arriving at prison wearing Dodger caps. Perhaps these were conscious strategies linked to the appeals for humanity, and for clemency, by rendering the Rosenberg family human and American while the state built a picture of vicious, alien, Communist (and Jewish) criminals.

The trial and the political period in which it was set was dominated by figures like J. Edgar Hoover and Joseph McCarthy and by a junior figure who became a violently conservative and repressive figure in American political life, Roy Cohen. The hatred of civil rights and gay rights and left progressive thought was virulent in certain parts of the larger culture but exemplified and embodied in these men. That we now know that Cohen and Hoover were also closeted gay men only adds to the sense of alienation and confusion. Some of this alienation is captured in Tony Kushner's *Angels in America*, which in presenting the tragic heart of the AIDS epidemic in the 1980s, brings together the 1950s and the 1980s, the Cold War, and the social and medical tragedies of AIDS in a scene when the specter of Ethel Rosenberg arrives at the deathbed of Roy Cohen, dying of AIDS. A ghost, a visitation, a hallucination: this is *nachtraglichkeit* in action, the re-remembering and reconstituting of continuous traumatic effects even where we remember only isolated and fragmentary slices of history.

Amidst these intense political debates and battles of image and word, the Rosenbergs themselves remained silent. It was generally believed that Ethel was on trial, convicted, and under a death sentence in the hopes that the couple or at least she would break and name names. Neither one gave names. The many abuses and misuses of evidence in the trial and the passionate determination of the state and the government to convict and prosecute the Rosenbergs occupied historians and political theorists for decades. Much of the evolution of thinking about the Rosenbergs appeared in the wake of the Rosenberg children, named Meeropol for their adoptive parents, who emerged from obscurity to speak on their parents' behalf and to write a book *We Are Your Sons* (1986).

To go back to that June Saturday in 1953, I of course hunted down a newspaper and read with great agitation a terrible account. Julius was executed first as it was said that he was weak and fragile emotionally and Ethel was stronger in temperament and more emotionally robust. I will return to this idea later.

I do remain puzzled as to what had alarmed my father. What was this? We were in Canada, a thousand miles from Sing Sing. My father was not at all political in any way I might discern. He was a veteran, marked by his time in the war, and yet, also, full of charm, easy going, more normally a newspaper reader of box scores and baseball stats. I think my father was expressing what must have been a pervasive feeling of horror, some deep, visceral fear triggered by the reports in press, radio, and movie news of the circumstances surrounding the execution of Ethel Rosenberg, a botched job that led to a gruesome and horrible death.

I think my father was reacting to the grotesque details of that execution, details that were, at the time, widely distributed. The decision to make these lurid and ghastly details public would have remained in the hands of the state, which had just discharged the execution. That decision surely was part of the politically motivated project of terrorization. As a result of repeated administration of electricity, and because she was too small for the equipment she was attached to, her death was slow and laborious and a grisly mess of smoke and burnt flesh. Ethel Rosenberg was almost literally burned at the stake.

Ethel Rosenberg

About Ethel's constructed place in this story, there is increasingly less and less confusion. At the time of the trial, some observers took her silence for disdain and wickedness; her husband's was seen as more enigmatic. Not initially arrested, she was by the time of the trial and certainly in the aftermath increasingly and bizarrely seen as the lynchpin, the wicked witch of Communism.

In retrospect, one sees how so many details of the prosecution and the trial were calculated and very often invented. A key element that figured in the trial was a jello box, which the prosecution claimed had been used as a signifier and identification mark for communications and meetings by the spies. There was no such box ever found so Roy Cohn held up a model jello box by way of illustration, but clearly also a way to insert a fabricated piece of evidence. It was a box of red jello. Think of this jello box as an element in a dream. This simple kitchen product, this simple American product, is used to pervert and attack America. I would read the deep agenda here as the project to identify and accuse and criminalize the immigrant, Jewish (jello was decidedly not kosher), Communist (red jello), and female (the domestic worker). Slowly, inexorably the woman comes to personify betrayal.

In looking more closely at how Ethel was positioned both in the legal discourse and in the public space, I see that Ethel is taken up as a projective object in many ways. Martyr, demonic woman secretly in control, mother, saint. Half a century of exposure to political analysis and opposition and decades of psychoanalysis have barely given me tools to think about the long shadow of that event in 1953 my father had wished to shield me from.

One crucial question underlies this chapter. What does it mean that Ethel Rosenberg is transformed from a very minimal figure on the sidelines of the espionage ring, to the center of the conspiracy? What cultural trope is at work here? Just prior to the execution, Eisenhower wrote to his son: "she is the vicious one." When trying to explain his refusal of clemency, Eisenhower spoke privately to his son. "She is strong minded, the apparent leader. It is the woman who is the strong and recalcitrant figure, the man who is the weak one."

Yet, it was widely known by all – both the members of her family and the state agencies that pursued her – that her involvement was slender, minimal. The FBI note on her is "in delicate health, not involved in the 'work' " = code word for espionage.

Retrospectively we see how doomed she was. In 2008, the transcript of the grand jury testimony was released following a lawsuit brought by a number of historians who wanted to understand better the evidence that undergirded the prosecutions. Scrutinizing the testimony of 36 of the 46 people called to the grand jury, as many had suspected, testimony about Ethel's involvement to the grand jury was fragmentary and on its own would not have led to an indictment.

The crucial testimony is that of Ruth Greenglass (Ethel's sister-in-law, a party member and someone with a code name in the Soviet documents on US spying, which the US had already decoded). In Greenglass' *grand jury* testimony, Ethel is a shadowy figure on the edge as the two couples feel the FBI closing in and wonder, hopelessly, where they might flee to. In the trial, both Greenglasses name Ethel as the typist of the notes the conspirators were drafting. Ruth Greenglass was in fact a typist. After his release from jail her husband David Greenglass, who had testified at the trial that Ethel was the typist, acknowledged that he had changed his testimony to protect his wife at the expense of his sister and apparently under guidance from the prosecution.

The damage however was clearly done. Transformed between the grand jury testimonies of the Greenglasses to a whole new level of involvement in the actual trial, Ethel Rosenberg begins on the edge, liminal, and in the end is toppled over the precipice into the inferno. Certainly informed about what was going on, she is never even named in the decoded spy manuals which the US already knew of (called the Venona documents). Interestingly, some commentators noted that jurors found Ethel Rosenberg's silence a sign of disdain and criminality, not dissociated shock. From the onset of her crisis, she is already not the right kind of woman.

Intergenerational Transmission: In the Culture and in the Family

This chapter and several talks I have given in the last five years were composed explicitly in reaction to the moving documentary *Heir to an Execution*, made by Ivy Meeropol, the granddaughter of Julius and Ethel Rosenberg and the daughter of Michael Meeropol, their older son. The intergenerational transmission of trauma, the wound of history that I am writing about here is a collective and social trauma as well as a wound with multigenerational elements in the Rosenberg family. I am going to focus on intergenerational trauma that is cultural and social as well as familial.

The execution of the Rosenbergs was a tragedy within a family, as Ivy's film *Heir to an Execution*, shows, but the trial and execution of the Rosenbergs and the period of repression and fear that surrounded those events shaped a postwar generation, silenced political and progressive thought, creating what Bion would call – K, the collapse of thought.

The film, the granddaughter, we the audience, we ask the question that is perhaps not fair and certainly not answerable. Technically, we ask this question of both the Rosenbergs, but upon deeper excavation I think we mostly direct it to Ethel. Was it worth it? What is worth dying for? Why did you leave your children? There are many different positions as speaker and as addressee and many assumptions (perhaps some of them naïve) about agency and about gender that run through these questions.

It is striking that both in the hands of the state and in our queries several generations later, Ethel's femininity and her maternality are the site of criticism and sanction. It is not just the state that demonizes Ethel Rosenberg, but indeed for almost everyone she carries the stigma of the rebellious woman (whatever her character actually was), a woman who could fail her children.

Were the Rosenbergs simply and fatally caught? Or is there any way to see their fate as chosen, as deliberate? In respect to Ethel Rosenberg's situation, we come quickly to the difficulty, some might say the impossibility, of female agency and the certainty of maternal responsibility, certainly in that historical period, and even now a continuing question.

The feminist sociologist, Gilda Zwerman, wrote a dissertation (1997) looking at 1970s-era women on the left, particularly far left and often violent focused groups (Weathermen, May 19th). What she found were radical politics in relation to the state and political life and deeply conservative stances in relation to gender.

I have always thought that the split in women who did or did not enter far left movements had something to do with feminism, with the politics of self interest and not the politics of guilt. By many accounts, women in the Communist Party in the pre and postwar era had very difficult paths. Zwerman's sample of 1970s women radicals showed that these women often had longer sentences than men in similar circumstances, were more likely to lose children, paying, in short, a very steep price.

Zwerman was struck by the discrepancy between gender politics and other radical ideology, a contradiction that fatally compromised the Weathermen and other far left groups for many men and women. This is always a hard question to approach. It is easy to see the sexism, the hatred of women capitalized and used to inflame popular sentiment against the Rosenbergs with a focus on the evil of the woman. But there is also the sexism with which the Old Left and the New Left was riddled. Could one see Ethel Rosenberg in this light? In this way, we might see Ethel Rosenberg as a spectral figure in the conscience and consciousness of many generations of political and socially conscious women. She is a medium, a lightning rod for an intergenerational transmission of sexism (regardless of politics) in which a woman is dangerous if strong, failed if nonmaternal, and endangered by any belief in the conventions of gender (quietness, loyalty, or perhaps obedience).

I think of Ethel Rosenberg as an iconic object. Part of the iconography is her actual death, the attack on the body, the violence of this execution. Julius' image is much more abstracted. Enigma remains. Her impassive face and posture were apparently read by the jury as indication of a vicious character. Julius' managed expression was not read in this negative and sinister light. I see the impossibility of this woman's stance here. In thinking about the intergenerational transmissions of trauma within multiple cultures and subcultures one might see the pervasive contempt and hatred of women and the violence of the state's suppression of dissent as a kind of funeral dirge, music in a minor key that floats or rolls just under the surface of awareness.

Second wave 1970s feminism opens the portal on that pervasive low and high-grade violence. We are very accustomed to our naming and finding of sexism and repressive forces in the culture before the 1960s, but to read of the rhetoric of the radical 1960s groups (Echols, 1989;

Alpert, 1973, Sales, 1973) write powerful unsettling accounts of the internal and social and gender politics of the left in these eras is to find stunning evidence of the potent demeaning of women that dominated the practices of those groups. Yet another form of unconscious transmission despite the official and potent voices in women's liberation.

When I think of the genealogy of lost women in this history of the left, there are figures in the Old Left that I do not know but in the 1960s I think of Diana Oughton, a young woman, caught up in the Weathermen, a woman who is blown up when she and other Weathermen are building bombs in a townhouse in NYC. Similarly, another figure from that incident was later arrested for a politically motivated robbery in which policemen were killed. That woman, Kathy Boudin, and her partner, then served long and in the partner's case ongoing prison sentences. They undertake that action while also the parents of a 14-month-old child.

These narratives were repeated in European leftist movements in the 1960s (Baader Meinhof, Red Brigade) in very similar patterns. While there is some writing and some filmmaking on these experiences of women in the extreme and often violent forms of left wing politics, these ideas mostly stay under the collectively attuned radar. Can one not ask of all these figures what Ivy Meeropol wanted to ask: How could you leave your children? And recognize, even in our advanced era of feminist analysis, it is a question addressed more usually and centrally to the mother.

Perhaps inevitably, the horror and danger that this execution posed for progressive thought and action backfired. Even if only at an unconscious level, everyone, I feel, understood something of the danger of such power and so, perhaps inexorably, the seeds of transgression were sown as well as those of conformity and fear. At a personal, familial level, precisely because my father tried to shield me, I remember every detail and in a certain way, that moment at the age of 12 was the point at which, I see retrospectively, I experienced a first encounter with state-imposed terror. Sixteen years later, to me and many young people, opposition to the US actions in Vietnam made terrible sense, binding us in a geneology. Ethel Rosenberg also sits in that geneology.

I believe that we were a generation for whom the executions in 1953 would have been primarily part of unconscious transmissions delivered within families and within the larger culture. Left wing families would have felt this most acutely. Perhaps tragically, perhaps rightly, I think that, as a generation, we could not knit together the Old Left of the 1950s and the anti war movements in the 1960s. These integrations across generations were activated but not without tension. Some aspects of the Rosenbergs' execution and perhaps some struggle in regard to the Communist Party and its often contradictory impact on individuals may be operative here. How well did families and children's interests fare in the zeal for political work is a controversial and painful subject. I think of Bion's concept of the caesura (Bion, 1962; Civitarese, 2008), the site of gaps and crossings, the place where experience is both continuous and discontinuous. The gap between the 1950s and the 1960s cultures is one such space.

For the generation coming into political consciousness in the 1960s, the Rosenbergs' actual and figurative children, the emergent political structures were infused and spoiled by the preceding generation's traumas and triumphs. We were living immersed in the tides of oppression and state terror that had been operating since the end of the Second World War and we felt the impossible divides between that fearful world and our own hypomanic one. Into this moment of caesura, the memory of those harrowing days intrudes.

Heir to an Execution

Ivy Meeropol's documentary plays out these matters in a familial context. She makes a documentary to ask the questions that would have been perhaps unaskable by the Rosenbergs' children. Why did no family member (Julius had a number of siblings) step forward to care for the children? And later in the film, daringly, she asks why did Ethel not save herself for the sake of her children?

Why did Julius and Ethel not make that decision together? Did they make their decisions freely? Where were the rest of the families? She pursues these questions in dialogue with many of the Rosenbergs' allies and comrades from the 1950s and the prewar heyday of the Communist Party. She pursues it within her own family. It is however striking that the question about the fate of and damage to the children is asked most acutely in relation to Ethel.

Four moving scenes stand out for me, in an overall deeply heartfelt and brave film. There is an early scene in which two of the grandchildren, one a lawyer and one the filmmaker, stand in the empty courtroom in NYC where the trial took place and the lawyer grandchild confesses that as a young person growing up she sometimes imagined that she would have been the lawyer at their trial saving them. Talk about an errand.

Later in the film, there is a scene shot in LA where Ivy meets up with a long-lost, never before met cousin, a grandson of one of Julius Rosenberg's sisters. They begin to talk and suddenly both of them are weeping. The LA cousin is confused. He feels ashamed and guilty, he says. He is carrying the agony and guilt of his mother who had declined to step in after the execution and take in the orphaned boys.

There is another striking moment when the two brothers, now men in middle age, go to visit the apartment on the Lower East Side from which first Julius and later Ethel were arrested. This would have been the last place where the family lived together and so the last site of memory of parents who could function as a place of safety. Michael is animated and talking fast. Robby moves through the spaces in a state of what I would term dissociation. One understands the hot spots from where trauma is initiated and the dissociative process that guarantees it will be transmitted under the radar of consciousness.

Late in the film there is an interchange that I want to consider in the context of intergenerational transmission of trauma. It is a moment in the film, which I realize, over the years of thinking and writing about the death of the Rosenbergs, I have never been able to integrate. Ivy Meeropol is interviewing a colleague and ally of the Rosenberg, Miriam Moskowitz, a woman under dangerous attack for her wartime and political activities. Moskowitz was indicted for giving aid to the Rosenbergs and served two years in prison. Ivy poses a question. It is *the* question. Why didn't Ethel save herself? She had children, Ivy Meeropol presses on. Moskowitz is agitated but firm. "It is an impossible question. It could not be. You cannot ask that question."

It seems clearer that the question, unaskable, is asked and asked again. We can wonder why this is asked only in relation to the mother. Unspeakable, unassimilable guilt and sadness is carried and buried in the question it is impossible to ask and equally impossible to ignore. The question and the painful affects such a question carries is part of the intergenerational legacy that is carried in progressive American (and international) circles. How do you carry the personal and the political? There is a long lineage and legacy of the impossibilities and necessities for women in political and social action and the meaning of political action for women still embedded in patriarchy.

Encrypted Secrets, Mandated Errands

I have come to feel that that pronouncement: "It is an impossible question" marks a place where trauma remains locked in. I have thought about
this increasingly as I have been researching the trajectory of other figures
in that period and the challenges they faced. When Morton Sobell, a man
convicted along with the Rosenbergs, but not sentenced to death, came
out of prison, he toured to promote a book he was writing. The Meeropol
sons were supporting his efforts and so we arranged that Sobell would
come to my university in Toronto to speak. He was impressive and also
so clearly marked and injured by years in prison. He wanted to take his
moment of exposure and speak about prison reform. He did not re-open
the matters that sent him to jail. He wanted, he said, to continue a progressive line of opposition to oppressive acts and now for him these
involved men and women in prison. In Ivy Meeropol's documentary, he
is very old. Clearly suffering the aftereffects of a stroke, still he remains
enigmatic about guilt or innocence. Only scant months before his death
does he speak about his involvement in espionage. What is being
avoided, buried, and also recalcitrantly rising into awareness?

I want to end with my current best thoughts on what the silences, late
stage confessions, refusals, gaps, and absences carry. I suspect among
many of the period of the trials and the 1950s at varying degree of closeness to the situation must be carrying overwhelming amounts of guilt.
Survivor guilt in particular. I think this process can be tracked in thinking
about the Rosenbergs' choices, or their powerlessness. It has to be seen
in the context of two other couples intimately implicated in their story.
Ethel's brother and sister in law become the fatal weak link in the
network of spies, the ones finally the FBI can break. Many motives have
been suggested here, most visibly that Ruth Greenglass had only recently
given birth. When Ivy poses the question of his parents' choice to
Michael Meeropol in the film, he turns the question back to his daughter
the filmmaker. What would that have been, how could they have acted
differently? Would you want to be the Greenglasses? Unthinkable. Yes
but we know that everything unthinkable is always also being thought.

There is another couple in this long saga, a more recently visible set of
players in this tragic story. There was an atomic spy who remained at
liberty, sheltered in England at Cambridge in the postwar era whose
widow has recounted their lives within this time period. The man's name

is Ted Hall. He was the youngest scientist at Los Alamos, recruited into the party by his Harvard roommate and involved in espionage and passing atomic secrets and key scientific data to the Russians on what he defined as moral grounds. Unlike David Greenglass who was a very low-level techie, he was a ranking scientist and would have had serious data to deliver. His argument was that there should be no secrets in science and that these secrets would lead to dangerous assymetries in politics. He continued to manifest these views for the rest of his life.

There is interestingly a position within the American left that argues the role of the passing of information about the atomic bomb actually improved the chances of peace. Staughton Lynd:

I am a lifelong advocate of nonviolence. When I first read John Hersey's *Hiroshima*, I was horrified. But I believe the argument could be made that to whatever extent Fuchs, Gold, the Greenglasses, and one or both Rosenbergs hastened the development of a Soviet atomic bomb, it may have tended to preserve the peace of the world during the crises of the Cold War.

(Lynd, 2011)

Here is Ted Hall's obituary from *The Guardian* (December 19, 1999):

Theodore Hall was the American atomic scientist discovered by the United States authorities to have been a wartime Soviet spy – but who was never prosecuted. The information he gave Moscow was at least as sensitive as that which sent Julius and Ethel Rosenberg to the electric chair. The Americans decided not to charge Hall because of the security and legal difficulties. With the tacit consent of the British security authorities, Hall spent more than 30 years as a respected researcher at Cambridge University until he retired in 1984, aged 59.

Here is an excerpt of an interview with Joan Hall describing the evening of the Rosenberg's execution.

We watched from the sidelines in horror.... We had been invited to a gathering at the home of a colleague of Ted's in Westchester. We were driving up from Queens where we lived. The road took us parallel to the Hudson River past Ossining the town where Sing Sing

Prison is. It was eight o'clock [the time of the executions] as we drove by. The sun was setting.... I absentmindedly switched on the radio and believe it or not, they were broadcasting the last movement of Mahler's Ninth Symphony, a farewell symphony which is some of the most sad, heartbreaking music that exists. So we rode along listening to Mahler and watching the sun go down and feeling indescribable. We didn't say anything, not a word.

(Joan Hall, 2002 interview)

There are many ways to parse this material. It seems oddly dreamy and certainly quite dissociative. This couple, so clearly implicated in the activities for which the Rosenbergs are being executed, at that very moment, find themselves drifting down the Hudson River past Sing Sing. Uncanny would be the mildest term one might muster.

So, we can see the challenges and terrors of the 1950s period of repression and state crackdown. McCarthyism and the power of HUAC to control individual and collective destinies was very entrenched in the postwar period. I have been arguing that our history both as citizens and as analysts was shaped by the 1950s. That period, characterized by the collapse of freedom to think, the danger of activism, would take several decades to repair. In ways that psychoanalysts understand very well, it has been hard to even see what was missing.

A Thought Experiment

In that context, let me close with a thought experiment. Three couples. All three active in progressive work, committed in varying degrees and ways to opposition to the state. Two couples are limited by funds and resources and unable to flee. One couple turns states evidence and their testimony is instrumental in the death sentence imposed and carried out on the Rosenbergs. One couple remains silent, stoic, and this stance costs them their lives. One couple, believing in the need to share scientific information, and not to make power so asymmetric by having secret weapons, remain 'at liberty,' are protected by the very state groups that might have persecuted them and live 'normally' as productive scientists and educators. They literally drive by the site of the Rosenbergs' execution, despite their moral stance about freedom of access to scientific data. All had young children at the time of the Rosenberg arrests.

Perhaps, even this account endows more agency than was actually ever really in play. Perhaps imagining choice is an illusion that somehow these decades of state surveillance and management have not dispelled for many of us. Were the Rosenbergs simply and fatally trapped? Is there a way to see their fate as choice? Regarding Ethel Rosenberg, I find myself always at the same conclusion: the impossibility of female agency and the certainty of maternal responsibility, in that historical period, on the left and on the right, and a bedeviling question to this day. It haunts Ivy Meeropol's film and her quest.

I ask the reader a different but related question than the one Ivy Meeropol posed and Miriam Moskowitz refused. What would you have done? Which path would you have trod? Would you be silent? Silent on principle or for reasons of self-preservation. Would you sacrifice others to preserve safety and family for your children? Or does the state remove these questions, make them ridiculous? Alternatively, is there a critique of the role of the Communist Party in certain kinds of doctrinal demands. Was this family sacrificed? Many people, growing up in the culture of the party, surmised deeply that children always came second. Or second at best. Gilda Zwerwin found the protection of family low on the priorities of women in extreme far left movements whom she interviewed. Is this conflict part of our traumatic intergenerational legacy whether it is generated out of the attacks by the state or by Stalinist practices on the left, or by a political vocation to fight oppression? Something like these moral and existential dilemmas led Levinas (2005) towards a concept of our responsibility to the other. How would that look in this context?

References

Abraham, N. and M. Torok (1994) *The Shell and the Kernel: Renewal in Psychoanalysis.* Chicago, IL: University of Chicago Press.

Alpert, J. (1973) "Mother Right: A New Feminist Theory." *Ms* Magazine. August.

Apprey, M. (2015) "The Pluperfect Errand: A Turbulent Return to Beginnings in the Transgenerational Transmission of Destructive Aggression." *Free Associations: Psychoanalysis and Culture, Media, Groups, Politics* 77: 15–28.

Bion, W. (1962) *Learning from Experience*. London: Karnac.

Civitarese, G. (2008) "'Caesura' as Bion's Discourse on Method." *The International Journal of Psychoanalysis* 89: 1123–1143.

Echols, A. (1989) *Daring to be Bad: Radical Feminism in America*. Minneapolis, MN: University of Minneapolis Press.

Guralnik, O. & Simeon, D. (2010). Depersonalization: Standing in the Spaces Between Recognition and Interpellation. Psychoanalytic Dialogues, 20: 400-416.

Guralnik, O. (2014). The Dead Baby. Psychoanalytic Dialogues, 24: 129–145.

Hall, Joan. (2002) Interview. www.pbs.org/nova/venona/. February 5, 2002.

Levinas, E. (2005) *The Humanism of the Other*. Urbana, IL: University of Illinois Press.

Lynd, S. (2011) "Is There Anything More to Say About the Rosenberg Case?" *Monthly Review* 62(9), February.

Meeropol, R. and M. Meeropol (1986) *We Are Your Sons*. Urbana, IL: University of Illinois Press.

Ritter, A. (2015) "Theories of Trauma Transmission After Ferenczi: The Unique Hungarian Contribution." *Canadian Journal of Psychoanalysis* 23(1).

Sales, K. (1973) *SDS*. New York: Random House.

Schrecker, E. (1999) *Many are the Crimes: McCarthyism in America*. Princeton, NJ: Princeton University Press.

Zwerman, Gilda. (1997) "Participation in Underground Organizations: Conservative and Feminist Images of Women Associated with Armed, Clandestine Organizations in the United States," in *International Social Movement Research* Volume 4. Ed. Donatella Della Porta. London, England: JAI Press.

Chapter 5

The Endurance of Slavery's Traumas and 'Truths'

Janice Gump

Conveners of the Wounds of History Conference asked participants to address the manner in which our forebears' traumas continue to shape our lives, haunting our psyches, relationships with others, and cultures. The African Americans' most agonizing traumas occurred during slavery, and through intergenerational transmission continue to cause pain. Given the endurance of racist modes of thinking and relating, however, African Americans must contend not only with what has been bestowed, but with present forms of racism as well. I shall discuss the wounds of slavery as well as the compounding of those wounds through contemporary racial insult.

When we think of the oppression of Africans and the genocide of Indians, African Americans and Indians are the subjects of such reflections. But as we all know, it is whites who brought these traumas about (Frankenberg, 1993; Grand, 2015; Sterba, 1996), and the values and psychologies which made those acts possible need to be understood as well. It is not just that such attitudes and behaviors determined actions toward the noted groups in the past: these values and behaviors have determined whites' perceptions of reality (Frankenberg, 1993), now as well as then.

Whites too have suffered trauma, and just as generations of African Americans and Indians were impacted by their traumas, so too have generations of whites been affected by what they endured.

Finally I contend that this history has been one of the elements determining white males' management of painful affects.

All of us, then – whites, Indians, blacks – have been determined by trauma, even if in different ways and to differing degrees. Moreover, to a large extent, this effect has taken place in unconscious processes. For example, while African Americans are clear about racism and know something about slavery, to a large extent we are unaware of how lasting and determining its traumatic effects have been. And whites to a large degree are unaware of the manner in which their fundamental beliefs constrict and distort their thinking. I am concerned with what both groups don't know, not only of the other, but of themselves.

In the midst of preparing for the Conference I was reminded I had agreed to respond to a paper which, it turned out, was due at the same time. The paper was a thoughtful discussion of Lynne Jacobs' white privilege (2014). That's interesting, I thought, but what did white privilege have to do with African Americans, with me? Well, quite a lot, I discovered.

The fact of the two deadlines proved serendipitous; for it was in the process of writing the first paper that I discovered a certain repair of self, and a clue to the question of speaking across difference. I will share some of that paper with you.

The paper on privilege evoked memories of my days at the University of Chicago Laboratory School. Four African Americans, of whom I was one, integrated the 6th grade. It was the beginning of an intellectual journey which opened the world to me, and which brought about aspects of my life I can't imagine living without.

As the years went by I came to be deeply puzzled by the comparative confidence, light heartedness, and what, at eleven, I thought of as happiness in my white friends. What did they know that I did not? Was that difference due to their socio-economic class, to their parents? And might I come to possess what was so effortless for them?

I could see differences between our parents, our homes, our financial resources. I was pretty certain my parents were more burdened. My mother could be short, was critical, and seemed always to have more to do than she could manage. But my friends' parents weren't always "nice." They lived in houses largely near the University, we in an apartment in the black part of town. Both my parents were highly intelligent, had had some college, though never obtained degrees. But my feelings about class were largely assuaged by knowledge of how that difference had come to be.

My father's vocational options had been severely constricted by racism. I heard stories, as on occasion I slept in their bed until my father came home from the night shift. In hushed tones (they thought me asleep), he would relate the trials of a Negro janitor amongst white factory workers, many of whom had just migrated from the South, all of whom held jobs from which he was barred.

It is not the stories I remember, but my father's somber voice, my mother's rapt attention, and affects hovering like presences in the darkened room: tension, anger, fear, a kind of wonderment, a profound solemnity which perhaps was grief, and a helplessness evoking a profound dread. Those experiences were like none other in my childhood, so grave, so grown-up, so disturbing were they. They transmitted information about the danger of the world, from whom it might flow, and how destitute we might be before it.

Was rage too dangerous? Or had it simply been displaced, because we, his family, certainly experienced it.

I could not metabolize what was being done to my father. How could a man *this* intelligent, *this* good looking, *this* civilized be treated so abominably? Only at the end of his career, when he became the first African American vice-president of a major brewery – Anheuser Busch – was his work level appropriate.

Perhaps my father's severe depressions should be attributed, as my mother did, to what-it-meant-to-be-a-black-man in this country in the 1930s and 1940s. But what had been the impact of being sent from Montgomery, Alabama, his home, to San Francisco at the age of eight, for in California he might obtain an education and exposure denied him in Alabama? He was to live with an uncle, a porter on the railroad who was therefore rarely home. The owner of the rooming house in which they lived refused the role of substitute mother.

Somehow my father largely raised himself. A local Jewish shopkeeper, the owner of a small store my father frequented, asked him if he was being given supper. Dad must have said something like "sometimes," for the shopkeeper instructed him what amongst his snack-like offerings might be more nutritious than potato chips.

And what of my mother's depressions? The one I recall most keenly occurred when my brother and I were quite young, though there are briefer memories of later ones, when she would take to her bed and cry, and my brother and I would stand at her bedside imploring, "Don't cry, Mommy, don't cry"? To what could they be attributed?

At sixteen she had emigrated from Little Rock, Arkansas to Chicago, where she had come to live with her older sisters. I don't know if her mother accompanied her at the beginning, but at some point she was present in her daughters' homes as well. Prior to this relocation, one of my grandmother's married daughters had become pregnant. She lived in the South, and no hospital would accept her. She gave birth, and died. Whenever it was that my grandmother came to Chicago, she brought with her her depression, undoubtedly caused by many factors. The depression deepened, and she was "put in an insane asylum." After a period of time she was found strangled on her bed. It could not be determined if she had purposefully wrapped a sheet around her neck, or if it were an accident; murder as the cause of her demise was not mentioned. I learned of the nature of her death through my cousin: my mother had told me none of this.

As I wrote I was impressed as never before with the severity of my parents' wounds. I had known my father's history since I was a child, but now something was different. With the gift of the paper on privilege, the reading it inspired, and my understanding of trauma, I could speak to that child within who could be assuaged neither by good grades, when she got them, or leadership. That child had decided there must be something wrong with her. There was, but it was not due to some mysterious, inherent deficiency, the shamed child's assumption. In this country, with its history and that of her parents and ancestors, there was no possibility she could have been happy, light, or carefree, as were her white peers. This history and the affects it aroused provided me with insight I had not previously possessed.

My analyst, singularly aware, in part because he was Jewish, and in part because he was highly sensitive to the social and political surround, taught and led me through much. His greatest gift was his holding, which made it possible for me to feel a depth of pain my life had been constructed to deny. But neither he nor I could appreciate the trauma that infused my life.

With an enhanced understanding of trauma's impact, Jacobs' (2014) depiction of her large and small fortunes enraged me. Perhaps it was the comparison of our innocent childhoods. I was faced with a chasm of difference. *Could* I bridge this gulf enough to write? It didn't take long to realize that my anger and its aftermath were gifts.

I had known and written of slavery (Gump, 2000, 2010, 2014) but now I could imbue that knowledge with affects previously less available. I shall share some of my thoughts and feelings with you.

The Wounds of Slavery

A violent disruption with all he had known initiated the African into slavery. Men, women, and children were kidnapped and forced on often long marches to the sea. There, in holding camps, they awaited the slave ships. A black journalist wrote not long ago of his visit to one of these dungeons, where he could still feel the dampness of the dirt floors, be frightened by the oppressive darkness, and assaulted by the foul smell.

The Middle Passage followed:

> They were packed like books on shelves into holds which in some instances were no higher than inches. "They had not so much room," one captain said, "as a man in his coffin, either in length or breadth." Here, for the six to eight weeks of the voyage, the slaves lived like animals.
>
> (Bennett, 1966, p. 40)

In the past I have used the Middle Passage as an introduction to the nature of New World slavery. While it makes graphic the horror of this particular aspect, in truth the horror began in Africa. Slavery existed in Africa – as in Europe and Asia and along the Mediterranean – for centuries prior to the North Atlantic slave trade (Davis, 2006; Patterson, 1982). The idea that Europeans enslaved Africans *in* Africa is a myth, Davis maintains: It was Africans who captured and transported slaves to be sold to Europeans. The historian John Thornton (as cited in Davis, 2006), maintains that while Europeans used *land* as a source of revenue-producing property, slaves and wives were the only form of private, revenue-producing property recognized in African law.

Survivors of the Middle Passage arrived physically weakened, and vulnerable to disease. They were housed in desolate barracks, separated by sex. Little effort was made to clothe, house, or feed them adequately. The booming slave trade made 'New Negroes' expendable, as others could readily replace them. And given their susceptibility to disease in the new environment, efforts to assure their health seemed futile. Within a year of their arrival 25% of the slaves were to perish (Berlin, 2003).

There were countless instances of trauma during slavery – the sale of family members typically never to be seen again; beatings; rape; forced labor to an injurious degree; prohibition of learning; and most wounding of all, subjugation. I will not discuss them here, however. The inauguration of slavery and my parents' histories are sufficient for a discussion of the effects of slavery's traumas, as well as its enduring impact upon both whites and blacks.

I shall initially write of the wounds slavery wrought upon African Americans. I will explore those wounds with respect to the effects of trauma, processes of attachment, the development of the self, and shame. Following that analysis I will discuss the psychological cost to white Americans of creating and maintaining an 'Other' upon whom deficiencies of the self might be projected, as well as the effects upon whites' capacity to metabolize pain.

Trauma

Stolorow and Atwood (1992) maintain that "the *essence* of trauma lies in the experience of unbearable affect" in a *context* in which the attuned responsiveness of a caretaker is unavailable (pp. 52–53). Interestingly, they argue that the intolerability and intensity of affect experienced is not "solely, or even primarily" based upon the severity of the injury sustained (p. 53). Rather, it is the absence of *attuned responsiveness* to "assist in its tolerance, containment, modulation, and alleviation" (p. 53) that renders painful or frightening affect unbearable, which renders it traumatic. A failure of attunement leads to the sequestration of such affects, which become "a source of lifelong inner conflict and vulnerability to traumatic states…" (p. 54).

Stolorow's conception of developmental trauma (Stolorow & Atwood, 1992) is similar to the description of trauma discussed above, but differs in the following ways. In developmental trauma a child's intense affective state disappoints the caregiver, or causes the caregiver to rebuff the child's pain, thereby producing in the child an acutely painful reaction. Yearning even more now for attuned responsivity, the child again seeks containment but finds what he perceives as the caregiver's experience of *him* as damaging or unwelcome. These authors argue that the traumatized child must dissociate such painful affect from his ongoing experience. Such feelings are now no longer available, meaning that that part of *himself* is no longer available, at least at a conscious level. Not only do they "become a source of lifelong inner conflict and vulnerability to traumatic states" but even more significantly, they lead to the "establishment of invariant and relentless principles of organization" (pp. 54 and 55): *This* is the nature of the universe, *this* is who I am, and *this* is how others will relate to me. These principles "remain beyond the influence of reflective self-awareness or of subsequent experience" (p. 55). It is to be remembered that such reactions, which are largely unconscious, exist to maintain the relationship to the caregiver.

Attachment

Bowlby understood attachment as a genetic set of behaviors determined by the infant's need for survival. Its function was to protect the infant from predators through the proximity of a caretaker. Though varying, these behaviors had functional equivalence, as all were directed towards the goal of proximity. Whether a child ran or crawled towards the mother, the end of all these means was proximity (Cassidy, 1999).

Proximity makes change possible in the infant's internal state, say from hunger to satiation, or in the environment, through the removal of a threat. However, cognition and affect are also determinates of attachment behaviors, as the child produces mental representations or "working models" of experiences with attachment figures, the self, and the environment. The quality of the child's attachment, i.e., whether secure or insecure, is determined by the caregiver's availability and responsivity: Caregivers who are both responsive and available produce children who are securely attached.

What is crucial is the child's "expectation" of the mother's availability and responsivity, that is, the child's representational model. Those whose working models are such that availability and responsivity are not dependable are "insecurely attached." According to Cassidy (1999) Bowlby asserted that " 'the extent to which the mother has permitted clinging and following ... or has refused them' " (p. 7) is what determines security or its lack (Cassidy, 1999). Cassidy notes that empirical data have been found to support Bowlby's assertion.

In its most fundamental aspect attachment refers to a process in which a mother is both attentive and responsive to an infant's bodily movements, facial expressions, and eyes, etc. When a caregiver is aware of and responsive to the infant's communications, the child develops secure expectations of the caregiver's and ultimately others' responsivity.

Bowlby's ultimate formulations of attachment extended far beyond the infant's early manifestations of security issues, though research makes clear that other determiners of motivation need to be added to demonstrate its continuing relevance (Lyons-Ruth & Jacobvitz, 1999). This lifelong impact was made possible through the "'mental representations' or 'working models' of the attachment figure, the self and the environment, largely based on experience" (Cassidy, 1999, p. 7).

The Developmental Significance of Trauma and Attachment

Trauma refers to an important interaction which has gone seriously awry, i.e., one in which a caregiver fails to provide needed attunement to a child's painful affects. Trauma theorists provide outcomes of such malattunement, which, though specific, are necessarily general, such as an inability to regulate affect, enduring vulnerability to traumatic states, a deep sense of shame due to a sense of internal badness or defect (Stolorow & Atwood, 1992), or a fragile sense of self (Brandchaft, 1994). These are, then, *principles* of subjectivity which will guide and determine behavior.

Attachment differs from trauma in that it is both broader and at the same time more explicit in its prediction of outcomes. Bowlby's predictions about the effects of security or lack thereof were specific and clear, leading to a vast body of research, particularly after the disorganized category of attachment was identified. For instance, such family risk factors as maltreatment of the child, parental bipolar and major depressive disorders, and parental alcohol intake have been found associated with disorganized attachment behavior in infants.

My recognition that both trauma theorists and the originators of attachment designate these early caregiver/infant interactions as the *origin* of the significant consequences they describe was of considerable moment. These highly similar if not identical processes are critical to development and produce lifelong consequences, containing as they do the seeds of who we are to be, how we will relate to others and they to us, and the manner in which we shall construe the world. Their pertinence to slavery is immediately apparent.

For example, there can be little question that the tearing of us from all we had known and been must have been traumatic. There is little reason to believe that the first Africans to arrive here were insecurely attached. Van Ijzendoorn and Sagi (1999) reviewed studies conducted in non-western areas of the world, several of which were African. These investigators were interested in the effects of multiple caregiving upon attachments to a single provider and found that multiplicity of caregiving produced secure attachment in proportions comparable to Western findings. But the traumas of capture, of passage, the selling block, and slavery midst the absence of containing others must have significantly diminished earlier senses of security. Such unbearable traumas *had* to affect the parents' capacity to provide the holding from which attachment stems and initiated the generational transmission which I encounter in the patients with whom I work today. Further, parents who were slaves could provide only limited protection of their child's experience of trauma, and certainly were unable to protect them from the traumas they would endure leading their slave lives. Ultimately the question which needs to be raised is one of resilience: from whence did it come, and how was it preserved?

I have not here explicitly written of trauma's transmission (for fuller discussion see Gump, chapter 9 in Demons in the Consulting Room, edited by Harris, Klebanoff & Kalb, 2017) nor of the transmission of attachment styles. I can hope, however, that my focus on the caregiver/infant interaction conveys how determining of the adult self this interaction will be.

I have written as if only people of color are to be explained. But the issues I raise cry out for explanation: How *did* whites believe their enslavement of blacks legitimate, even generous, and how today do so many maintain racism and violence towards us is appropriate? Certainly whites themselves have extensively written their answers to such questions. Loewen and Sebasta (2010) have compiled a substantial and impressive collection of documents written around the time of the Confederacy, presenting Southern arguments for the Confederacy and the Civil War. These documents remove any question of the centrality of slavery as the motive for that war, and in so doing justify and argue slavery's necessity. In what follows, however, I will present Ruth Frankenberg's (1993) understanding of the oppression of blacks, whose brilliant thinking answers some of the questions I've raised.

Whiteness: A Refreshing Perspective

Frankenberg (1993) argues that racism is typically thought of in terms of those against whom it is directed, rather than as a system which impacts *everyone* within it, pervasively, deeply, and for the dominant group, often unconsciously. She writes,

> [W]hiteness refers to a set of locations that are historically, socially, politically, and culturally produced and, moreover, are intrinsically linked to relations of domination. Naming 'whiteness' displaces it from the unmarked, unnamed status that is itself an effect of its dominance ... [D]ealing with racism is not merely an option for white people ... racism shapes white people's lives and identities in a way that is inseparable from other facets of life.
>
> (p. 6)

Frankenberg (1993) expands the meaning of whiteness through the construct of 'social location.' Social location refers to one's proximity to power and resources. It determines how one sees and understands the world, what is meaningful, and what is insignificant or wrong. Further,

> The truth claims of those who are centrally socially located are often treated as *prima facie* valid, whereas those of others more often need to be argued or justified ... Because their world-views are not subjected to questioning, those who are centrally located are least aware of their position.
>
> (Jacobs, 2014, p. 747)

Further, Jacobs contends that the closer one is to the center of power and resources, the more one considers one's views self-evident, and the less one is aware that those views have been determined by one's location, rather than truth.

White Trauma

Slavery provided not only the possibility of becoming powerful and wealthy, but the possibility of esteem for a group of immigrants who, for the most part, had been at the other end of the socio-economic scale. Painter (2010) writes that "before the African slave trade burgeoned in the 18th century, between one-half and three fourths of all whites Britain shipped to the Western hemisphere arrived as unfree laborers" (p. 40). This element consisted of vagabonds, beggars, orphaned children, and convicts, an uncontrolled group which committed crimes and chaos of many sorts. The English were seriously concerned about this group, and decided ultimately to ship them, along with those already indentured, to foreign lands.

Further, early colonists encountered significant trauma. For example, of the 100 colonists shipped to Jamestown, VA in 1607, only 38 of them remained alive some eight months later when a second group was brought to join them (Lane, 1999). And many contend that though indentured servants had contracts stipulating length of service and what was to be given them in exchange for their labor, their conditions were no better than that of slaves (Painter, 2010).

Later immigrants came for reasons of religious or ethnic oppression, famine, and other traumas. "It would take too much time," wrote Davoine and Gaudilliere (2004), "to list all the countries from which refugees fled in order to start a new life and forget [the catastrophes which led to their flight]" (p. xxii). And many suffered trauma once they arrived, given their living conditions, discrimination, and the uncertainty of employment.

Both early on and later immigrants worked hard to distinguish themselves from slaves. Slaves thus served an important function, for here was at least one group to which they were indisputably superior.

Joseph Miller (2004), who emphasizes the role that capitalism played in the phenomenon of slavery, opened me to an aspect of slavery I have failed to consider sufficiently. While we know of slavery's economic determination and consequences, we tend to respond to its personal, cultural, and social ramifications, and not to its primary reason for existence. For one's value to reside so singularly in the capacity to produce, and so minimally in humanness, makes more understandable a class of people whose primary concerns were wealth and power. America was not only a safe haven, providing refuge to whites fleeing the limitations and traumas of their original homelands. It also offered the possibility of wealth and power, the possibility that one day those attributes might be descriptive of *them*.

In a recent *New York Times* article Timothy Egan discusses England's reaction to famine-racked Ireland in the mid-19th century, during which "at least a million Irish died" (Egan, 2014). British rule that attempted to strip the Irish of their language, their religion, and their land had produced a wretched peasant class, subsisting on potatoes. "A great debate raged in London. Would it be wrong to feed the starving

Irish with free food, thereby setting up a 'culture of dependency'?" The English nobleman in charge of easing the famine certainly thought so, declaring that "Dependence on charity is not to be made an agreeable mode of life."

Further in Egan's article he quotes Paul Ryan, a US Congressman, as saying, "We have this tailspin of culture, in our inner cities in particular, of men not working and just generations of men not even thinking about working or learning the value and the culture of work." In other words, blacks, like the Irish of the nineteenth century, were poor due to character defects.

However, Ryan's ancestors on his father's side *came* from this ravaged Ireland in order to avoid the famine. Egan (2014) quotes the Irish historian John Kelly (2012) who wrote that "Ryan's high-profile economic philosophy is the very same one that hurt, not helped his forebears during the famine – and hurt them badly." It is not, Egan writes, that Paul Ryan has forgotten why they left Ireland: He "never learned." I suggest that what Ryan "never learned" – and perhaps was shielded from knowing – was the *anguish* of his forebears, leaving him, then, unable to recognize it in others.

I have discussed white trauma not because whites are unaware of the fact of it, but because they are too often unknowing of its anguish. Michael Lerner, in a 1994 editorial for the *Washington Post*, speaks of Americans' innocence, of their optimism and wish for goodness, and of their difficulty in knowing and coming to terms with despair, with the limitations of the way in which the environment may be treated, with the harm that our foreign policy has done abroad, or unregulated economic policy does domestically.... Some have argued that this difficulty is the inability to come to terms with death. I suggest it is more about how to experience and endure riveting pain, *in life*. The metabolization of traumatic affects is clearly wanting. More than denial is at work.

My Narrative

My paper on privilege was a journey of discovery, for I now knew of what a childhood *might* be composed. When I thought of us as children, the difference between my life and Jacobs' seemed huge. And this was the case even though my life was privileged in a number of respects, and the traumas of my family clearly less weighty than those of many African Americans.

Frankenberg's (1993) 'outing of whiteness,' stripping it of its super-ordinate position, placing it in a category that differed from mine in terms of power, its maintenance, and its history *but nothing more*, made it possible for me to access a rage I had not before known. That affect, and reflection, deepened my understanding of racism and self.

A colleague was curious about the nature and content of my rage, how it had empowered me, and I was thus prompted to consider it more carefully. But I no longer felt it. Had the statement been hyperbolic? As I called to mind the moment when I grasped the difference between the author's childhood and my own, I remembered hatred, rawness, a bitter clarity. In time I discovered that though I no longer experienced those affects, something within me had shifted. That shift was sufficiently noteworthy to lead me to write about it immediately following an incident which revealed something of its nature.

Driving to work one morning, I turned a corner from one of the bucolic streets in my neighborhood onto a busier one. A large utility truck stood on one corner, and a fat bellied, mustachioed worker stood on another. He was white, and looked at me in a manner I experienced as unfriendly, no, contemptuous. I was puzzled: I had slowed appropriately, did not turn too close to him, could discern nothing I had done wrong. Then I smiled, even chuckled. Who was this man? What had he come from that he might look at me as he did? Now I knew. If this was his work, it was likely his forebears had similarly labored. And going all the way back (with no knowledge of course) I imagined they could have been indentured, or Irish, fleeing famine. And without question there must have been a time when it became urgent that his ancestors distinguish themselves from mine. It might even be that they had to so do for hundreds of years. The culture assisted profoundly, depriving my ancestors of freedom, and later, permitting the economy to differentially reward those like him, telling him that of course he would be hired for positions they could not obtain, not have to live amongst them, or force his children to go to school with theirs.

The shamed, bewildered child in me, searching for what she had done to elicit the utility worker's reaction – that child was no longer present. *I* was not what was wrong: I was amused I should have felt so demeaned. Rather, the issue lay with the culture, a culture which elaborated upon the projections Europeans cast upon first seeing the African, characteristics which could not – heaven forbid – be descriptive of them. Slavery was a cruel materialization of those projections, providing rich images and notions about who and what black people were, and what, therefore, white people were. How dare we somehow come to dwell in such a neighborhood as this, and he in the one he must early on and yet still inhabit?

And I – at least for those moments – had broken free.

This shift in my subjectivity derived from my experience of rage, taking a form indebted to Frankenberg (1993), whose clarity disrobed whites of centuries of philosophy, convictions, political and financial power. I called the shift 'a-right-to-be.'

Difference

Both Jacobs (2014) and I hold reflection and narration to be promising paths. The communities in which this is to occur differ, but overlap. The refusal of the powerful, on the whole, to *acknowledge*, let alone *hold* the feelings of the un-empowered had dire consequences for the slaves' "sense of self" (Brandchaft, 1994). The refusal to recognize slave affects was fundamental to slavery – "How *you* feel about the chains on your feet, the pain from your whip lashing, that I am selling you away from your wife and children is of course immaterial." The degree to which slaves' feelings were irrelevant *had* to impact the self of the slave mother, thereby diminishing her capacity to respond to her infant's affects, to her capacity to bring about a securely attached child.

I am also clear that whites are a part of the community I shall address, for hopefully I can provide perspective and knowledge that become part of new formulations. Both whites and blacks need to know the 'other,' though given slavery we are ahead, for our lives depended upon how we were to behave with them in the most minute as well as broad areas of life. Understanding the other provides context, and only through context may we approach the complexity of reality.

The task of change is not simple, either for whites or blacks. Jacobs (2014), along with an African American colleague, attempted several times to offer in their institute an elective on Frankenberg's (1993) theory. When the course was described in terms of racialization, few signed up. When they 'disguised' the course content they got a class. At some point one brave candidate said that although she was glad to have taken the class, she was angry that we did not advertise at the outset that the class would study primarily racial themes. We asked her if she would have signed up if we had said that. She said 'No.'

(Jacobs, 2014, p. 757)

Reaching African Americans is complex, in part because what needs to be addressed is that aspect of our history from which it has been necessary to be protected. I am referring, of course, to the affects which slavery produced.

The progeny of slaves had parents who, due to their traumas, were in varying degrees compromised in their ability to provide what all children require when experiencing painful, frightening affect: the attuned responsiveness of a caregiver. The cost to the child was significant and enduring, consisting of difficulty in affect toleration, modulation, and integration, but also sensitivity to later trauma, which would evoke the original, unbearable affects. Further, Stolorow (2007) maintains, as noted previously, "[f]rom recurring experiences of malattunement, the child acquires the unconscious conviction that unmet developmental yearnings and reactive painful feeling states are manifestations of a loathsome defect or of an inherent inner badness" (p. 4). I believe this latter consequence a significant source of our shame, which I shall discuss below.

The transmission of these deficits began early, and it is unlikely any children of slaves could have entirely escaped. And of course from the moment the African was captured, the larger cultural context in which he lived not only failed to provide containment, but continued to traumatize.

Shame

Our ability to integrate the meaning of slavery has been limited by an intense level of shame. Shame may be conscious or unconscious. Hurmence (1998) compiled excerpts of slave narratives in *My Folks Don't Want Me To Talk About Slavery*. An ex-slave tells an interviewer, "My folks don't want me to talk about slavery. They's shame niggers ever was slaves" (p. ix). It is hardly surprising many of us came to feel, largely unconsciously, that slavery must be due to *our* inherent deficiency.

As discussed above, one outcome of repetitive malattuned responsivity causes the child to believe there must be something wrong with *her* to be responded to in the manner she has been. Such 'truth,' transmitted by parents, is of enormous power, and is accessible neither to reason nor reassurance, given that it is unconscious. And of course, white culture has explicitly and implicitly continued to assert our defectiveness. Though we recognize and fight against such 'truths,' their internal destructiveness may not be as readily apparent or erased as it might seem.

In the End...

Given who my mother, her sisters, and their mother appeared to be, I have no question of the pain transmitted them, even though I don't know its particulars. Something in their family led one sister to give away both children she conceived, as infants I believe. I experienced what I now recognize was an absence of responsivity in my mother toward me. Something deep and powerful seemed amiss in these women. And I was shocked to learn from my cousin how little my mother had told me of her own mother. I now see how much her life had been an effort to avoid experiencing her sorrow.

My father's departure from his home at age eight stemmed from the past, given the condition of blacks in the South, and his parents' wish for him to have more than the South would permit him. *His* feelings were not that important, a transmitted relic of slavery. It is extremely unlikely he would have become the vice president of a large, national firm had he remained. But had they known what it cost him – the sense of abandonment, the deep depressions, his rage, I wonder would they have acted as they did.

I am clearer about what was transmitted to me and my siblings. There were many ways in which my parents led us to believe we were unimportant, or were defective: My father's response to many of our wishes, "Who *cares* what you want?" led me to believe my desires/feelings were of little consequence; and thus that *I* was of little consequence; my mother's refusal at times to wash or iron my brother's clothes, an enactment materializing her disapproval and distaste for this child; and her seeming disinterest in me – in truth, her malattunement – leading me to feel "she doesn't love me."

Such lack of attunement from my mother was, I can now appreciate, transmitted from her mother, and though I know little of my grandmother's history, I know enough about the primacy of the processes I have discussed to know that she too must have experienced transmitted trauma. I wonder if she committed suicide in the asylum where she was placed.

I know little of my mother's father, except that he was important in the community where they lived, and that my mother seemed afraid of him. He was not portrayed as someone who would/could be emotionally available.

While my personal history evokes a desire to know more, as well as sorrow, my recent ability to place me in this broader context has been transformative. When I write "context" I refer to the psychological, psychoanalytic theorizing which makes clear how devastating and enduring have been the traumas African Americans have experienced.

References

Bennett, L. (1966). *Before the Mayflower: A history of the Negro in America 1619–1964* (Revised Edition). Baltimore, MD: Penguin.

Berlin I. (2003). *Generations of captivity: A history of African-American slaves.* Cambridge, MA: Belknap.

Brandchaft, B. (1994). To free the spirit from its shell. In R. A. Stolorow (Ed.), *The intersubjective perspective* (pp. 57–76). Northvale, NJ: Jason Aronson.

Cassidy, J. (1999). The nature of the child's ties. In J. Cassidy & P. R. Shaver (Eds.), *Handbook of attachment: Theory, research, and clinical applications* (pp. 3–20). New York: Guilford.

Davis, D. B. (2006). *Inhuman bondage: The rise and fall of slavery in the New World.* New York: Oxford University Press.

Davoine, F., & Gaudilliere, J.-M. (2004). *Beyond history: Whereof one cannot speak, thereof one cannot stay silent.* New York: Other Press.

Egan, T. (2014, March 15). Paul Ryan's Irish amnesia. *New York Times,* Sunday Review.

Frankenberg, R. (1993). *The social construction of whiteness: White women, race matters.* Minneapolis, MN: University of Minnesota Press.

Grand, S. (2015). *The other within: White shame, Native-American genocide.* Cambridge, MA: Psychology and the Other Conf.

Gump, J. (2000). A white therapist, an African American patient: Shame in the therapeutic dyad. Commentary on paper by Neil Altman. *Psychoanalytic Dialogues, 10,* 619–632.

Gump, J. P. (2010). Reality matters: The shadow of trauma on African American subjectivity. *Psychoanalytic Psychology, 27*(1), 42–54, doi: 10.1037/a0018639.

Gump, J. P. (2014). Discovery and repair: Discussion of Lynne Jacobs' paper. *Psychoanalytic Inquiry, 34,* 759–765.

Gump, J. P. (2017). The presence of the past: Transmission of slavery's traumas. In Demons in the consulting room: Echoes of genocide, slavery and extreme trauma in psychoanalytic practice, edited by Harris, Kalb & Klebanoff, Oxford, UK: Routledge.

Hurmence, B. (Ed.). (1998). *My folks don't want me to talk about slavery: Twenty-one oral histories of former North Carolina slaves.* (13th printing). Winston-Salem, NC: John F. Blair.

Jacobs, L. (2014). Circumstance of birth: Life on the color line. *Psychoanalytic Inquiry, 34,* 746–758.

Kelly, J. (2012). *The graves are walking: The great famine and the saga of the Irish people*. New York: Henry Holt & Co.

Lane, A. I. (1999). *For whites only: How and why America became a racist nation*. Washington, DC: 21st Century Press.

Lerner, M. (1994). In "Gump" we trust. *Washington Post*. Retrieved August 14, 1994, from www.washingtonpost.com.

Loewen, J., & Sebasta, E. (2010). *The Confederate and Neo-Confederate reader*. Jackson, MS: University Press of Mississippi Press.

Lyons-Ruth, K., & Jacobvitz, D. (1999). Attachment disorganization: Unresolved loss, relational violence, and lapses in behavior. In J. Cassidy & P. R. Shaver (Eds.), *Handbook of attachment: Theory, research, and clinical applications* (pp. 520–554). New York: Guilford.

Miller, J. (2004). Slaving and colonialism. *Journal of Colonialism and Colonial History, 5*(3), doi: 10.1353/cch.2004.0095.

Painter, N. (2010). *The history of white people*. New York: W.W. Norton.

Patterson, O. (1982). *Slavery and social death: A comparative study*. Cambridge, MA: Harvard University Press.

Sterba, J. P. (1996). Understanding evil: American slavery, the Holocaust, and the conquest of the American Indian. *Ethics (106)*, 424–448.

Stolorow, R. (2007). *Trauma and human existence: Autobiographical, psychoanalytic, and philosophical reflections*. New York: Psychoanalytic Inquiry Book Series, V 23.

Stolorow, R. D., & Atwood, G. E. (1992). *Contexts of being: The intersubjective foundations of psychological life*. Hillsdale, NJ: The Analytic Press.

van Ijzendoorn, M., & Sagi, S. A. (1999). Cross-cultural patterns of attachment. In J. Cassidy & P. R. Shaver (Eds.), *Handbook of attachment: Theory, research, and clinical applications* (pp. 713–734). New York: Guilford.

Chapter 6

Dialogues in No Man's Land*

Ofra Bloch

This article attempts to lose the abyss between the offspring of victims and perpetrators. In chronicling a journey from New York, to Berlin, to Jerusalem, the author seeks to engage not only the contemporary legacy of the Holocaust but also the roots of her own othering of Germans and Palestinians. She seeks answers to controversial but crucial questions: Will Germans and Israelis move towards a less confining and ideological notion of their identity, or will they instead find themselves unintentionally perpetuating a cycle of fear, hate, and oppression? Can Israeli Jews and Palestinians break down the walls of blindness between them? The article proposes that mutual recognition and acknowledgement of intersections of experiences can undo the process of dehumanization done by former and present generations on each side.

I grew up hating Germans. I never thought it required any explanation.

When I was a child, I used to go with my great uncle Binyamin to buy a block of ice because he didn't have a fridge. We would carry the dripping ice block home, losing half of it to the heat, while laughing our hearts out at his jokes about his time in the concentration camp. I especially liked the stories in which he used to trick the camp commandant and make a fool out of him. Once I asked my mother if she and Dad had ever been to such a camp. She told me they hadn't. "How come?" I asked. "Weren't you good enough to be sent there?"

---

* Reprinted with kind permission: This chapter first featured under the same title in the journal Contemporary Psychoanalysis as part of a Special Issue 'The Evolution of Witnessing: Emergent Relational Trends in Holocaust Studies,' Volume 51, Issue 2, 2015. Reprinted by permission of Taylor & Francis, LLC.

It was only afterward that I learned that Binyamin's wife and two children died in that camp.

I belong to the first generation born in the newly-established State of Israel. Being born in that time meant growing up in an environment of constant war and the aftermath of the Holocaust. Loss was a common phenomenon; it was only later in life that I realized that its magnitude and prevalence were extraordinary. Many of my friends grew up in a deafening silence concerning the past. It was as if they had been snatched from the fire by parents with numbers tattooed on their arms, destined to fulfill the legacy of those who had perished. Other friends were sons, daughters, brothers, and sisters of soldiers who died in the war. The survivors were living reminders of the helplessness of the victims, and were the basis for the post-war attitude among Israelis that the "new" Jew being raised in Israel would never succumb to the enemy. The generations of Israelis after the Holocaust continue to hold tight to the victim identity and narrative, all the while claiming moral superiority because of it. This was the environment in which my deep interest in the loop between 'other' as subject and 'other' as verb originated.

My reality has always been saturated with Holocaust particles that spelled out a message of indefinite hate of the other. I inhaled it, as one does oxygen, but there was never space to exhale it until I emigrated from Israel. "Never Again" and "Remember and Don't Forget; Remember and Don't Forgive" were two messages I heard over and over again. At the beginning of every Holocaust Memorial Day, our national day of mourning, we stood in silence listening with bowed heads to a two-minute siren that was heard all over Israel. Yet, there was never a siren to mark the end of the day, implying, to me, that the mourning should continue, should never end. The Israeli leadership tends to make a cynical use of the Holocaust: Israelis are told repeatedly that another Holocaust is around the corner, and any criticism of the State of Israel by a person who is not Jewish constitutes anti-Semitism. If the criticism comes from within, the person is labeled a 'self-hating' Jew. This approach not only cheapens the memories of the Holocaust but also manipulates the PTSD symptoms of Israeli society, creating a permanent state of hypervigilance and paranoia. The past hovers above the Palestinian-Israeli conflict and feeds a vicious cycle of 'othering,' and those who were 'othered' continue the tradition of 'othering.'

For many, many years, the anger I felt towards Germans was always present. I spent three days in Germany in 1977 and then had to flee because I felt terribly uncomfortable, even slightly paranoid. I saw a Nazi behind the front desk of every hotel, a Nazi on every street corner. I could not stand the sounds of people conversing in German, because the harsh tones of the language made me think of Nazis barking orders to send Jews to be slaughtered. In the years that followed, my feelings did not change, and I remained unaware of how I was casting Germans in the role of the 'other' only because they were Germans, perpetuating a tradition initiated by their own forbearers who dehumanized and othered the Jews.

For the last 20 years, I have had hanging above my desk the famous photograph of the Russian soldier raising the flag over the Reichstag in 1945. Every morning I wake to find it there, along with the conflicted feelings that it continues to provoke. On the one hand, it stands for something decisive: the fall of Nazi Germany and the total ruin that seemed like a necessary obliteration, a just outcome that could allow the German people to construct a civilized nation where nothing like the Holocaust could ever happen again. On the other hand, it is not decisive at all. There is no triumph, and it is not an end to anything. The image remains clouded by the larger incomprehensibility of the Nazi era and the Holocaust, and for me, by memories of places I have never seen.

In the summer of 2012, I found myself feeling a somewhat mysterious and urgent need to travel to Germany and enter that frame of the photograph above my desk. I began to think a lot about the perpetrators' descendants and how they might need to have their voices heard – not to take or assume guilt for their ancestors' actions, but to have their own struggles acknowledged and legitimized. I decided then to make a film about it, which I named "Afterward." All I knew at the time was that it was unacceptable for me to go on with my life harboring this dread of Germany and its people. I was aware of the pernicious way in which hate can cycle into more hate; I could sense that I might have already passed on some of my fear and misgivings about Germany to my sons.

I told myself that I was going to Mars without a compass or a guidebook to help me find my way. What did I want? I could not define my goals or what I was looking for. I do not know that I wanted anything. Yet, I had a visceral yearning for proximity and eye-level encounters with second- and third-generation Germans, and I was hoping to stay open to whatever came along. I was not aware then that my journey would start in Germany, and continue on to Israel and Palestine, where I would focus on the unique experience of post-Nakba (The Catastrophe) generations of Palestinians, an event that defines their collective identity. I would find that getting to know German and the Palestinian narratives does not diminish or belittle the magnitude of the Holocaust, but has the potential for opening up what has felt like a collapsed space for the possibility of empathy and compassion in me. The following notes are some of my thoughts about the experience of being the 'other' and seeing the act of 'othering' in myself.

Before the Interviews

I'm due to fly to Germany in a week and I'm anxious. The journalist I was going to interview has dropped out. He's been known for being critical of Israel, and he is concerned that once again he'll be accused of being an anti-Semite because of his views. Another scheduled interview subject, D., has dropped out as well because her mother doesn't want her to discuss the family on film that might be shown one day in Germany. It's hard to know what to make of D.'s decision not to talk to me about her grandfather 70 years later. D.'s mother was a child during WWII when her father, a soldier in the Wehrmacht, was fighting on the Eastern front. When visitors asked her where her father was, the little girl would point to his framed photo on the piano. In it, he looked handsome and joyful on the back of a horse. After her father returned from the war – having lost his leg and high spirits – if asked where her father was, she would still point to the photo. I realized that this child, who grew to be D.'s mother, still has difficulty accepting the reality of which her father was a part. She still keeps his memory framed in that photograph on the piano, with him on top of his horse.

I can feel empathy for D.'s mother, but I find it very disturbing that D., a member of the young generation in Germany, feels – because of her loyalty to her mother – that she has the right to opt for silence. I wonder, again, how much these sorts of denials will stand in the way of my interviews.

Ruth – A Writer

I sit waiting for the interview to begin. My palms sweat as the crew sets up cameras, lights, and microphones. The woman I will call Ruth takes her place across from me. Twenty years ago, I would not have imagined myself sitting here facing a German woman.

RM: It was so hard to learn how to speak to Jews through the fear of getting punched in the eye, and also hearing these stories and what is it that you say? I mean, what can you say? You can say thousands of things, but also you cannot say anything.

I don't share it with Ruth, but I think she knows it's very hard for me to learn how to listen to Germans through the fear of my own rage and aggression, through my sorrow and pain. Who would I be with them? Who would I be to them? As I was to discover, I was different in each interview and each subject would unearth different emotions for me.

Ruth shares a quote from Hitler, "And they will never be free again, all their lives." Part of not being free is not being able to really understand what is going on around you, but at the same time, being so much a part of what surrounds you that you cannot ask questions and wonder. It becomes normal. As I listen to her, I ask myself: Will either of us ever be free from the legacy of the Holocaust? Do we want to let go? Is it even possible?

Ruth's Father

Ruth shows me a photo of her father who was an officer in the Wehrmacht during WWII and spent five years as a POW in a camp in Siberia. She laughs when she says to me, "My father was a hero." She continues,

I'm sorry I'm laughing about that now, but I felt a great compassion for my poor father. I have to say that as a child, it was a story about suffering, and it was my poor father who had gone through all of this.... Later it became more complicated ... our relationship really became quite unbearable, and there was a time when I didn't want to hear about his suffering anymore. I had on my mind one particular testimony from a woman who told how they were put in an open cattle car and at some point they were ordered to step out of the wagon and to put down all the children, because all the children had frozen to death. The women had not been able to protect them with their bodies, and so all these children were frozen and they put all these little bodies on a heap and were ordered to get back on, and the transport continued. And she was talking about how she had parted with her son, and she was saying how happy she was that she didn't have her child with her on that occasion. And I had that in mind and I didn't want to hear about how horrible my father's trip back from the POW camp was, and I said to him, 'You know how we transported people?' and I think I walked out.

As Ruth tells me about this memory I am reminded of a recurrent dream in which I am on an overcrowded train headed to a concentration camp. We arrive at the camp and I hear shouts of "raus, raus…" People are shoving each other to get off of the train as quickly as they can. I am carried along with the crowd and jump out onto a ramp and stand in line. When I arrive at the head of the line, an SS officer approaches me and snatches my glasses from my face. He breaks them in two and the world suddenly becomes a blur for me. I feel relieved that I do not have to see the brutality of the unspeakable. Could it be that this was my way to avoid witnessing my own annihilation?

Ruth tells me that one thing that has helped her over the years was her impression that her parents were not immediately implicated. She didn't think that either of them was actively involved in what the Nazis called the "Final Solution," and that is a great relief to her. Ruth wonders what her grandfather, who was driving a locomotive during the war years, had transported in his train. I find myself hoping together with her that it was only coal.

My Father

I remember asking my father what he did in the War of Independence of 1948. He told me that he was stationed in Jerusalem, which was under a siege, and how hungry he and his fellow soldiers were. At some point he saw no choice but to order the soldiers in his unit to shoot … a chicken. They finally had something to eat. When my father returned from the next war, the Sinai War of 1956, he told me that he went through training as a medic. He demonstrated to me how to carry a wounded soldier and also showed me some yoga positions. I could never make sense of why they would teach him yoga in the army, but pretty soon my whole family was able to sit in a lotus position and raise our bodies up in the air by leaning on both hands. I don't know if my father told me the whole truth about his participation in the various wars, but if – as a child – I was disappointed that he was no hero, all of a sudden, as an adult, the idea that he might have been too much of a chicken to fight the enemy became comforting.

Our Mothers

Ruth's mother, who was a nurse in Berlin during the war, told Ruth to make sure that all the hangers in the closet faced in one direction. She tells me,

> I still do that and the reason is that when there is – and I didn't pick that up then – that when there is a fire, you can grab everything with one hand and lift it out of the closet, and my mother was telling me that people had done that during the air raids, and then you wrapped it in a curtain and you threw it out of the window into the street and that's how you saved your clothes. And then you ran down yourself and picked up your bundle. But of course when there is one hanger pointing in the wrong direction...

My mother used to sing me songs of war. She would sing and I would cry and when she was done, I'd ask her to sing it all over again. One particular song spoke of a bereft mother who, as she stood weeping on the grave of her second son, declared how she had already lost her first son in battle and that nothing would break her and nothing would ever make her leave this land. I would be bawling at this point, but I could then sense a new hope in my mother's voice as she sang about a young, tall man who stepped forward and told the grieving mother that he was there to fight the hated, bloodthirsty enemy and be her son as well. I knew of course who the enemy the song referred to was.

And what about the Palestinian mother? The one often ridiculed by the Israelis for comforting herself by believing that her son who blew himself up while killing Israelis is a martyr. Isn't she hurting as well? Aren't her tears as bitter as those of an Israeli mother?

On Israeli TV I see a Jewish Knesset member comparing the grief of a Palestinian mother to that of an Israeli mother, and insisting upon the moral superiority of the latter.

Ruth and I

Ruth tells me about the fall of the Berlin Wall. She was born in the year the wall was erected, a child of the Cold War, so she has never had a longing for any lost territories like the generation of her parents. But then things started to move and she describes it as if the blood circulation went back into limbs that had become numb. All of a sudden, it became possible to go places and the freedom to move about felt wonderful. It became possible to ask, to see, to understand how "frozen," in her words, the situation had been. "I also think it needed to be frozen. I think it needed to be held in place for a very long time because people would not have been able to ask the questions ... to have access to themselves, to have access to their memories." Ruth remembers the chaos, the joy, the crowds in the streets, and the feeling that something monumental was happening; yet she speaks of the wall continuing to be, even though it doesn't exist anymore, the organizer of her geography.

I also grew up in a divided city. The border went through the middle of Jerusalem separating East Jerusalem and the Old City from West Jerusalem where I lived. Walking by the border that splits buildings, I could see Israeli soldiers and Jordanian legionnaires with sniper rifles on top of the buildings, children playing nearby as if it were a normal situation – and it was, for that part of the world. I used to come to Notre Dame, a monastery that stood on the border. It faced a no man's land that was filled with barbed wire, land mines, and dirt. I would climb to the roof, from which I could see East Jerusalem. I can still remember the excitement and my pulse quickening as I watched the others, the Palestinians, going about their daily lives, exactly like we Israelis did in West Jerusalem.

There was great joy when Israeli forces conquered East Jerusalem and the Old City during the Six-day War. Shortly afterward they referred to it as the liberation of Jerusalem, and the reunification of the city is now celebrated yearly. I was just about to graduate from high school and my friend and I hitchhiked on a bicycle with an improvised platform on which we sat, and got to the Old City for the first time. We entered a café and ordered Turkish coffee and asked to try the nargileh (hookah pipe). They let us try on embroidered Palestinian dresses that were soon to become a popular fashion statement. I didn't realize then that I was under the protection of Israeli soldiers, visiting a foreign land. That would come later. I did feel confident enough to play a few games of backgammon with some Palestinian men in the café and win a game or two. In my romantic mind, I imagined that they respected me as an equal.

In 2008, I visited Israel and saw for the first time the Separation Wall. It's a barrier set on the outside of the Green Line (1949 Armistice) and it cuts into the West Bank and annexes Palestinian land that has been used to build Jewish settlements. Israeli friends tell me that the wall was built to prevent terrorists from entering Israel, and that it is a way to establish a new de facto border. I hear from Palestinians that this barrier is an apartheid wall and that it has been built as a form of collective punishment.

Horst – A Sculptor

Horst says to me, "The first time I heard about the Holocaust was through the silence." Horst tells me that as we hear water gushing underneath our feet, standing at the Aschrott Fountain Memorial in Kassel, Horst's first "counter-memorial." The fountain was destroyed by the Nazis in preparation for Adolf Hitler's visit to Kassel, because a Jewish merchant funded it. Horst rebuilt it as negative form, upside down. He says that if the thousands of Jewish citizens of Kassel could be brought back, he would rebuild it in its original form.

Horst says that the problem with memorials is that people regard them as redemptive – once they are finished, people feel they have done their duty, paid their dues, and that it is time to move on and develop a new national feeling. All this coincides with the time when the last survivors die, and when memory is transformed into books. Horst's purpose in building counter-memorials, emphasizing the absence and the void, is to make people angry. They can only sense the water falling down into the ground, nothing else, and therefore are turned into participants who must ask questions. In this way the story and the history come back, and the fountain serves as a stimulant to repressed memory.

I find myself deep in thought about void and absence. I learned as a child that when the Jewish pioneers, one of whom was my grandfather, arrived in Israel, the land was empty of inhabitants. It was due to their hard work that the land turned into a green oasis. I was told that the lack of forests was because the Bedouins' goats ate all the leaves off the trees until the Zionists came, planted trees, and created new forests. As a matter of fact, when my grandparents immigrated to Palestine from Canada in 1923, the women of the Hadassah chapter of St. Thomas planted three trees in their honor. By the time of the War of Independence, there were some Arabs living on the land, but – as the story goes – they ran away from fear. It was only later that I understood that when new life began on that land, the life of some 750,000 Palestinians living on that very land ended, when many were forced to emigrate and become refugees.

Horst's father told him stories about his childhood, but never about his time being employed as a high-ranking official forester during the occupation in Riga. Horst was the only one among five siblings who started asking his parents questions in 1968 and found out that his father administered the forests around Riga where the Rumbula massacre took place on November 30th and December 8th 1941, in which 25,000 Jews were killed.

It was years later that Horst learned the real story. When he found out that the Jews of Kassel were transported to Riga and that most of them died in the Rumbula massacre, Horst realized that not only was he dealing with the story of the Aschrott Fountain, he was also dealing with his own family story. The boundaries between the private and public spheres are blurred now, as they were in 1941. I register that November 30th and December 8th are the birthdays of my sons, but I don't say it aloud.

On Holocaust Memorial Day, on January 27, 1996, as part of an art installation, Horst projected an image of the gate of Auschwitz with the sign "Arbeit Macht Frei" ("Work Makes You Free") onto the Brandenburg Gate, and so both gates were together for one memorial night. By this, he meant to say that Germany cannot use its national symbols as other countries do, that there is a break in identity. Horst tells me how when he walks with his dog along the railway and hears the trains, he always thinks about the trains of deportation.

Early on, in my typical Israeli childhood, the word "train" lost its innocence. Trains led to one place only: the concentration camp.

Later on, other objects became a receptacle for additional related associations. Once, when I offered a bowl of cherries to a friend who survived the Holocaust as a child, I pointed to two cherries attached to each other on the same branch and remarked, "Look, twins!" He replied instinctively, "Mengale's twins," and to me this seemed normal. On a recent visit to Israel during the month of August, I had a taste of Holocaust humor. When I complained to a friend about the terrible heat, she answered without batting an eyelash: "You think this is hot? In Auschwitz it was hotter."

Sophie – A Physical Therapist

During a break in my interview with a woman I will call Sophie, she calls her father and asks him if he had ever talked to his mother about what happened to the Jews during the Holocaust. Her father replies they did not talk about it because they were not directly affected. Her grandmother replied that they were aware that occasionally people had disappeared, but not aware of the monstrosity or the vastness of these crimes. Sophie seems distressed; she tells me how much she wants to believe the person she has loved the most, how she didn't want to destroy the image she had of her, and that this is the reason she didn't pry. It is difficult for her to imagine that people would not have known, yet her grandparents were very simple people and not politically engaged, so she thinks maybe it is possible that they weren't so aware of what had happened.

Sophie tries to hand me various documents used by her grandfather to prove his Aryan background, but my skin protests – or this is how it feels to me – and I refuse to touch them. I view them with my eyes as Sophie shows them to me and can see the signature of Goering at the bottom of the letter below a "Heil Hitler" and the Nazi swastika decorating the rest of the documents. I do not understand why it is bearable to see this, but not to touch the paper.

I'm aware that Sophie's grandfather worked in a factory during WWII. I search the name of the factory online and easily discover that this factory used slave labor and inmates, mainly Jewish women and girls, from the nearby concentration camp. I can sense how Sophie is afraid to taint her grandmother's memory. I find it hard to share my knowledge with her. I'm afraid of my own anger, and I'm aware of the envy I feel of her privilege to choose not to know. Do I have the right to interfere with that?

Every day, when I returned home from elementary school to eat lunch, the "The Search Bureau for Missing Relatives" program was on the radio. Everyone in Israel listened to this program, day after day, after day. I would hear about people like Sarah Lieberman from Radom, who was looking for her sister Leah Spector, last seen in December of 1942 in the Warsaw Ghetto, or about Isaac Finkelstein from Krakow, who was looking for his cousin Mendel Finkelstein, last seen in Sobibor in July of 1943. It was not my choice to listen, but that was the background noise of my childhood.

At the end of the interview Sophie says: "You know, I feel ashamed a little bit in front of you, because here you are, and this has been such a part of your life and your history, and now you're sitting with a German and the German keeps saying, 'Well, I don't know, we never talked about it.'" At that moment I feel ashamed myself. Who am I to judge? In the late 1970s, I made a decision not to visit the West Bank and Gaza anymore, believing that it was a way to protest the occupation. However, in making that choice, wasn't I also choosing not to know about the way the Palestinians were living? To remain ignorant of their reality? To avoid seeing the other?

Thomas – A History Teacher

In my interview with Thomas, I ask him when he found out that his father was an officer in the SS. He tells me that he was brought up knowing because his father spoke about it a lot when Thomas was a boy. Thomas had contradictory feelings listening to his father's stories,

> He had many scars on his body, and he rolled up his trousers, and took his shirt off, and he showed me. And I was disgusted in a way and also fascinated, and it was the same thing with these stories. I was caught in between. On the one hand, I was disgusted. I was just, like, 'Oh, wow, this is being a man. To be a man, strong! Not being afraid. Going, fighting. Wow. I want to become a man myself.'

I imagine the yearning and fear of Thomas as he encounters the scarred body of his SS father and I can sense my own conflicting feelings as well. I both relate to his experience of longing, and am keenly aware of my own disdain and repulsion for the man who shaped Thomas' psychic landscape.

Thomas talks to me about the transmission of trauma between generations and in the course of the conversation he says that he would kill himself immediately, and even defend his suicide to his children, if he would ever find himself blind. Thomas's father was blinded for one month during the war. Perhaps, he says to me, this is his worst fear, a fear that he cannot face.

OB: So, Thomas, blindness is the scariest thing.
TC: Yes.
OB: And your father was blind for a month. But he was blind in other ways too, for a longer time than a month. And I'm just wondering whether this is also part of your response.
TC: This is, um … This is an accurate picture. Yeah. Could be. Perhaps. This is my legacy. My legacy is to look.
OB: And what legacy would you like to give your children?
TC: …I don't speak about that. Not in front of camera, I don't. I don't want to…

Thomas' eyes are tearing up. He gets up and leaves the room. Not one word is uttered in the room in his absence. It is as if the camera crew and I are compelled to respect his silence.

Thomas' last encounter with his father happened shortly before an SS reunion. Thomas visited with his wife and daughter, and his father told him he had no time to talk because he was preparing for the meeting. When Thomas and his family were about to leave, Thomas called to his father, "Hey, Father, your granddaughter and we are going! Say goodbye, please!" His father came down the stairs and said, "You're not educating her right. You're not raising her in the right way. You do not teach her the important things in life." And Thomas asked him what was important, and his father said, "It's duty. It is obedience. And it's subordination." And he went up the stairs and Thomas never saw him again. Thomas' father died shortly thereafter.

As I observe how Thomas' father was an SS father to him, I think about the transmission of trauma and how the Israeli born children in the 1950s, without realizing it, enacted the role of the Nazis to the immigrant children of survivors. A kid who wasn't tanned and muscular like the rest of us, a kid who was dressed in shorts longer than ours, who was too polite and well mannered, was referred to as "soap." The term, derived from rumors that began circulating during the war that the Germans were manufacturing soap from the human fat of dead Jews, conveyed an unspoken message of criticism – common at the time – that Holocaust victims went to their deaths like lambs to the slaughterhouse. In Israel, after the war, there was palpable prejudice, even feelings of shame, among Sabras (Israeli born), which these newly arrived Holocaust survivors engendered.

After the interview, Thomas writes me an e-mail and says that, in talking with me so openly, he felt like a traitor of the SS soldiers. I find that I was prepared on some level for Thomas to tell me that he felt like he betrayed his father, but hearing him express a conflict about being a traitor to the SS soldiers hurts. I realize that Thomas has forgotten who I am and was not cognizant of the effect his words might have on me. He has not seen me. I write back to him that perhaps his first loyalty is to himself.

Ingo – Former Leader in the Neo-Nazi Movement

On the day I interview the ex-leader of the East German neo-Nazi movement, everything seems to be going very smoothly. I ask him difficult questions about his past, and he answers openly, giving a lot of details about his own personal acts of violence and about neo-Nazi activity in the early 1990s. I am unaware that this encounter with these atrocities is making me, in a sense, go into hiding. Writing about it here allows me to realize that I was feeling as if, like in my nightmare, my glasses were broken; everything became blurry. And, as I describe this to myself, and pronounce 'not-see' in my Israeli accent, it sounds like I'm saying 'Nazi' – a reminder to myself that the ability to 'see' is a necessity in the struggle against evildoing.

Ingo received a jail sentence of twenty months in 1987 for trying to escape from East Germany. That was when everything changed for him. He was put in a cellblock with old WWII criminals like Henry Schmidt, who used to be the Gestapo chief of Dresden and was responsible for the deportation of all Jews from Dresden and Leipzig. Schmidt refocused Ingo's hatred of East Germany and communism and explained to him why it had been essential to get rid of the Jews.

Ingo tells me that it might have been any other movement, Scientology or Hare Krishna, that swept him up. He needed a home to belong to and help to survive the jail conditions. Later on, after the fall of the Berlin Wall, he met Michael Kuhnen, the leader of the neo-Nazi movement in West Germany, who saw the potential in Ingo to be an Aryan posterboy because of his looks and quick mind. He appointed Ingo to be the leader of East Berlin. In this position, Ingo met neo-Nazi leaders from other countries. He remembers that the Austrian neo-Nazi Gottfried Kassel painted a Star of David inside of his toilet and decorated his apartment with black and white photos of the Warsaw Ghetto. He painfully tells me about a board game, in which the goal was to bring four figures marked as Jews to Auschwitz. The fastest would be the winner. Ingo can barely repeat the words of the song they used to sing: "Smash him in the face, he's just a Jew." He stops dead short and tells me: "I'm sorry, I can't repeat it anymore. This is as ugly as it gets."

OB: How does it feel to physically attack someone? Can you remember that sensation?

IH: Well, I can remember. If you fight in the name of an ideology, it gives you the greatest feeling on earth. I can tell you that. You feel justified; you feel right. You are not thinking about whether the person is weaker or alone and you are standing in front of him with five people. It does not make a difference.

OB: I read in your biography that there were a few instances in which you referred to the feeling of being violent, and in one of them you speak about kicking somebody on the ground and feeling godlike, because it's in your hands.

IH: That's the right word. It's in your hand. You have the power over this person, and if there is some ideology behind it, it makes it even more important and right. It makes it absolutely OK to do that. There are no limits at all.

I was aware before the interview that Ingo left the neo-Nazi movement in 1995. Together with a policeman who investigated him, Ingo established an organization called EXIT, with the purpose of helping people get out of extreme right-wing organizations and aiding the parents of young people who are drawn to that activity. But I feel numb and not present during this part of the interview. There is a quality of the unreal to the whole situation: I am hearing awful things and feeling nothing. Before the end of the first part, I ask him how it feels for him to be interviewed by a Jewish woman and he answers that he doesn't think in those categories about people.

At that point, still feeling dissociated, I feel compelled to ask for a break, not even knowing why I so desparately need it. I need air. I go for a walk by myself in the courtyard, and as if from nowhere, I begin sobbing. I have no words to go along with the tears. All I know is that I have never felt so Jewish in my life. All of a sudden, without having put up a fight, I AM the Star of David in the toilet. I'm a Jew not by choice. I'm chosen. It does not matter that I don't want to have my identity be a reflection in the eye of the other. I can be undone in a split second and I feel myself disappearing. There is only space for the Nazi.

When we resume the interview, I feel a strong sense of urgency – as if it is a matter of survival – and I tell him that I need to address something first of all. I explain that I DO think in those categories, and I don't want him to behave as if he is color blind, and that I am very much Jewish and am happy to belong in that category. I'm talking to him from a deep place – a feeling of being annihilated and being denied my identity. I can clearly see him sensing that something is wrong, and I ask him to imagine how it is for me to interview him. Then I share with him the sense of the unreal, along with the real fear that I am feeling in his presence. This exchange opens the collapsed space between us. Remembering how he once found refuge from his difficult childhood on the roof of his grandmother's building, I suggest we climb to the roof to finish the interview. (Looking back, I still can't believe that I climbed a narrow and shaky ladder in order to take a stroll on the roof of a building with an ex-neo-Nazi.) Ingo shares with me how shocked he was by my reaction to him and how he has never had that kind of conversation before. He tells me that he has spoken a lot in public about his experiences, but that he has wound up telling me things he hasn't told anyone before. He says that he was convinced that, after so many years, he could put his past behind him, but that talking to me has made him realize that he cannot and that it's going to stay with him forever. There is such a sad look in his eyes; I feel enormously sorry for him.

A few days later I received an email from Ingo:

Dear Ofra,
Well, I had many thoughts after we left. I thought that it actually was a pity that we didn't continue because, for some reason, I felt there was a lot unanswered. Don't get me wrong, not in the way you asked me, more in between ... I think we would have had a chance to go much deeper in many ways and I felt too that I was willing to do that. As I said before, I have done a lot of interviews but this was by far the most interesting one. For the first time ever, I had the feeling that I have an opportunity to get something off my soul and that gave me a great feeling, but also made me sad while realizing what all this actually means.

Later, reviewing the footage of our interview, I again had such a bout of weakness that I had to lie down. I managed to sleep for 25 minutes, and when I opened my eyes I was thinking about the tattoo of "Germania" on his shoulder that he showed me and how I could see the small blond hairs on his skin underneath the faded tattoo (he used to have three little swastikas but they are unrecognizable now) and the visceral sensation of an "other" that flooded me by that sight.

Standing on the roof with him I felt empathy: I could see the 2-year-old in him who was given to a group foster home for four years, I could feel the pain of the 6-year-old who was beaten by his stepfather whom he thought to be his real father, and I could sense his deep regret and sorrow about his past deeds. I was also very much in touch with my own lingering physical and emotional fear being in his company. It still seemed unimaginable that I could have been in such proximity to someone who had called himself a Nazi.

The Bavarian Quarter

On May 19, 1943, the Bayerisches Viertel (Bavarian Quarter), along with all of Berlin, was announced by Reich officials to be "free of Jews." The memorial "Places of Remembrance" in the Quarter designed by Renata Stih and Frieder Schnock consists of 80 double-sided custom signs (text and image panels). The text side shows the content of Nazi laws and regulations by which the disenfranchisement of the Jews was promoted in

Germany. On the other side of the panel, there is a pictorial representation. For example, Jews were not allowed to buy shaving cream or soap starting in 1941 and forbidden to have house pets from 1942 on. That would have meant that if you are a Jewish man and you lived in that period, you would have had a long beard and no cats or canaries, and if you are a Jewish woman, you wouldn't have been allowed to use the pool from 1938 or participate in a choral group from 1933 on.

The road to Auschwitz started in 1933, when Jewish teachers were suspended from public schools, and ran through 1938 when only comrades of German blood, or related descent, were allowed to become allotment-gardeners, into 1942, when cigarettes and cigars were no longer sold to Jews and Jews were forbidden from buying newspapers and magazines. The one that pierces my heart is the one that forbade Jews to buy flowers. What mind could have come up with that?

I decide to interview people randomly, on the street, in the Bayerisches Viertel. Walking through the Quarter, looking at the signs, my emotional reaction to those prohibitions, which tore so deeply into the fabric of daily life of Jews, is so overwhelming that all traces of my ordinary shyness drop away; I approach passers-by and ask them to translate for me into English what is written on the various signs. I would have never believed before that I was capable of such an act. I find myself feeling a level of rage that becomes hard to control when I converse with the Germans who translate the signs for me. On one occasion, when a man passes by with his dog and refuses to be interviewed, I yell at him, "Isn't it terrific that you are allowed to own a dog," and when a young man tells me, "It used to be a Jewish Quarter," I snap sarcastically, "Obviously, not anymore."

The Return

When I returned from my shoot in Germany, it became clear that I needed to talk to and interview those who have been the other 'others' in my life – the Palestinians. The 2014 Gaza War made it imperative. There are many narratives offered to explain the Gaza situation and they are categorized – depending on whom you talk to – as right or wrong, true or false, when in reality, there is a multiplicity of very nuanced narratives. Listening can lead us to find ourselves in the experience of the other, to discover the other in us, give birth to new possibilities. It would be so much easier and less agonizing if I could see and trust just one narrative, but that creates a permanent wall on which to bang my head and would blind me to the experience of the 'other' forever. I "know" the Israeli soldiers who died. By that I mean that their faces are so familiar that they are etched in my heart; they look so much like my two sons who live, as do I, in the relative peace and safety of the US. At the same time, I can also call up the image of four Palestinian boys playing ball on the beach in Gaza before being killed. I probably played with their parents who were children when I was visiting there in 1978. I do not live under rocket attacks from either side, but I lived through a few wars in Israel and I do believe that people can get out of the suffocating hugs of "just" and "no choice" wars once they start listening to each other's narratives.

I wanted to come back from Germany waving a moral flag or bearing moral conclusions. Instead, it became an opportunity for self-examination. When I was told in the delivery room that I had a son, I turned to my husband and said, "We can't go back to Israel." I did not want my son to participate in an unnecessary war like the Lebanon War of 1982, which was happening at that time. While I have always held the view that the occupied territories gained in 1967 need to be returned to the Palestinians, who deserve to have their own state, I was never fighting for it in the trenches. Going to demonstrations and having political arguments in cafes do not require much courage.

This summer, reading the news of a Palestinian teenager burnt alive, in apparent retaliation for the murder of four Jewish boys, I caught myself being shocked that there are Jews who are capable of such an atrocity. It is then when it dawned on me that I, too, had bought into the narrative that we the Jews are the 'the chosen people,' which in reality only breeds indifference to the plight of the other and causes a profound lack of empathy.

I was asked by several people, why now? It was a question I could not answer then. The answer, which I dissociated at the time of the shoot, became conscious about a year after my return from Germany. I wanted to understand how 'they' deal with shame, guilt, and responsibility – emotions that have flooded and bothered me by the mere fact that I am an Israeli, struggling with a myriad of ambivalent feelings concerning the possibility or impossibility of having a democratic state that allows all Jews in, but does not shut the door in the face of others.

I came back from Germany burdened by the realization that 'evil,' for lack of a better word, can be unearthed in each of us, given the 'right' conditions, regardless of our religious or ethnic background. It is the capacity to become a bystander who stops asking questions, sleeps well at night, and remains silent in the face of moral collapse. It is about emotional blindness. Being just is not an innate privilege of the victim, and knowing about the past is not going to change who we are. I can only hope for something on a smaller scale, an act of humanizing the other, a small attempt to undo the 'othering' I personally have done.

On my last day in Berlin, I went to the Jewish Museum, to view an exhibition named "The Whole Truth And Everything You Wanted To Know About Jews." The exhibition is referred to as "The Jew In The Box," because there is a Jewish volunteer sitting in a glass box, enclosed on three sides, who answers questions from the visitors. I was curious to find out what types of questions were asked of the volunteers – and not surprised to find that most of them were focused on Israel. The two volunteers that I watched were kept busy defending the positions of the Israeli government concerning the Palestinians. I was about to leave when a church group of teenagers from ages 12 to 14 arrived and presented questions. One stepped forward: "There are prejudices against Jews, and I wonder if they are partially correct? If they are true – partially…"

Afterward

After filming in Germany, I return home and contact several Palestinians. Among them is Ibrahim, a devout Muslim from Ramallah. He views all acts of violence against the Israeli occupier as a legitimate tool in the Palestinian struggle. He believes in the Right of Return for the Palestinians and in a one binational state solution. We have an initial meeting on Skype and I experience an almost visceral sensation of his hate for me. I AM an Israeli, after all, and therefore a perpetrator in his eyes. Our conversation is respectful, but I am unable to shake the awareness of the gulf between us.

I want the voice of Gaza, a place I'm forbidden from entering by both Israel and Hamas, to be heard. I eventually meet Basel, a 20-year-old photojournalist from Gaza who has recently arrived in the US to attend college on a Magnum scholarship. He is so young in years, yet already a veteran of three wars and one Intifada. His photographs are evidence of what he has seen, and experienced.

Another Palestinian with whom I speak is Bassam, a native of East Jerusalem and a veteran of the Israeli jail system, where he spent seven years for having thrown hand grenades at Israeli soldiers when he was seventeen. In 2005, he co-founded Combatants for Peace, an organization of former Israeli and Palestinian combatants leading a non-violent struggle against the Occupation. In our first meeting on Skype, Bassam tells me that he believes that the Israeli oppression is a consequence of the Holocaust and therefore he undertook to learn about the Holocaust in order to understand the Jewish experience. When he first read about the concentration camp and the crematoria, Bassam found himself feeling angry that the Jews did not fight back as they were led to the gas chambers. On January 16, 2007, an Israeli soldier shot and killed his 10-year-old daughter, Abeer, a loss as grievous as anything from his study of history. And yet, Bassam didn't pick up arms against her killers. Instead, he opened his heart and embraced the enemy – the one hundred former Israeli soldiers from the organization he had founded – who built a playground in Abeer's memory.

It is hard to learn how to listen and speak to Palestinians. When I hear Bassam's story, I fight hard to keep myself from crying. I'm afraid it will come across as if I'm hiding behind redemptive tears. In some way, I find it easier to deal with Ibrahim's hate. When I look into Basel's eyes, I feel shame and responsibility for the sort of knowledge he has, having experienced things that no young person should have to endure.

I also meet Professor Mohammed Dajani, an academic and a moderate Muslim leader, who tells me that many Palestinians think of the Nakba – the 1948 exodus and forced immigration of over 750,000 Palestinians from the land that was to become the State of Israel – as the child of the Holocaust, a product of the European and American feelings of guilt, at having closed their doors on Jewish immigration before and during WWII. He says that the Holocaust is not being taught in Palestinian schools and when it is mentioned, it is often claimed to have been exaggerated, in order to generate sympathy for Israel and get more control over the world. In 2011 Mohammed was invited, along with other religious leaders from around the world to visit Auschwitz. It was the first time that he confronted the horrors of the Holocaust and he felt that he should not be a bystander; rather, he has chosen to work to relay this horrible experience to the Palestinian people. He believes it is historically and morally wrong to deny the Holocaust or to ignore it. Mohammed tells me that as a political scientist he believes that "showing empathy for the suffering of my enemy might elicit from my enemy empathy for my suffering." He tells me that when his Palestinian students ask, "Why should we study about the Holocaust or recognize it when the Israelis are making it illegal to study about the Nakba or celebrate the Nakba?" he tells them that it is important to understand the psyche of the Jew, of the Israeli, of "Never Again," and their fear that the Holocaust can happen again at any time, which at least partially explains the Israeli obsession with security. Mohammed ended up taking a group of Palestinian students to visit Auschwitz and speaks of their reactions. It was important for the students to emphasize that learning about the Holocaust is not meant to provide an excuse for the occupiers or an attempt to suppress their nationality and their cause, but is their way of being more humanistic. Upon his return Mohammed encountered hostility from his community. He was viewed as a traitor and threats were made on his life, which culminated in an assassination attempt when his car was torched. He resigned from his job and because he did not feel secure in East Jerusalem among his people, he came to the US to be a fellow in the Washington Institute. It represents another sort of an exile for him. When Mohammed is asked, "What was more hurtful, to be labeled a traitor, to be referred to as a collaborator, who has supplied the Occupation with a cover of normalcy, or to have lost his career," his answer is "neither." What hurt the most, he says, is the silence, the silence of his colleagues, his friends, the faculty, the intellectuals within Palestine. I sit across from him at my home where the interview is taking place and I can feel his deep loneliness.

As I prepare to go to Palestine and Israel to interview Palestinians, I find myself facing repeated false starts. I spend long hours searching for subjects, but when I reach out to them, I either get no response at all, or, if I am able to establish contact, people disappear with or without explanation. I keep wondering whether the boycott movement has a negative impact on their interest in talking to me. I think about what language to communicate with them in. Does the language of the Occupier, Hebrew, hurt their ears? I have a running monologue in my mind, in which I explain to them that I was merely born in Israel and I have been living in New York for 35 years, that I am an American – but then I catch myself making this false apology. After all, I did serve in the Israeli army during the War of Attrition between 1968–70, the war nobody ever talks about.

It took the form of limited artillery duels and small-scale incursions into Sinai as Egypt tried to compel Israel by means of long engagement to withdraw from the Sinai Peninsula. The war ended up with no obvious victor after great economic and human expense.

During my army service, I was assigned to the artillery southern command; my job entailed typing the coordinates of military targets based on aerial photography for our cannons. At that time I used to have long conversations with my friend Leah, during which I would argue that Israel must return the Occupied Territories. She said that the Liberated Territories would never be returned. Today, she still holds to the same views, while I have recently started thinking that maybe it is getting too late for a two-state solution, with all the existing settlements, and that the effort should be focused on creating one state with equal rights for both peoples.

While serving in the army I managed to see Hanoch Levin's satirical play, The Queen of the Bathtub, which – in contrast to Israeli euphoria and self-congratulation in 1970 – ridiculed the nation's pride and mocked the war and the Occupation. The play encountered extended public uproar, riots and a storm of protests unprecedented in Israeli theater history and closed down after 19 performances. Levin had confronted national beliefs that were accepted as truths. To this day, I remember how I was criticized for going to see the performance and how the play parodied Avraham's sacrifice of his son and implied that Israeli parents were doing the same. It shook the earth from underneath me.

At the time, I did not really comprehend that real people were being killed as a result of my fulfillment of my army duties. I had the mind of an 18-year-old and lacked the intellectual or emotional depth needed to truly process the multilayered reality that surrounded me. I also did not fully understand what it meant to live under occupation, with restriction on every aspect of daily life.

I wonder if perhaps I am still the enemy and that talking to me feels to my prospective interviewees, an act of normalization that in a way supports the Occupation. I find myself telling my subjects that I want their voice to be heard, their narrative to be known and understood, and that facilitating this is my own tiny attempt at reparation. As a matter of fact, I suspect that I am asking for their help in order to make me feel better about myself. Going to demonstrations and signing petitions can only go so far. I have an urge and yearning to take an extra step, but I'm struggling with the nagging notion that I'm tapping into their generosity in order to achieve a measure of peace of mind. I think of the journey I have made since I started work on this project, which began with my interviewing second and third generation Germans, and how it has evolved to include the Palestinians as well. I understand now that it was with the help of the 'others' that I was allowed to grow and learn about myself and the world that surrounds me.

I realize that a conversation is not going to undo the intense feelings that are engulfing us. We need to do more than that. We have to take risks, and break down walls, and discover each other's humanity. We don't need to love or even forgive each other, but we must create a potential space for 'I-Thou' experience that allows for multiplicities of narratives and requires each of us to enter the experience of the other and own our part and contribution to their pain.

It is during these kind of encounters in real time, which belong forcibly to the present, when it becomes clear to me that it has never been – for me – about forgiveness and reconciliation, but about seeing and being seen as well.

Acknowledgements

I thank Adam Bloch, Theresa Claire, Sue Grand, William Tipper, and Sharon Zane for their insightful comments and encouragement.

Chapter 7

Racialized Enactments and Normative Unconscious Processes

Where Haunted Identities Meet*

Lynne Layton

Some years ago, long before I understood much about the transgenerational transmission of trauma and how it might be enacted in the clinic, I reported on several racialized enactments in my work with an Asian-American man, Michael (Layton, 2006). My work with Michael continuously challenged and perplexed me, and, through it, I began to recognize the unconscious racial and cultural underpinnings of some of the very ways I think about certain "basics" of analytic practice: dependence, independence, happiness, and love. Revisiting that work now has brought me more in touch with the many ways in which our dialogues were haunted by the transgenerational transmission of trauma present in each of our histories.

At the time of writing, I was working with a model of gender identity formation that I referred to as a negotiation model (Layton, 1998). I thought this model could account both for the narcissistic wounds incurred from living in a sexist culture and for the kinds of gendered experience we all have that make us feel good about being men or women or something in between. I called it a negotiation model, because I wanted to capture the way we constantly negotiate identity both from what Benjamin (1988) and others call doer-done to relations and from relations of mutuality. In part, I was writing "against" postmodern and Lacanian theories that suggest that identity categories are necessarily coercive and oppressive, that no version of gender or racial identity is healthy. At the same time, I wanted to give the coercive aspects of identities their due, because so often psychoanalytic theory ignores the psychic effects of the power hierarchies in which we live. The negotiation model accounts psychologically for the defensive and regressive use of identity

* Reprinted with kind permission: The present article is a shortened and re-worked version of Layton, L. (2006) Racial identities, racial enactments, and normative unconscious processes. Psychoanalytic Quarterly LXXV(1):237–269. Permission to reprint has been granted by John Wiley and Sons.

categories (see Dimen 2003; Goldner 1991; May 1986) as well as the progressive use of identity categories (for example, in liberation struggles and in the resiliency oppressed groups manifest in spite of the hateful projections to which they are subjected).

I next wanted better to understand the regressive and foreclosing use of identity categories, and that work led me to elaborate a concept I refer to as "normative unconscious processes" (Layton 2002, 2004a, 2004b, 2004c, 2005, 2006, 2014). With this term, I refer to the psychological consequences of living in a culture many of whose norms serve the dominant ideological purpose of maintaining a power status quo. My assumption is that racial, class, sexual, and gender hierarchies, which confer power and exist for the benefit of those with power, tend not only to idealize certain subject positions and devalue others, but tend to do so by splitting human capacities and attributes and giving them class or race or gender assignations. Such assignations cause narcissistic wounds that organize the desire to belong to one group rather than another, and these wounds become lived as a complex amalgam of class, race, gender, and sexual identities. Coercive norms form the crucible in which we "become" gendered, raced, classed. And these norms operate both within distinct large groups and between them. Working-class white women or middle-class black women, for example, grow up with norms particular to their social location, but no social location exists without reference to all the others, and all identities must take up *some* cognitive and affective position toward dominant cultural ideals (Layton, 2015). Power hierarchies create and sustain differences that mark out what is high and low, good and bad, pure and impure, and there is certainly a general tendency for those not in power to internalize the denigrating attributions that come at them (see Dalal 2002; Moss 2003; White 2002). I understand the narcissistic process that emanates from these wounds of culture to be bipolar in nature: fragile selves, wounded by traumatic failures in caretaking, oscillate between self-deprecation and grandiosity, idealization of the other and denigration, longings to merge and needs radically to distance (Layton 1988; Shaw, 2013). Nonetheless, it would be a mistake to think that norms are internalized without conflict (Layton 1998, 2004a). Because the hierarchies split and categorize *human* attributes and capacities, we find in the clinic and in our lives unceasing conflict between those unconscious processes that seek to maintain those splits and those that refuse them. The ones that seek to maintain the splits are those that I call "normative unconscious processes."

Normative unconscious processes refer to that part of the unconscious that pulls to repeat affect/behavior/cognition patterns that uphold the very social norms that cause psychic distress in the first place. The familial and cultural transmission of racial as well as class and sex and gender valuations is generally deeply conflictual, precisely *because* the categories are products of splitting human capacities and needs. Enactments occur when the therapist is unconsciously pulled by the same norms as those pulling the patient, or when the therapist is pulled by destructive norms. Such enactments are of course more easily unraveled if we are aware of these norms and how they operate.

Normative unconscious processes, then, are one of the psychic forces that push to consolidate the "right" kind of identity and to obfuscate the workings of unequal power hierarchies. They protect the psychic splits that cultural norms mandate, and they do so because the risk of contesting them is loss of love and social approval. But let us not forget that the result of splitting is to keep what has been split off near. Repetition compulsions are the very place where the struggle between coercive normative unconscious processes and counter-normative unconscious processes are enacted. And since all identities are relational and not individual possessions, these repetitions are stirred up and played out in relation. In the clinic then, we are likely to find patient and analyst engaging all the time in enactments of normative unconscious processes. The concept of normative unconscious processes helps to clarify the inextricable link between the psychic and the social: the regimes of power that define relations between the genders, between the races and classes, and between those with different sexual desires condition the very way we experience dependence and independence, separation and individuation, affects such as shame, and a host of other psychoanalytic staples not usually thought of in social terms.

Race and Ethnicity: Beyond Black and White

What exactly *is* racial difference? While physical differences might anchor our notions of racial difference, what it actually is, in its oppressive mode, has to do with the power to split asunder human capacities and call some white and some nonwhite. It has to do with ideological means of maintaining power differentials, of assigning, as Bourdieu (1984) might say, distinction to one group of people and lack of distinction, or at best second classness, to others. When we look more closely at the content of racial splitting, as I shall in the vignette below, we find all sorts of effects of these splitting processes: cognitive effects, effects in the way attachment and agency are defined and valued, and effects in emotional states, expression, and range.

On the other hand, drawing again on the negotiation model of identity, racial difference also has to do with whatever the people labeled "racially other," i.e., nonwhite, collectively and individually have fashioned historically from being so labeled. Racial identities and the relation between dominant and subordinate identities are not closed systems; subordinate groups' identities are never fully determined by the power of dominant groups. Social and political life in modernity involves ceaseless struggle between subordinate and dominant groups over the power to define such things as race (Hall, 1982; Laclau and Mouffe, 1985). Thus, aspects of the identities nonwhite groups fashion for themselves are healthy, at times psychologically healthier than the psychic states of those who identify with the split cultural ideals of whiteness.

Feminist literary critic Susan Stanford Friedman some time ago (1995) drew attention to the fact that when "race" is evoked in the U.S. context, what is meant is black and white. Friedman lays out a complex map of relations between whites and nonwhites that goes beyond the black/white binary and, in fact, disrupts it. Friedman focuses not only on relations among multiple racial positionings, but also highlights the fact that the same person can be privileged along one identity axis, e.g., class, and lack privilege along another, e.g., gender (on the lived experience of intersectionality, also see R.M. Williams, 1997). Since her essay appeared, much work has been done on the varied experiences of Asian-Americans in relation to whiteness (see, for example, Eng and Han, 2002), some of which influenced my work with Michael.

What I was not fully conscious of at the time of writing the 2006 paper is the effect on clinical work of the way that the interrelated histories of the privileged and the socially marginalized mark each other. Thus, I had not yet explored how we become complicit in each other's suffering (Layton, 2009, 2015; Grand, 2007, 2013). We can only begin to understand the workings of complicity if we explore how our identities are constructed in relation to one another and how our small histories, part of a shared BIG History, have been affected by the intergenerational transmission of trauma. As the editors of this volume put it, the complicities and connections emerge in haunted dialogues. Thus, I return to the vignettes between me and Michael with a greater sense of the Big History in which we were both operating and how it marked our encounter. The therapy is over, so I cannot explore with Michael what I only now am able to contemplate. But I can speculate a bit more and raise some questions that might have been raised.

In the vignette, I explore a series of enactments with Michael, enactments in which normative unconscious processes pulled me (all too comfortably) into the position of "whiteness." After examining the clinical significance of the ambivalence of stereotypes, I go on to discuss the increasing discomfort I felt with this patient as I "explored" what I considered his tendency to self-abnegation. I look, too, at the way gendered, classed, and sexual histories/identities intersect with race. And, finally, I look at the patient's struggle to know what love is, a struggle that showed the ways that love—as well as many other constructs that analysts rarely think of in cultural terms—is itself racialized.

Clinical Vignette

Michael was a gay Asian-American male in his mid-thirties who entered therapy because he couldn't get his last boyfriend, a white middle-class male, out of his mind. He was worried that this would get in the way of his new relationship and hoped therapy, which he had never tried before, might help him extirpate disturbing thoughts of the ex-boyfriend, particularly the compulsion to compare himself unfavorably to the ex and to feel socially inept in relation to him. Michael had long felt socially inept, and at least part of the origin of this feeling was that his mother, who strongly values family and education, did not let him have much of a social life outside the family. In a situation not atypical in contemporary middle-class Asian-American culture, he was expected to focus single-mindedly on schoolwork (a scenario that is currently causing clashes between middle-class white parents, newly concerned about stress on their children, and middle-class Asian-American parents, worried about the degree of excellence their children need to attain to succeed in white culture).

His mother and father had both emigrated from Asia to a suburb of a big city in their early twenties, and Michael considers many of his thoughts and feelings to be a product of his non-Western culture—and he values them as such. Nonetheless, Michael felt he had problems with self-esteem, and he also hoped therapy might help with that. At the same time, he was clearly conflicted about being in therapy from the outset. It seems that one of the ways his parents differentiated themselves from "Westerners" was by feeling superior about their capacity to be private people; Westerners, the parents felt, talk too loudly, too publicly, and too long about their private business. They also make far too much of their emotions. Michael often thought so, too. Michael's lived experience illustrates the splitting and, in this case, racing and nationalizing of human capacities: in the family, emotion and rationality were split and labeled "Western" and "non-Western," respectively. This is not the way capacities are usually split by dominant Western groups, to be sure, but if the parents saw their best shot at success in being rational and scientific, then it served them psychologically to distinguish themselves from "the other" in terms of superior rationality.

Yet, how much more complex these things are than they first appear. It turns out that Michael's mother could herself become highly "irrational" at times, yelling, screaming, and imposing rules that to Michael made no sense. Surely, her rages had something to do with losses she had incurred in emigrating and the racism she encountered in her new country. I regret now that I had gathered no knowledge of her history and so now can only speculate on what had driven her and her husband to emigrate, but in such cases, the motive is often to offer a better life to one's children, a motive that often puts great performance pressure on the children (Eng and Han, 2002). Ironically, her rages only heightened Michael's identification with rationality and against emotion. Note that I use the term "rationality," not reason. The split versions of reason and emotion that marked this family convey the histories of loss, racism, and whatever else went on in earlier generations in the homeland. Indeed, where we find inexplicable rages and angry outbursts, we often find traumatic histories. For example, Bodnar (2004), speaks of an African-American female patient, Lisa, who was prone to inexplicable rages. Eventually, the patient gets in emotional touch with the history of her paternal grandfather, a bootlegger and alcoholic in the Jim Crow South. Terrified as a young man by frequent lynchings, he had tried to keep himself and his family safe by going into a business that would provide whites with something they wanted: alcohol. He also beat his children, in no small measure to keep them from enacting the kind of missteps with white people that he knew had the potential to lead to their murder. In reaction to his own father's beatings, Lisa's father sustained his sanity by demanding that the family live in the rigid world of white good/black bad. And the effects on Lisa came out in the treatment as her world collided with Bodnar's white working-class ways of splitting and racing/gendering human capacities. I imagine Michael's mother's seemingly irrational rages may well have had similar origins in historical and present trauma.

In high school, Michael was aware of longings to be part of the white in-crowd, but he also joined his Asian friends in denigrating the popular kids' practices, for example, how whites seemed to keep switching love partners but only took partners that were within their same-raced group. He figured that he was the only one of the Asian kids who longed to be part of the white crowd: as he told me, it isn't logical that the Asian kids would denigrate something they really longed to be a part of (I pointed out to him that this was precisely what he was doing and perhaps logic wasn't all that it was cracked up to be). Because of his longings, he must have felt a certain degree of alienation from his friends as well, which exacerbated his feeling of being socially inept. What is striking about Michael's ambivalent place between the Asians and the Caucasians, East and West, is that it left him quite uncertain both about what he felt and the value of what he felt, for it pulled him into denigrating the very thing he longed for.

From the first sessions, I saw two grids begin to form, one that associated certain attributes with white Westerners and others to superior Asians, and another that denigrated Asians and idealized white Westerners. These stereotypes were not just racial and ethnic; they were nodal points that stitched together race, ethnicity, gender, and sexuality. Michael and I were both aware of the grids, and, at one point, he laughed and said "I rely on stereotypes a lot, don't I?" I invoke Michael's way of splitting and racing attributes, sometimes with whiteness in the superior position, sometimes in the inferior, because it stirred a lot of thought and feeling in me and a lot of questions about how best to work with him. It also kept me conscious of my own ways of categorizing and judging, and made me wary of some of the certainties with which I found myself operating. The therapy raised a number of issues about the way intersecting identity categories are lived and the way power differentials create differences: differences in emotional range and expression, in the relation between emotion and cognition, in modes of separation and attachment, in one's very experience of love. I do not take Michael to be representative of Asian-Americans; rather, I draw on our work together to explore in more depth the way histories and ideologies of race, ethnicity, gender, and sexuality intersect and are lived and enacted in treatment.

As I mentioned above, Michael both idealized and denigrated Caucasians, which put me now in a superior, now in an inferior position. Conscious of his tendency to stereotype, what was unconscious was the splitting upon which this rested, and the trauma that caused the splitting in the first place. Splitting and projection may be universal mechanisms of defense, but racism creates the wounds that marshal such defenses and it is within a racist field that people enact the repetitions that simultaneously keep the wounds fresh and seek to heal them (see Dalal 2002; Layton 2002). Michael's ex-boyfriend, in fact merely a mid-level corporate employee and not a higher-up, incarnated in Michael's fantasy everything Michael wasn't: handsome, dashing, well-dressed, athletic, a corporate success, and, most important, socially suave and popular. Michael's attraction was clearly a mix of sexual desire and desire to HAVE what he thought the ex-boyfriend had. To be the right kind of male in Michael's economy, one had to be white. The fantasied ideal of "whiteness" that organized Michael's desire was upper class, worldly, popular, and, as the boyfriend was not fully comfortable identifying as gay, at least semi-straight and homophobic.

Michael denigrated what he thought of as Asian masculinity, and didn't think he could be attracted to an Asian male. He felt that neither white men, the ones worth having, nor Asian men were attracted to Asian men. At the same time, he and his Asian friends had disdain for what they saw as the ex's culture of self-serving false sincerity. As Bourdieu (1984) has noted, one of the central mechanisms of the aspect of identity formation built on a repudiation of otherness is to claim virtue for one's own social group; the Asian friends served the function of saying "who wants to be white anyway?" Whites are selfish. Indeed, the ex and his friends pretended to be concerned for others, Michael said, but really they were always manipulating social scenes to get what they wanted. Michael even complained that his loving current boyfriend had that white Western way of thinking of himself first—in restaurants, Michael observed, his white friends would pour water or tea for themselves when they wanted it, whereas he and other Asians he knew would always pour for everyone else, and only pour for themselves last. So here was yet another stereotype, that white Westerners are self-absorbed and Asians more polite.

The Ambivalence of the Stereotype

While the content of Michael's beliefs and observations is important and tells us the way that he and his family split and racialized human capacities, I want to look a bit more closely at the form the stereotyping took: the oscillating idealization and denigration. In academic critical race theory, much has been written, from a psychoanalytic perspective, about the ambivalent nature of the stereotype. In my view, such ambivalence derives neither from an originary destructive instinct, nor an originary split in our feelings about the breast/parent, nor in an originary refusal to acknowledge limits and loss. Rather, I think it derives from the psychic effects of racism (Boulanger 2007): from the fact that dominant identity categories are defined by dividing up in binary pairs human capacities and attributes that can only develop and thrive in tandem, such as dependence and independence, connection and agency, emotion and reason. Such dividing determines the ways in which we love, hate, create. And the reason why such divides exist has little to do with human nature. It exists so that those in power, those with the power to define the proper identity, stay in power. The oscillation between denigration and idealization that marks Michael's stereotyping is characteristic of narcissistic process, and it is part of my argument that racism and other cultural inequalities can produce not just narcissistic injury but narcissistic character and defenses. Michael frequently gets caught in his web of projections, now disdaining what he in fact longs for, now disdaining what he feels he is. Is the fantasy behind the ambivalent stereotyping process a fantasy of a "lost" wholeness no one ever can or did attain (Bhabha 1994)? Is the love-hate relationship with whiteness rooted in originary destructive and libidinal drives, torn asunder by racism (Balbus 2004)? I suggest that fantasies of lost wholeness and racist-driven splitting and projection arise from the ashes of racist-driven narcissistic wounding that leads us to seek a place, a fantasy space, where we might no longer be vulnerable to hurt, humiliation, and isolation. The ex, who incarnated "whiteness" and whose rejection of Michael only made him more desirable, represented such a fantasy space for Michael. In this fantasy space, which Michael resisted relinquishing with all his might, he would either be loved by the ex or more like the ex—and he would never again feel the pain of inferiority.

Whiteness

Michael came to therapy with me, an upper middle-class (currently, not by origin), Jewish female analyst who, certainly at this point in history, would be designated "white." A major stake of discourses that reinforce racial difference is their power to define who can lay claim to whiteness/ wholeness and who cannot. In their article on racial melancholia, Eng and Han (2002) argue that different stereotypes haunt Asian-Americans from those that haunt African-Americans. They focus specifically on the psychic effects of the model minority stereotype. In their view, many middle-class or upwardly mobile Asians become melancholic because to be successful in white America often requires a rejection of part of who they are. Further, Eng and Han assert that while Asian-Americans can become wealthy and successful in their fields, they can never become white; if the inclusion that comes with whiteness is what they covet, the psychic mission is doomed to failure.

Michael felt he had the wrong attributes, including body type, to be the right kind of man. The attachment to the ex-boyfriend that Michael could not relinquish reminded me of the psychic positions Benjamin identified in *The Bonds of Love* (1988), two versions of narcissism that emerge from splitting and gendering human capacities such as connection and assertion. For, in this relationship, Michael had taken up the self-denying submissive position typical of dominant white femininity in its relation to dominant white masculinity. His wish seemed to echo the Kohutian (1971) formula, "You are perfect and I am part of you." All this felt obvious to me, and I felt that in the course of therapy Michael would probably come to see that he did not so much want the boyfriend as he wanted what the boyfriend represented and he lacked. What was less obvious to me until later was that in the many interchanges about his desire, Michael had put me in, and I had unconsciously assumed, the position of "the white one." While it is certainly true that in our particular historical moment I am called and call myself white (as opposed to historical moments when Jews were considered nonwhite), it is also true, as Lacan might have said (1977, 1998), that whiteness embodies a fantasy of wholeness (invulnerability) to which NO ONE can lay claim.

My pretense to incarnating whiteness is precisely the kind of normative unconscious process that sustains racial inequality. It contains an intergenerationally transmitted imperative, held by all four of my grand-parents, to escape, via assimilation, the traumas of Eastern European pogroms, Western European associations of Eastern Jews with dirt and darkness, and American anti-Semitism (see P. Williams, 1997). My "wish" to occupy the position of what I would call "invulnerability" (rather than wholeness), a collusion with Michael's wish, demonstrates that racism and class inequality do not only split the psyche of the subor-dinate; they also bolster the fantasmatic position of the dominant—and BOTH parties want to hold to the fantasy that, again, as Lacan might say, SOMEONE has the phallus, someone is invulnerable to pain and loss. The fantasy attained by splitting does more, however, than just bolster my identity. By claiming the whiteness they, as immigrants, so longed for, I, in fantasy, secure my attachment to my ancestral ghosts, keep them alive, remain loyal to them. To be recognized as white was, and to a large extent still is, to be recognized as American, to be safe and loved.

It seems to me important to think about how, technically, we might reckon, in our work, with the splitting inherent to racial categories without fostering a fantasy of wholeness. It was while listening to a talk by Leary (2003) one evening that I suddenly realized I had that very day adopted the position of whiteness vis à vis my patient. We had been talking about the function the boyfriend had served for him psychically, the connection to whiteness that the relationship had brought him, and I recall saying something like, "And you can never be white." Thinking of the Eng and Han article, I recall saying to myself something like "Poor guy. He'll never be white and he shall have to mourn that." So long as I was putting myself in the place of whiteness, I must have been acting somewhat superior, which probably enabled me to tolerate his envy and idealization, and to empathize with his feelings of inferiority. But I did not realize that I was in some ways re-enacting the very scene of humili-ation by sustaining a superior stance. Indeed, while I well know intellec-tually that "whiteness" is a fiction, a cultural ideal created by repudiating undesirable attributes labeled non-white, I unconsciously held onto the privileged position because it enabled me to keep a certain distance both from my own ethnic vulnerabilities and from the pain caused this man by racism, not to mention homophobia. In doing so, however, I was in fact enacting the humiliation of racism and the projection of vulnerability that underlies it. Once onto my collusion with the norm that splits white and nonwhite, I began to ask different kinds of questions: for example, what was whiteness to him, what was desirable about the attributes he associated with it, and how had these attributes fallen into the category of "not-me?" More importantly, I asked him if he was assuming I was white and what that meant to him. While acknowledging the privilege I have from the fact that I am associated with whiteness, I yet tried to transmute the categories of "white" and "Asian" into what they stood for in a racialized culture and our mutual racialized imaginations. In consequence, at the same time that whiteness as a narcissistic structure was either denigrated or idealized, there arose a third space of whiteness in which Michael used the fantasy that his ex and I held "whiteness" in order to be able to explore what he had coveted and what he had shut himself off from in life.

On Politeness and Self-Absorption, Emotion and Reason

And now for the content of the stereotypes and how that content played out in treatment. On numerous occasions, this treatment not only confronted me with my own stereotypes, but it also rendered both conscious and problematic some of the assumptions of health that I hold, assumptions that also get enacted unconsciously in treatment and that serve to sustain a particular power status quo. As I mentioned above, Michael's Western/Nonwestern binary at times seemed to take the form of what I was familiar with as a male/female binary. One day he told me that his ex-boyfriend had pointed out to him that whenever Michael walked down the street and someone was coming in another direction, straight at him, it was always Michael who deferred and moved to the side. Michael also sometimes wondered why he did not feel anger in situations in which he knew his Western friends would be angry. He often noted that Westerners seemed angry a lot, that they, for example, would say they were having a bad day rather than just say that some random thing hadn't worked out (like the weather was bad). In other words, he felt Westerners had an irrational way of seeing non-personal events as personal. More than once, I thought that if Michael had been a white female and told me some of the things he did, I'd know right away that we were dealing with problems with self-assertion. But what made me less certain, for this case and perhaps for all, was that I happened to read an article by Rothblum et al. (2000) that brought to my attention the possibility that some of the tension in the therapy, his ongoing discomfort with being in therapy, might have had something to do with my conscious and unconscious assumptions and how I was enacting them. In the article, the authors argue that the basic tenets of attachment theory, for example, that secure attachment promotes freedom to explore, are not universal but rather are a product of Western psychological assumptions. Contrasting Western with Japanese child-rearing practices, they note that while Western parents encourage their children to assert themselves, to figure out what they need and ask for it, Japanese parents tend to anticipate the child's needs and fears, to create an environment in which the needs are met without the child having to ask. The Japanese mother, they argue, fosters emotional closeness, while the Western mother fosters exploration and autonomy. Where the Western ideal of competence values getting what you need yourself vs. depending on others to meet your needs, in Japanese child-rearing, the focus is on coordinating your needs with the needs of others. In the West, babies are encouraged to explore and are encouraged to be oriented to the environment; in Japan, babies explore less and are encouraged to be more oriented to their mothers, more dependent. While in the West there is a value on linking attachment and exploration, in Japan the primary link is between attachment and dependence. This serves the Japanese value of accommodation or social fittedness. "These terms," the authors write, "refer to children's empathy with others, their compliance with others' wishes, and their responsiveness to social cues and norms" (p. 1099).

For Michael, many things made therapy difficult, not least of which was the idea that he was supposed to start the sessions. He told me that he felt it was pushy to talk just about himself; it made him feel as though he was intruding on me. I would interpret this as a problem with self-assertion, but perhaps that's not what it was at all! As an assertive little girl, who, at some point, acquiesced to cultural demands to be a good, self-abnegating girl, I myself had spent much of my analysis struggling with whether or not my agentic desires were selfish, and these struggles surely influenced my interpretations. And yet, as someone caught between two cultures, it was obvious that Michael struggled, just as Eng and Han suggest, between being like a Westerner and being like his family. Am I, then, to be the cultural agent that makes Michael more comfortable operating within Western norms, in effect taking a side of the conflict? Or is my job merely to point out the diverse norms, the conflict, and let Michael find his path? Consciously, I believe my job is the latter, but I fear I fairly frequently perform the former, relying on the ideals of health that my Western training has championed, ideals incorporated not only in technique but even in "the frame." I suppose one could argue that such performances are conscious, for, after all, I can state for you what the ideals are. But it is my view that while the ideals may be conscious, the splitting and devaluation they rest on is not. Repeatedly performing the norms of my profession, I maintain the approval/love of my peers while sustaining a certain distribution of power.

Michael presents a dilemma he's having with his current boyfriend. He doesn't really know whether or not he loves him; he knows he's loved but that's not enough. I ask him what his feelings are. He knows he loves his parents because he wants them to be happy and wants to do what he can to make them happy. Is that a feeling, he asks? I float a hypothesis that there is something that inhibits him from feeling and knowing what he feels, and I think it has to do with the way feelings have been identified as Western and bad. He repeats his sense that Westerners react out of proportion when bad things happen, and he's *glad* he doesn't. But sometimes he'd like to get angry—and he's not sure he should. In fact he does feel angry sometimes—he mentions a new game he's playing, where he waits a little longer before moving out of the way when someone walks toward him. He guesses that because the ex had remarked on how he always moves out of the way, he thought there must be something wrong with it. But he *does* get angry that others don't step out of the way. It's not fair. And it's rude. He's glad he's like he is—but is he getting stepped on?

I struggled in this treatment because my working hypothesis, based on some things Michael said that showed a desire to express more emotion, was that the whole Western/non-Western binary was one way he kept himself inhibited, kept himself from integrating emotion and reason. I also felt that his mother's yelling fits, sometimes paired with humiliation, made emotion frightening for him. And yet, I certainly agreed with him that Western forms of assertion (at least their East coast version) often crossed the line into rudeness and incivility. In the next session, I spoke to Michael about some of my confusions. He was talking about the fun he'd had the past weekend with a visiting friend, a man who laughs a lot at Michael's jokes. He remarked that he generally feels responsible to show his guests a good time and isn't very focused on whether or not he's having a good time himself. Because I again read this as self-abnegation, I brought up the confusions I've been feeling about the Western/non-Western dichotomization. I told him I'd been concerned that, like the ex-boyfriend, I may have been pathologizing something about these values of civility and duty that guide his behavior, and I told him that my therapy culture tends to understand some of these ways of being as self-abnegation. I mentioned that I was pretty sure that if I were seeing a Western female, I would move in the direction of seeing the behavior as self-abnegating. I said, "I suppose what matters is whether or not you find that these ways of being get in your way; do *you* want things to be different?" He then revisited some of the examples of Western rudeness, and in the new rendition, matters were more complicated, more East-West: he said that when he pours tea, he is aware that if there isn't much in the pot, he might not get any; this does in fact bother him. Indeed, he said that the responsibility to make others happy also is self-focused: if the friend doesn't like what you thought would constitute a "good time," you feel devalued as well as guilty. He then noted how often his ex-boyfriend would leave him alone at a party, and how the boyfriend would rationalize his behavior by asserting a value on independence and a disdain for clinginess. But, Michael said, "after I told him more than once that I was uncomfortable in those situations, he shouldn't have left me alone." "Indeed," I say and realize at the same time, "it isn't about which value system is right; it's about being in tune with your partner, conscious of his vulnerabilities." At this point, I decided to ask if he was having any feelings about my upcoming vacation, since he had mentioned being left alone. The rest of the session focused around his question of whether or not he really needs therapy: he associated to the first therapist he saw, the one who referred him to me over a year ago, and expressed a feeling that she was much more conveniently located than I am and that he'll be glad to be able to sleep in and to think, in my absence, about whether he should stop therapy. He then associated to his friend's girlfriend not being very good looking, even though the friend is quite attractive. And when I asked what this might have to do with what came before, he concluded the sequence by saying his new boyfriend doesn't think he really needs therapy. "I think the issues I have, a lot of people have—and I don't think others are in therapy with such issues." I'm thinking that this expression of his discomfort with therapy relates to all of what came before about what's Western, what's not, and I say, both defensively and non-defensively, that many are in therapy for just the issues he brings. And then he tells me he wouldn't pay the fee if his insurance weren't paying, and he feels guilty about that. He just found out his insurance ends in two months' time.

This material is so full of suggestive moments that I hesitate to offer an interpretation, and I imagine that others might have more interesting things to say about it than I do. But my best guess is that Michael may have felt wounded when I suggested a connection between his psychology and that of Western femininity. Had I inadvertently feminized this Asian man who was already sensitive to the feminizing stereotype—both as a gay man and as an Asian man? Perhaps my way of framing things made Michael want to point out to me that he really is much more assertive and self-focused, more masculine, than I think. Perhaps the next association, about abandonment, did not have as much to do with my impending vacation as with the way I had wounded him. Like the ex, I perhaps should have known that what I said would make him uncomfortable. I venture this guess because the material that came after, about whether or not he should quit therapy and whether or not it was worth paying for, had a somewhat hostile edge. It was also not lost on me that the therapist whom he'd first seen was not only closer to his home, but was also quite young and beautiful—was he perhaps trying to wound me by questioning *my* femininity? Why had I framed my intervention in gendered terms? Was I perhaps unconsciously enacting my own dissociated racism and homophobia? Was I imposing my own struggle with sexism on his painful struggle with Orientalism and homophobia? What did it stir up for me to sit with a man who did not assert himself in ways I associate with masculinity? Was I pathologizing his lack of assertiveness because I do not find desirable men who are not assertive?

I would be remiss not to add, however, that Michael's conflict about therapy had other roots as well. A major issue with the current boyfriend was that he didn't value processing, and Michael was coming more and more to see how much he valued it. I believe he found his desire for insight somewhat taboo, perhaps even associated with both the degraded feminine **and** the degraded Western.

What is Love?

Another theme that Michael struggled with during the therapy was the question, what is love? This was a presenting problem in the therapy, but

I also invoke it to demonstrate how the constructs we tend to see as most universal and psychological, least culturally inflected, are in many ways simultaneously socially and psychically constructed. Earlier I noted that Michael didn't feel sure he was in love with his current partner, and I also noted that he felt he wasn't very desirable, a feeling the ex-boyfriend heightened but the current boyfriend completely contradicted. The current boyfriend had only had two male partners in his life, and both were Asian. My patient wondered about white men who only desire Asians—he averred that generally only fat and old white men were into Asians. And Michael wondered why he was never attracted to Asian men either.

Countless works of fiction convince me that love is a social construct as well as a feeling, and that racism can destroy or severely interfere with capacities for love. No work perhaps gets at the socially constructed nature of love as well as David Henry Hwang's *M. Butterfly* (1989). In this play, a French diplomat falls passionately in love with what he thinks is a diminutive, female, Asian, opera singer whom he has heard sing the title role in Madame Butterfly. Early in the play, the opera singer tells Gallimard, the diplomat, the tragic story of the American sailor who seduced and then abandoned the Japanese Butterfly, who, in her desperation, committed suicide. And then she taunts him for finding the story beautiful, denouncing it as an Orientalist fantasy dear to the Western imagination. In a powerful speech (p. 17), she searingly underscores the way power relations infuse love. She asks Gallimard to imagine what he might say if he heard the story of a blonde homecoming queen who had fallen in love with a short Japanese businessman who treated her cruelly. In her lover's long absence, this white Butterfly refuses to give her love to anyone else; she even turns down a marriage proposal from a handsome young Kennedy. The Japanese businessman remarries, and when the homecoming queen finds out, she kills herself. She insists that Gallimard would no doubt find this girl to be insane, underscoring her point that the only stories Western white men like himself find compelling and beautiful are those in which an Oriental woman dies for the love of a cruel Western man. And yet, this is just what the play enacts, the revenge of the short, thin, Asian male against Gallimard, the white Westerner. Gallimard falls madly in love with his Butterfly, who turns out to be a transvestite Asian male. Desperate to preserve the Orientalist fantasy of true heterosexual love, where men are dominant and women submissive, Gallimard transforms himself into the female Asian Butterfly at the end—and kills him/herself for love.

And no writer perhaps better shows the damaging toll that racism takes on love than Toni Morrison. In one of her short stories, "Recitatif" (1983), two girls, one black and one white, are left at an orphanage because their mothers cannot care for them. One mother is physically ill; the other is mentally ill. We do not know which girl is black and which white, and Morrison, intentionally mixing up signifiers of class and race, makes her readers face our own racial stereotypes as we frantically try to figure out who's black and who's white. But the story moves us through the girls' lives and shows us how, at every historical point, racism frustrates their possibility of re-finding the mutual care and protectiveness they had once shared when, on first meeting, each recognized in the other the vulnerability caused by maternal abandonment.

Such literary works suggest why Michael could only love white men, especially those who could not or would not be sexual with him. The Big History of intergenerationally transmitted racism, in which identities are constructed in relation to other identities and marked by differential power relations, also constructs possibilities for love and thus the very nature of love relationships. As the therapy went on, his membership in a gay, Asian activist organization seemed to decrease his homophobia, and he began to be attracted to men from certain Asian subcultures, not his own. It seemed to me that here was an example of the way that essentialist categories and identity politics can in fact facilitate growth and defeat internalized racist and sexist prejudice.

But there is more to the story of love and ethnicity in this case. For Michael, love was less a feeling than a sense of duty. He came to understand that the passion he experienced for the ex-boyfriend had to do with the boyfriend remaining inaccessible and rejecting. His only experiences of passion were on that model of unrequited love (my interpretation was that his desire was fueled by his wish to have what the fantasied ex-boyfriend seemed to have). Otherwise, of love he knew only that he loved his parents, because he wanted them to be happy and because they sacrificed themselves for him. He wanted to sacrifice for them, and he called that love. At the beginning of therapy, he reported that he only cried in movies during scenes of parent-child love, never adult-adult love. In his view, adult-adult love was never pure: in merely desiring the other, you are asking for something back for your love. During the treatment, I was never sure if he simply didn't love the boyfriend, and was at best enjoying how much his boyfriend loved him, or if we were dealing with an inability to love that had to do with several other kinds of things: the inhibition on feeling and being "irrational"; the self-denigration and internalized homophobia (I don't want to be a member of a club that wants me as a member); and the confusion that seemed always to ensue when the other knew what s/he wanted of him. Indeed, it seemed to me that the legacy of mother's control, which he experienced as love but also as control, was to make him unsure of what he felt whenever the other *was* sure. I thought that the constraints on his freedom that he so disliked growing up had become rationalized as a "true" kind of love, a selfless love.

And then I came across a paper on filial piety (Gu 2004) in the particular Asian culture from which my patient hailed. The author of this paper argued that the Oedipus in this culture is different from the Western Oedipus. Specifically, it is marked by a loyalty between parent and child that transcends the loyalty between spouses. Once again, I was decentered by recognizing that my patient's desire was not simply defensive, perhaps only defensive when seen in my particular frame. Am I so jaded that self-less love seems absurd to me? I certainly didn't hear his rendition of his mother's love as selfless; to me, it seemed her sacrifices were as much aimed at having her son achieve what she and her husband couldn't as they were about her son being happy. But I suppose I should ask: What's happiness got to do with it? Is the idea that we are meant to be happy yet another Western value? I leave the reader with my confusion, not with answers. But I hope I leave you with a sense of how every psychological category we contemplate is rife with hauntings from the past—and how our engagements across difference actualize those hauntings.

References

Balbus, I. (2004). The psychodynamics of racial reparations. *Psychoanalysis, Culture & Society* 9(2):159–185.

Benjamin, J. (1988). *The Bonds of Love*. New York: Pantheon.

Bhabha, H.K. (1994). *The Location of Culture*. London and New York: Routledge.

Bodnar, S. (2004). Remember where you come from: dissociative process in multicultural individuals. *Psychoanalytic Dialogues* 14:581–603.

Boulanger, G. (2007). *Wounded By Reality: Understanding and Treating Adult Onset Trauma*. New York: Routledge.

Bourdieu, P. (1984). *Distinction*. Cambridge, MA: Harvard University Press.

Dalal, F. (2002). *Race, Colour and the Processes of Racialization*. Hove and New York: Brunner-Routledge.

Dimen, M. (2003). *Sexuality, Intimacy, Power*. Hillsdale, NJ: The Analytic Press.

Eng, D.L. and Han, S. (2002). A dialogue on racial melancholia. In *Bringing the Plague*, S. Fairfield, L. Layton, and C. Stack, eds. New York: Other Press, pp. 233–267.

Friedman, S.S. (1995). Beyond white and other: relationality and narratives of race in feminist discourse. *Signs* 21:1–49.

Goldner, V. (1991). Toward a critical relational theory of gender. *Psychoanalytic Dialogues* 1(3):249–272.

Grand, S. (2007). Maternal surveillance: disrupting the rhetoric of war. *Psychoanalysis, Culture & Society* 12(4):305–322.

Grand, S. (2013). God at an impasse: devotion, social justice, and the psychoanalytic subject. *Psychoanalytic Dialogues* 23:449–463.

Gu, M.D. (2006). The filial piety complex: variations on the Oedipus theme in Chinese literature and culture. *Psychoanalytic Quarterly*, LXXV (1): 163–195.

Hall, S. (1982). The rediscovery of ideology: return of the repressed in media studies. In M. Gurevitch et al., eds., *Culture, Society and the Media*. NY: Methuen, pp. 56–90.

Hwang, D.H. (1989). *M. Butterfly*. New York: Plume.

Kohut, H. (1971). *The Analysis of the Self*. New York: International Universities Press.

Lacan, J. (1977). *Ecrits. A Selection*. London: Tavistock.

Lacan, J. (1998). *The Four Fundamental Concepts of Psychoanalysis*. New York: W.W. Norton.

Laclau, E. and Mouffe, C. (1985). *Hegemony and Socialist Strategy*. London: Verso.

Layton, L. (1988). *An Empirical Analysis of the Self and Object Love. A Test of Kohut's Conception of the Self*. Diss. Boston University. Ann Arbor, MI: UMI, 1988. 8806495.

Layton, L. (1998). *Who's that Girl? Who's that Boy? Clinical Practice Meets Postmodern Gender Theory*. Hillsdale, NJ: The Analytic Press.

Layton, L. (2002). Cultural hierarchies, splitting, and the heterosexist unconscious. In *Bringing the Plague. Toward a Postmodern Psychoanalysis*, eds. S. Fairfield, L. Layton, and C. Stack. New York: Other Press, pp. 195–223.

Layton, L. (2004a). A fork in the royal road: on defining the unconscious and its stakes for social theory. *Psychoanalysis, Culture & Society* 9(1):33–51.

Layton, L. (2004b). Attacks on linking: the unconscious pull to dissociate individuals from their social context. Paper presented at the spring meeting of Division 39 of the American Psychological Association, Miami Beach, March 19. In: Psychoanalysis, Class and Politics: *Encounters in the Clinical Setting*, eds. L. Layton, N.C. Hollander, and S. Gutwill (2006). London: Routledge, pp. 107–117.

Layton, L. (2004c). This place gives me the heebie jeebies. *International Journal of Critical Psychology* 10:36–50.

Layton, L. (2005). Notes toward a non-conformist clinical practice. Paper presented at the spring meeting of Division 39 of the American Psychological Association, New York City, April 14.

Layton, L. (2006) Racial identities, racial enactments, and normative unconscious processes. *Psychoanalytic Quarterly* 75:237–265.

Layton, L. (2009) Who's responsible? Our mutual implication in each other's suffering. *Psychoanalytic Dialogues* 19:105–120.

Layton, L. (2014). Normative unconscious processes. In: T. Teo (ed.) *Encyclopedia of Critical Psychology*, pp. 1262–1264. New York: Springer.

Layton, L. (2015). Beyond sameness and difference: normative unconscious processes and our mutual implication in each other's suffering. In: D. Goodman and M. Freeman (eds.) *Psychology and the Other*, pp. 168–188. Oxford: Oxford University Press.

Leary, K. (2003). How race is lived in the consulting room. Paper presented to the Massachusetts Association for Psychoanalytic Psychology. Boston, October 29.

May, R. (1986). Concerning a psychoanalytic view of maleness. *Psychoanalytic Review* 73(4):175–193.

Morrison, T. (1983). Recitatif. In *Confirmations*, Baraka and Baraka, eds. New York: Morrow Press, pp. 243–261.

Moss, D., ed. (2003). *Hating in the First Person Plural*. New York: Other Press.

Rothblum, F., Weisz, J. Pott, M., Miyake, K., and Morelli, G. (2000). Attachment and culture. Security in the United States and Japan. *American Psychologist* 55(10):1093–1104.

Shaw, D. (2013). *Traumatic Narcissism*. New York: Routledge.

White, K.P. (2002). Surviving hating and being hated. *Contemporary Psychoanalysis* 38(3):401–422.

Williams, P. (1997). The ethnic scarring of American whiteness. In *The House that Race Built*, ed. W. Lubiano. New York: Pantheon, pp. 253–263.

Williams, R.M. (1997). Living at the crossroads. In *The House that Race Built*, ed. W. Lubiano. New York: Pantheon, pp. 136–156.

Part III

Reassembling Narrative and Culture

Bridging Otherness

Introduction

Healing Haunted Memories: From Monuments to Memorials

Donna Orange

Trauma concerns violence, intended or not. In our justified, and rightly psychoanalytic, concern to focus on traumatic experience, and most recently on transgenerational transmission (Faimberg 1996; Davoine and Gaudilliere 2004; Salberg 2015), we may miss the violation at its core. Something has ripped through bodies and minds, causing damage that destroys human beings and leaves their ghosts (Loewald 1960) haunting future generations (Harris 2009), down to the seventh generation, we have been told. "The fathers have eaten sour grapes, and the children's teeth have been set on edge" (Jeremiah 31:29). In less biblical and more clinical intensity, Sue Grand (Grand 2000, 2010) shows us how violence lives on, like a malignancy. Attachment fills the psychic holes children meet in their traumatized parents with terrors, unspeakable nightmares and daymares, impossible longings, disorientation. Memories of violence, more or less conscious in the parents and grandparents, become endless confusion for their children, grandchildren, and greatgrandchildren.

As many remind us, we psychoanalysts must return to Sandor Ferenczi who first understood how violence turned into confusion and shame in the first generation. He explained how the child, identifying with the perpetrator(s), takes on the perpetrator's point of view on herself, in a complex confusion of tongues, contextualized by radical abandonment. Ferenczi's healing project attempted to find the wounded child in his adult patients, and to name the violence. Likewise, today's psychoanalysis, including this book, has begun to name violence: the slavery system and its long inheritance; genocides; colonialism, child abuse and neglect, multiple forms of gender and sexual domination. Whether collective or personal or both, we want to know how this violence goes on and on, why it persists in ourselves—as familial memory, as "whiteness," even as obliviousness to our devastating climate emergency (Orange 2016a). We want to know how and why this violence continues decade after decade, and what to do about it.

From the four chapters in this section, overlapping the collective, the clinical, and the personal, approaching these questions by diverse paths, many approaches—not to say answers—emerge. Evie Rappoport tells us the story of one who inherits genocide herself meeting another massacre in Cambodia. Eyal Rozmarin uses his childhood reading of *War and Peace* to contextualize his readings of twentieth-century thinkers on remembering violence. Sandra Silverman relates a clinical narrative of mental violence, where gender and sexuality express the confusion of tongues. David Goodman shows in his own life how religious beliefs intended to be comforting can mask forms of violence. Each of these has its own integrity, and its own rich relation to the transgenerational transmission theme of this book. Over and over, however, the word and sense of *deception* surfaces.

"Everyone will agree that it is of the highest importance to know whether we are not duped by morality." So begins Emmanuel Levinas (Levinas 1969, p. 21), an author important to both Rozmarin and Goodman, as he begins his *Totality and Infinity* with a meditation on the ways that "winning" war suspends morality, totalizing all and everything. Duped, deceived, we have also been traumatized, entrapped by the violence that haunts us through the generations. As Rappoport reminds us, dictators like Pol Pot or Hitler deceive vast populations into suspending their ordinary moral sensibilities, and committing genocides, borne by the children and grandchildren of victims (Hoffman 2004) and perpetrators (Frie 2016) both. They resemble enormous versions of cults (Shaw 2014) as headed by malignant narcissists, deceiving their adherents into encouraging every kind of otherwise unimaginable violence to those they deem different and thus unacceptable to the regime. All of us, perhaps, become "duped by morality" into forgetting the possibility of such inordinate violence. Remembering, truly remembering, Rappoport implies, the other's traumatic destruction provides a renewed encounter with one's own.

Rozmarin, relating both family and intellectual history, tells more of the ways that our best efforts at memory deceive us. We carry traces, both personal and historical. To his photographer friend, he looks like a Rabbi. To this reader, he sounds like an intellectual with deep emotional roots in Europe (including European Russia), and in Israel. Haunted, he cannot stop thinking about the moment when his grandmother realized that everyone was dead. Traces of the past and traces of the infinite. Memory deceives us, and brings us back, forcing us to question everything we ever thought. We are the suicidal thoughts that come into God's head in a bad mood, Kafka tells him. Benjamin and Bloch offer him an angel of history and a spirit of utopia, but both already haunted, as if by the imminent "next catastrophe." Ultimately he turns to Levinas, "the tallest tree," not for comfort, but an attitude toward insoluble problems after what Derrida called "the worst," the ultra-violent deception. Escape from violence requires, it seems, also to Rozmarin, a radical turn to the Other.

In a gripping clinical narrative, Silverman shows us how deception traumatizes when a haunted mind takes over, through invasive violence (Williams 2010), the mind and body of a child. Unable to be at home in the body of a girl, or in the thought of transitioning to a male body, this patient struggles not only with gender trauma (Saketopoulou 2014), but with claiming her own life, from her mother and from her analyst. Her mother, more a possessive lover than the indispensable holding environment or primordial density (Loewald 1960, 2000), from which a child could differentiate, inhabits this young patient to the point that she/he cannot find a mind of one's own, let alone a body. More differentiated, but attached to mentalization theories and reluctant to encourage the patient to go her own way toward becoming overtly male, the analyst witnesses a courageous struggle, while engaging in her own. This story engages urgent clinical questions about how our patients teach us. Only through a yielding of her own theories and presuppositions in a gradual surrender (Ghent 1990) to the Other, can the analyst stand by her patient escaping from the violence of gender.

Finally, Goodman returns us to Ferenczi and confusion of tongues, the great traumatic deception. My young neighbors in New York's Upper West Side used to ask me, "Are you a Chanukah or a Christmas?" In later life I am lucky to feel myself, not so traumatically, to be both and neither. Born into confusion between his parents' Jewish heritage and life with their embrace of evangelical Christianity, he too was both, but this deceptive situation, as he tells us, imploded dramatically and traumatically in his life. When "religious" people blamed him, at age 16, for his mother's death from cancer, and his father abandoned him to fend for himself, he was left, like Dostoevsky's Ivan Karamazov, with a profound disillusionment that he calls an "attachment disorder with truth." Turning away from all the totalizing systems that had let him down and destroyed him, struggling through years of study and searching, he turned from searching for truth toward what Plato called "the Good beyond Being." In the work of Levinas, he found in the demand to respond to the face of the Other and to care for the suffering, the path he needed.

Profound and destructive shame often accompanies, as if built in to, deceptive traumatic violence. Duped by the leader, ideology, parent, creed, the consciously or unconsciously deceptive partner, one feels so humiliated to have believed and needed to believe. The victim now carries, often suicidally, shame that should belong to the perpetrators, a shame that impedes, or at least complicates, needed remembering and mourning. Primo Levi, Paul Celan, and Jean Améry are case examples (Orange 2016b).

Beyond deception and shame, each of these authors engages the question of how the haunting past can be usefully remembered. All agree that monuments, even if they are called memorials, do little or nothing beyond assuaging guilt in perpetrators. They place the crime out there, as if finished now by its public acknowledgement—a further deception, creating more trauma for those affected. By contrast these authors write of totems, memorials, and memorializing. Rappoport describes a glass tower filled with actual human skulls from the killing fields of Cambodia. She calls it a totem, creating an embodied kinship bond linking the lost generation to the collectivity of living human beings. Such remembering helps us to witness, to remember, to affirm our bonds with all human beings. Rozmarin writes of responsibility as creative memorial, quoting Levinas: "The presence of persons who, for once, do not fade away into words, get lost in technical questions, freeze up into institutions and structures" (Levinas 1999, p. 87). Silverman shows us how the dead monument to the mother's colonial takeover of her child becomes a living memorial, affirming what is still possible. Goodman transforms the dead cognition embodied in monuments to the dead, in dogmas, creeds, and systems into knowing as invitation, as demand, as responsibility to the other. As do our other authors, he makes his life a memorial that cries out never again, thus placing a spoke in the wheel (Bonhoeffer et al. 1970, p. 221) of the intergenerational transmission of trauma. Perhaps we could say that true memorials are turned toward the Other.

Readers will find themselves challenged, sobered, and enriched by the chapters in this section.

References

Bonhoeffer, D., E. Robertson, and J. Bowden (1970). *No rusty swords: letters, lectures and notes, 1928–1936: from the collected works [of] Dietrich Bonhoeffer, volume 1.* London, Collins, The Fontana Library.

Davoine, F., and J.-M. Gaudilliere (2004). *History beyond trauma: whereof one cannot speak, thereof one cannot stay silent.* New York, Other Press.

Faimberg, H. (1996). "'Listening to Listening'." *Int. J. Psycho-Anal.* 77: 667–677.

Frie, R. (2016). *Not in my family: German memory and the Holocaust.* London, Oxford University Press.

Ghent, E. (1990). "Masochism, Submission, Surrender—Masochism as a Perversion of Surrender." *Contemp. Psychoanal.* 26: 108–136.

Grand, S. (2000). *The reproduction of evil: a clinical and cultural perpsective.* Hillsdale, NJ, Analytic Press.

Grand, S. (2010). *The hero in the mirror: from fear to fortitude.* New York, Routledge.

Harris, A. (2009). "You Must Remember This." *Psychoanalytic Dialogues* 19: 2–21.

Hoffman, E. (2004). *After such knowledge: memory, history, and the legacy of the Holocaust.* New York, Public Affairs.

Levinas, E. (1969). *Totality and infinity: an essay on exteriority.* Pittsburgh, PA, Duquesne University Press.

Levinas, E. (1999). *Alterity and transcendence.* New York, Columbia University Press.

Loewald, H. W. (1960). "On the Therapeutic Action of Psycho-Analysis." *Int. J. Psycho-Anal.* 41: 16–33.

Loewald, H. W. (2000). *The essential Loewald: collected papers and monographs.* Hagerstown, MD, University Pub. Group.

Orange, D. (2016a). *Climate crisis, psychoanalysis, and radical ethics.* London, Routledge.

Orange, D. (2016b). *Nourishing the inner life of clinicians and humanitarians: the ethical turn in psychoanalysis.* London and New York, Routledge.

Saketopoulou, A. (2014). "Mourning the Body as Bedrock: Developmental Considerations in Treating Transsexual Patients Analytically." *Journal of the American Psychanalytic Association* 62: 773–806.

Salberg, J. (2015). "The Texture of Traumatic Attachment: Presence and Ghostly Absence in Transgenerational Transmission." *Psychoanalytic Quarterly* 84: 21–46.

Shaw, D. (2014). *Traumatic narcissism: relational systems of subjugation.* New York, Routledge.

Williams, P. (2010). *Invasive objects: minds under siege.* New York and London, Routledge/Taylor & Francis Group.

Chapter 8

Tower of Skulls

A Totemic Memorial to the Cambodian Genocide

Evelyn Rappoport

> First they came for the Socialists, and I did not speak out—
> Because I was not a Socialist.
> Then they came for the Trade Unionists, and I did not speak out—
> Because I was not a Trade Unionist.
> Then they came for the Jews, and I did not speak out—
> Because I was not a Jew.
> Then they came for me—and there was no one left to speak for me.
> (Martin Niemöller, 1946–1950)[1]

These poignant words, written by Martin Niemöller, a prominent Protestant pastor who was interned in Sachsenhausen and Dachau concentration camps from 1938 to 1945, capture the essence of the evolving force of tragic destruction and evil, which organizes and shapes genocide. Evil is a pernicious process that kindles a fire to destroy any vestige of "otherness" at an individual, group, and cultural level. More precisely, it is mass murder based upon primitive fears and terror of difference; fears which are disavowed and projected onto a demonic evil, which must then be destroyed by a greater evil (January, 2007). In genocides the primacy of groups and the politics of power dominate the primacy of any individual human being. Christopher Bollas (2011), in his article "The Structure of Evil," talks about genocide as the quintessential crime of the twentieth century, which on an individual level is exemplified by the serial killer, a perfect executioner in Western culture. Genocides are rooted in what Sue Grand (2000, 2010) calls the reproduction of evil, diabolical campaigns of mass murders and destruction of individuals and designated groups; massacres intended to destroy any vestiges of individual and group subjectivities of mind, body, and culture.

Cambodia – A Land of Contrasts

Cambodia, officially known as the Kingdom of Cambodia (Khmer) and once known as the Khmer Empire, is a land of incredible beauty, natural resources, and majestic, breathtaking temples. Yet it is layered with a history of war, strife, and one of the most brutal genocides of this century. Phnom Penh, Cambodia's busy capital, sits at the junction of the Mekong and Tonlé Sap rivers. It was a hub for both the Khmer Empire and French colonialists, and today is home to the ornate Royal Palace and Silver Pagoda, as well as to the National Museum. Phnom Penh has a diverse and exotic sense of "otherness." Its culture is rich with history and yet modern Phnom Pen is impoverished and decimated, held captive by the very same history of colonization and war.

Visiting Cambodia

In January of 2014, as part of a small group visiting Cambodia for the first time, I traveled a short distance from the city center of Phnom Penh, to the village of Choeung Ek, an area which today is known as the Killing Fields. Approaching the area with great trepidation, I found myself re-imaging visual fragments of the pictures of the killing fields, linking the name to the unimaginable evil and demonic practices that these grounds absorbed. Later, I learned that the Chankiri Tree, or Killing Tree as it was called, was a tree in the Cambodian forest against which children and infants were smashed because their parents were accused of crimes against the Khmer Rouge. The killing tree, a perversion of a vibrant tree symbolizing life, is now an iconic symbol of horrific brutality, corruption, and torture.

Nothing could prepare us, the tourists, for the ferocious cruelty of the landscape we entered. The memorial park at the village of Choeung Ek has been built around the mass graves of thousands of victims, most of whom were executed after they had been transported from the S-21 Prison in Phnom Penh. Many of these graves are visible above ground, and many are still in the process of being excavated.

There are no words to describe the repugnance and fear that arose within me while walking upon paths covered with decayed bones and looking up at scattered remnants of clothing hanging from tree branches. As I moved, step by step, feeling as if walking through a quagmire, I saw images of concentration camps of Auschwitz, Birkenau, Treblinka, Bergen Belsen, Buchenwald, and Majdenak; hauntings of the holocaust superimposed upon the landscape of the Cambodian genocide.

I was swept into a timeless space, a vortex of multiple genocides, the past of the 1930s and 1940s merging with the events of the 1970s all flashing in front of my eyes, penetrating my body, blending into confusing scenes of unspeakable, unimaginable, horrors and destruction. Pictures of lost members of my family, grandparents, aunts, and uncles who I never knew, came fleetingly to my mind's eye. Ghostly shadows became my companions as I experienced a continuous sense of confusion, disorientation, and nausea. These sensations, as well as deadening fatigue, were so pronounced that my face felt frozen and my eyelids so heavy that I could barely look at the exhibition graphic photos of tortured prisoners waiting to be shipped to final extermination.

Totems and Memorials

As I began to walk towards the stupa, a Buddhist structure, which housed the actual memorial, my knees buckled. Waves of fear washed over me when I crossed the threshold. Dissociating, I watched myself as if walking in slow motion, with my body detached from my will or agency.

Suddenly I was confronted with an enormous glass cylinder filled with skulls, piled high, one on top of the other. I then realized that these were decaying skulls of different sizes, skulls that were excavated in the fields and put on exhibition.

The placement of the skulls in the glass container loomed as a tower comprised of the totemic markers of those who had been massacred and defiled. Checking the definition of a totem, I discovered that a totem is an aesthetic object, an archetypal symbol that creates a kinship bond among a particular group or clan of living creatures, whether animal or human. This memorial of skulls, composed of tangible remnants of skeletal fragments of lives previously lived, symbolically linked each to the other, as well as to the collective, to the clan of human beings. This totem exemplifies what Marianne Hirsch (2012, p. 86) describes as "a repertoire of embodied knowledge," a living memorial of a lost generation erased from the annals of history.

The Reign of Pol Pot and the Khmer Rouge

Our tour group was transfixed as we listened to the details of the heinous atrocities inflicted by the Khmer Rouge from 1975 through 1979 under the reign of Pol Pot. Highly organized and executed mass killings of ideologically suspect groups were delineated, identified, and targeted as enemies to be destroyed. Ethnic minorities including Vietnamese, Chinese (Sino Khmers), Chams, and Thais, as well as former civil servants, government soldiers. Buddhist monks, secular intellectuals, and professionals were all deemed to be traitors.

The non-Communist intellectuals and the peasants all shared the fate of numerous other groups demonized by the Khmer Rouge. Anyone who could speak a foreign language was suspect, as were teachers, monks, and professionals. All were identified as "other" and targeted as enemies to eliminate. Indeed, even those who wore glasses or had a high forehead (evidence of being smart) were marked.

Children were brutally snatched from their parents, and family members dispersed and relocated to rural communes around the countryside. All familial ties were shattered and any form of communication was banned. Married couples were permitted limited visits with each other and individuals seen engaged in sexual activity were immediately killed.

It is estimated that between 2 and 2.5 million people were brutally tortured, dehumanized, and killed. Carrying out their diabolical campaign, the Khmer Rouge strictly isolated Cambodia from the rest of the world and then introduced the combination of executions, harsh labor, and calculated famine to create a brutal prison-nation where every person was an inmate of the state.

Regardless of age or gender, the work at these primitive, rural communes was backbreaking, unrelenting, and dehumanizing. Many starved to death or died of sicknesses related to malnutrition. Protestors and slackers were taken away and bludgeoned to death.

Almost all freedom to travel was abolished and all privacy was eliminated during the Khmer Rouge era. Even eating was restricted and became only a communal activity. All personal utensils were banned, and people were given only one spoon to eat with.

The plan of the Khmer Rouge was to grow rice to sell abroad for weapons, leaving the commune-bound Cambodians precious little to eat. The boy soldiers, who made up the army of enforcers, were given little ammunition. They were instructed not to waste their precious bullets on the subhuman creatures that were "other" and instead were encouraged to torture and maim slowly with the utmost agony, and only then to dismember and annihilate.

Perverse Ideology

Ben Kiernan (2003) compares the *Armenian genocide*, the *Holocaust*, and the *Cambodian genocide*. Although each is unique in its own right, they all share certain common features. It is evident that racism was a major part of the ideology of all three regimes. Although all three perpetrators were largely secular, they targeted religious minorities. All three also tried to use force of arms to expand into what they identified as a contiguous heartland. All three regimes also idealized their ethnic peasantry as the true "national" class, the ethnic soil from which the new state would grow. Fundamentally, in all genocides the goal of the empowered few is to strip select groups of their humanity and identity.

The Cambodian genocide was not driven by racial or religious hatred but by an ideology that had been incubated so fervently that it could be considered insanity. This constituted apartheid of the mind and corporal body, erasing all thoughts and markers of individual difference across multiple registers. Within a four-year time span, all of the non-communist inhabitants of Cambodia, regardless of race, ethnicity, or religion, were stripped of identity. Any hint of difference became taboo. Color in clothing was banned, as was the possession of any meaningful personal property or accessory whether a pencil, a mirror, a fragment of cloth, a picture. All personal items were banned and would be savagely ripped from the hands of any man, woman, or child. Homogenized and stripped of all social and emotional connections, everyone was reduced to the lowest, most basic primitive common denominator.

Personal Reflections

During this part of our trip, surrounded by ghosts, skulls, and skeletal remnants, I became dissociated and truly felt myself to be an alien, a foreigner in a foreign land. Even when I returned to the Phnom Penh, to the modern structures and breathtaking sites including Golden Pavilion and the Palace, I continued to feel lost and untethered, somewhat disconnected from the members of my group. I felt as if I embodied the foreign "other," unseen and invisible in plain sight.

The Spirituality and Transcendence of Angkor Wat

One hundred and fifty miles from the madness of the killing fields, I had my first glimpse of the majestic grandeur of the iconic temple of Angkor Wat built in the first half of the twelfth century. The central temple of the complex is estimated to have been constructed over 30 years by King Suryavarman II, dedicated to Vishnu (Hindu).

The entire complex is the world's largest architectural representation of the Hindu universe. It was originally constructed as a Hindu temple for the Khmer Empire, gradually transforming into a Buddhist temple toward the end of the twelfth century. The center of what was a massive temple city built, over the course of 600 years, by dozens of rulers who considered themselves part god, part king.

Symbolically, Angkor Wat is a miniature replica of the universe in stone, and represents an earthly model of the cosmic world. The central tower rises from the center of the monument symbolizing the mythical mountain, Meru, situated at the center of the universe. Its five towers correspond to the peaks of Meru. The outer wall corresponds to the mountains at the edge of the world, and the surrounding moat the oceans beyond.

Angkor Wat itself is surrounded by a 650-foot-wide (200 m) moat that encompasses a perimeter of more than 3 miles (5 km). This moat is 13 feet deep (4 m) and would have helped stabilize the temple's foundation, preventing groundwater from rising too high or falling too low.

Walking in darkness through the forest on the outskirts of the town of Siam Reap, we arrived on the edge of the moat of the temple complex at sunrise. We watched in awe as the darkness dispelled and the emerging light was reflected on the temples and towers of this majestic, incredible compound. At this place, in this moment in time, I was filled with inspiration and transcendence. I was privileged to witness this remarkable scene, an awesome, momentary experience of creation.

It was here, in this sacred place, that I heard echoes of the sounds of silence. I then experienced a whole-body sense of calm and healing. Suddenly, I was infused with energy, a visceral arousal surge, which began to dispel the fogginess and heaviness I was experiencing. For me, survival energy seemed to emanate from the figures etched in stone and the intricate carvings on the massive and formidable walls. I imagined generations of ancestors extending their hands, as in the carvings, transferring messages of hope and resilience to those who visit.

The dialectic tension between trauma and transcendence, between revulsion and revelation, was ever present throughout my journey in Cambodia. The proximity of structures representing multiple aspects of trauma and disintegration, to islands of inspiration and wonder was jarring. Moving between these states of being, I found that the people of Cambodia provided a link of connection to my own humanity and to the humanity of others. During my direct encounters with the local people, I was able to relocate and reorient myself both physically and emotionally. During these moments, my ghosts receded further into the background, and the presence in the eyes of those I met felt more in "the real."

Trans-Generational Transmissions

The population of Cambodia today is approximately 10 million with 90–95 percent of Khmer ethnic. An estimated 10 percent of the population lives in Phnom Penh. The Khmer Rouge reign of terror in Cambodia from 1975 to 1979 continues to haunt every surviving citizen both in memory as well as in the daily conditions of life which hold them captive. Today Cambodia is one of the world's poorest countries and the coexistence of the archaic with the contemporary is quite jarring throughout. The shock and destruction of the genocide under the reign of the Khmer Rouge continues to generate aftershocks that cover the landscape, and shape the psyche of the survivors and generations to follow.

The legacy of destruction, dehumanization, and cruelty is experienced across multiple registers in the infrastructure of the country. Extreme poverty, government corruption, crime, and child trafficking permeate the fabric of society. A small number of individuals, both in government and in the private sphere, once again hold the power while the majority are the "less than" who live in primitive and extremely limiting conditions. A generation was decimated; homeless children abound, as do elderly people who have no caretakers or sources of support.

The economic impact of the genocide is evident in present day Cambodia. There is a dearth of skilled workers and scant educated professionals in the workplace. Educational opportunities, although beginning, are still shockingly limited.

Fragments of memories blend with the sounds and voices of the city in a surround, which conveys a sense of absence, loss, and a flatness of experience. Not only do present-day conditions maintain the humiliation and degradation of those who did survive, but also these conditions explicitly and implicitly transmit these feeling states from survivors to the next generation.

The memories and raw sensory elements of genocide shape the psyche of the current population. Living history continues to claim victims, perpetrators, and witnesses across multiple physical and affective registers (Alpert, 2015; Grand, 2015). The process of destruction and dehumanization, humiliation and degradation, hallmarks of the Cambodian genocide, continue through the abuse of power, social oppression, and economic forces throughout the country

Resilience: Connectivity and Healing

And what of the Cambodian people in the aftermath of horror?

The Cambodian people are peaceful, loving, kind, and gentle. Everyone we met had a story about the horrors they or their family members endured under the regime of the Khmer Rouge. Some share little and speak without affect or inflection, while others offer detailed accounts of imprisonment, brutality, and conditions, which defy reality. And yet, the people we met were eager for contact with the outside world and grateful for any opportunity to learn and to work. Despite harsh conditions and years of helpless victimization they appear to be quietly resilient. In fact, the Khmer people are likened to the lotus flower, which grows in dirty, muddy water, and nonetheless blooms into a beautiful and usefully edible plant.

Our guides on this trip were all child-survivors of the Khmer Rouge. All appeared older than their chronological age, wizened, short and thin, their physical presentation bespoke of extreme malnutrition and deprivation.

One specific tour guide, Khim, a short, slightly built man with dark piercing eyes and glasses, appeared to be in his sixties but actually was in his late forties. He wore a black baseball cap, black baggy pants, and a grey, worn, collared shirt. He relayed his story in a soft monotone as he described how he was forcibly removed from his family and sent to live with a peasant family. That family worked him from morning until night. Even though he was in a constant state of terror and hunger, he maintained his silence, afraid that any sign of distress would result in greater punishment. After an undefined length of time, he was somehow "freed." With no place to go, totally alone, he set out on foot to return to his home. After days without basic sustenance, all the while trying to avoid stepping on land mines, he arrived at his town only to find his family home demolished and looted. There was no sign of any family member.

Throughout this tale he spoke with little affect. It was as if he was telling a story about a far, far-away land. It was only when he began to speak about his two young children that his voice became nuanced, and he spoke with inflection as he proudly shared his hopes and dreams for the future of his children. Like the others we met he did not speak of vengeance or of violence. He was, in fact, typical of the Cambodian people – peaceful, gentle, and spiritual.

The Cambodian people value family ties and connections above all. Respect is given to elders, and children are valued and cherished. The bonds of love continue to create a holding environment, a resource that enables healing to occur and love to flourish.

Humanitarian Aid

Help is being offered through NGOs, which are deeply committed to providing education and resources. Everyone we met who was part of an NGO told us the same story: they came to Cambodia to initiate a particular venture, met the people, heard about the atrocities they survived, and became entranced with the goodness they found. Buried in the mound of horror were sweet feelings and constant kindness. A number of founders relayed how they arrived to offer humane aid and found themselves unable to leave. They described how they fell in love with the kind and gentle people of this country who were extremely appreciative and grateful for any offers of help. They were impressed with their quiet determination and their family values, which, in spite of the efforts of the Khmer Rouge, continue to survive and flourish. Even after experiencing this enormous collective atrocity, the culture persists and traces of that heritage are evident within each person.

Perhaps this positive energy emanates from Angkor Wat, from a transmission of spirituality and belief in the Hindu tradition, and from the legacy, the living words of the Dharma of the Buddha.

The ancestral narratives, passed down largely through an oral tradition, consist of archetypal stories of the battles of the demons with the forces of goodness; wars in which good ultimately prevails over evil. This is particularly exemplified in the Ramayana, a series of complex mythological stories told in the form of an epic poem. In fact, the scene from the Ramayana depicted in the carvings of Angkor Wat is a long and fierce struggle between Rama and the demon king Ravana (10 heads and 20 arms) near the center. It is among the finest of the bas-reliefs at Angkor Wat. The battle takes place in Lanka (Sri Lanka) and ends with the defeat of Ravana, captor of Sita, the beautiful wife of Rama. The Ramayana shows and tells about the values of familial loyalty, trustworthiness, and filial piety. One of its strongest aspects is its clarion call for order in a world that fails to acknowledge it. This is a world in which the moral third (Benjamin) collapses, the very process that enables the evils of genocide to develop and conquer cultures.

Witnessing: Embodied Presence

Only now, in August of 2015, as I began to write this article, do I realize what the amassed skeletal heads of Cambodia represented. They, in essence, are the objects that retained the one symbol of the subjective human identity of the victims. The decayed heads and facial bones continue to hold the ineffable human element which the terrorists could not obliterate, even though they murderously defiled, tortured, and desecrated their victims' bodies.

In genocides personal history is destroyed, subjectivity and peculiarity are erased, and human subjects become "enumerated objects," nameless and unrecognizable (Grand, 2009, p. 178). Yet these bones and skulls, objects and remnants of skeletons, remain recognizable as human heads, heads once filled with life and knowledge. They are powerful, unforgettable reminders of the individualities and complexities of humanity. These heads live in the echoes of the memories of survivors and in the memory of all those who come to pay tribute. Some of the village people claim that they hear the skulls talking to them.

My experiences in Cambodia reactivated my own traumatic memories and hauntings, reconnecting me to my history and my family's stories of loss, separation, and survival, as well as to my own experiences of immigration and foreign landings.

In September of 2014, my sister, cousins and I flew to Leipzig, Germany, where we were privileged to pay tribute to the lost members of my family – the grandparents, aunts, uncles, and cousins who I never knew. My mother, born in Leipzig to an enlightened Jewish family, emigrated to Palestine in December 1937 at age 15, as part of a collective youth group. She was a fierce and passionate youngster unwavering in her commitment to the ideals of building Palestine. She was determined to join her peers on their great adventure of going to Palestine and completing their studies. Her parents reluctantly relented and permitted her to participate. In December of 1937, the entire family, as well as friends and neighbors, accompanied her to the central Leipzig rail station. With tears of sadness and joy they watched her depart on her adventure. This was the last time she would ever see her family.

Archives revealed that on October 26, 1938, my grandparents, aunts, and uncle were rounded up and deported from Leipzig on the first transport to Poland. They were "assembled" and immediately banished from that very same central railway station in Leipzig, in what later would become known as the "final solution." Unknown and unrecognized they disappeared without a trace, without a grave or even a marker, annihilated from history. Despite the precision of the record keeping of the Nazi killing machine, their whereabouts remained unknown; seemingly, they were not even significant enough to be recorded in their death.

Arriving in the city of Leipzig with a few family members, we came to re-witness and pay tribute to the spirits of my family, to those who were exterminated. With the assistance of a special task force dedicated to reconciliation, along with the cooperation of the German municipality, we dedicated seven stones to legitimize the memory of my family. These "stolpensteine" or "stumbling blocks" are 4×4 concrete blocks covered with a brass plate inscribed with the individual name, date of birth, address, and location of death of each individual. On September 9th at precisely 3:00 p.m. we gathered together to dedicate a stone for each of my seven family members in front of the home in which they lived.

One small stone for each soul. Each stone was installed and cemented by Gunter Demnig, the artist who designed, manufactured, and personally laid 60,000 stolpensteine in Germany. With a few officials and local pedestrians viewing our dedication, I quoted a passage, which read "there are people with hearts of stone and stones with hearts of people." I then added "the seven stones we place today have the hearts and souls of those who were lost to me long before I was born."

Despite shivering from fatigue, sadness, and a whirlwind of emotions, I sensed a wave of a return, a settling of shadows and ghosts as we brought our people as close to home as possible. Silently I recalled the last letter my mother received from her mother in 1941, a censored letter that was smuggled through South America to Palestine, in which my grandmother reported that "they had enough to eat and that all was well." At the bottom of the letter, the last sentence written in a child's handwriting in German read "we miss you a lot and love you so much." These last words were written by my mother's two younger sisters, Metta and Leah. They are parting words from the shadows, the last traces of my two aunts, who were killed in "occupied Poland" long before I was born.

September 2014: The Past in the Personal Present

Shortly after my return to New York on the afternoon of 9/11, I began to experience a deep and unrelenting sense of sorrow, which stayed with me for months afterwards. Often, I found myself in tears, saddened by moments large and small, and by fragments of early childhood memories. My filter was raw. A heightened sense of vulnerability and attunement to the suffering of others prevailed. I was aware of my own sensory sensitivities, my intensified startle responses, and the random waves of pain that I felt in what were otherwise fairly ordinary life moments and daily activities. Violent movie scenes became unbearable, as did stories depicting the torture of war and strife. I was mystified as to what was happening. And then I began to understand I was mourning and grieving for those I never knew...

Through my travels and experiences in East and West Germany, my visits to the concentration camps and graveyards of Poland, the cemeteries of Normandy, and the killing fields in Cambodia, I began to know, to feel, and to experience, both the presence and lived absence of my lost generation. Entering into these landscapes with the "disease" "of both the unknown and the familiar," I began to heal.

The "unthought knowns" (Bollas, 1987) of my attachment history have become more accessible, affectively connected, and even reconfigured within me, in the interior of my body and mind. At a certain moment, I realized that the visual images of the skulls in Cambodia were no longer grotesque and shocking as I remembered. Instead, I found myself linking these skulls to images to people, to individuals with heads and faces, with skin and bones, to the human heads, which once held their own memories as well as the wisdom of previous generations. The skull has become a universal symbol of mortality representing human aspirations to know the mysteries of the universe.

The powerful effects of war, genocides, terrorist attacks, and other life shattering events are transmitted from generation to generation. Researchers and neuroscientists are beginning to understand how environmental factors can alter genetic processes (i.e., acquired characteristics). This field of epigenetics is bringing evidence to support the process of "transgenerational epigenetic inheritance," that is, the intergenerational transmission of environmental factors which affect one generation transmitted to the next generation through DNA expression.

Continued evidence is emerging that indicates that the impact of trauma is held in the nervous system (Levine, 2010; Ogden et al., 2006; Scaer, 2014). Furthermore, environmental trauma, abuse, and/or neglect directly impact our brain/mind organizations. Specifically, research points to the impact of trauma as altering the brain's ability to flexibly update perceptions and representations, leaving a fertile area for unconscious repetitions and re-creations (Ginot, 2015).

Embodied memorials, affective connections, memories and narratives, all post-memory resources, can shape and re-contextualize fragments of traumatic memories into coherent, meaningful narratives. These embodied memorials are the experiential and affective links to the stories they tell of people and places in living history. These stories, reconstructed from fragments of memories, connect, hold, and re-enliven the bones and skulls. The nuanced details of individual and family stories are the flesh on the skeleton; together they transmit the energies of embodied human experiences.

The antidote to evil comes in the form of witnessing, remembering, and creating affective connections resulting in post-memorial transmissions. They move us beyond witness and bystander to the state embodied participant, sharing the felt sense of presence and absence.

Generational transmissions of trauma, or re-memory as Marian Hirsch writes, are emanations of experiences which erupt in flashes of imagery in the language of the body, in collective stories, which transform history cognitively and affectively, and as Eva Hoffman (2004) wrote, as living connections between proximate generations.

Only when we recognize, acknowledge, and share the events of the past, when the unspeakable is communicated, can we remember, locate, and place the "unforgotten" into the historical landscape of generations. Without recognition and acknowledgment, denial will continue to propel history to the collapsing past, present, and future into a timeless vortex of a living death. Without an antidote, on both an individual and collective level, the wounds of history will continue to bleed as scar tissue is ripped open again and again while history goes unheeded.

I conclude with the eloquent words of Marianne Hirsch (2012, p. 25):

The landscape of post memory is peopled by faces from the past, by images in and out of the family album, by photos of victims and survivors. Memory is mediated, cultural and also escapes from photographs to haunt the natural landscape of the present. The ghosts have become part of our landscape, reconfiguring the domestic as well as the public spaces of the post-generation. Despite these invasions, the woods themselves continue to replenish in the bright sunshine, the trees persist in reaching upward, indifferent witness to the layered connective histories projected onto them.

Death Toll in Genocides of the Twentieth Century

Namibia	1904	80,000
Armenia	1915–1917	1.2 million
Ukraine	1932–1939	7 million
The Holocaust	1937–1945	6 million
Cambodia	1974–1979	2.5 million
Rwanda	1994	800,000
Bosnia	1995	100,000

How many more genocides will we count in our and our children's lifetime?

Note

1 The first sermon delivered by Martin Niemöller containing the poem *may* have been delivered on January 6, 1946 at the Confessing Church in Frankfurt. Many versions of the poem circulated from 1946 through the 1950s.

Bibliography

Alpert, Judith (2015). Enduring Mothers, Enduring Knowledge: On Rape and History. *Contemporary Psychoanalysis*, 51(2), 296–310.

Benjamin, J. (2009). A Relational Psychoanalysis Perspective on the Necessity Of Acknowledging Failure in Order to Restore the Facilitating and Containing Features of the Intersubjective Relationship (the Shared Third). *Int. J. Psycho-Anal.*, 90, 441–450.

Bollas, C. (1987). *The Shadow of the Object: Psychoanalysis of the Unthought Known*. New York, Columbia University Press.

Bollas, C. (2011). *The Christopher Bollas Reader*. The Structure of Evil (pp. 155–178). London, New York, Routledge.

Frosh, Stephen (2013). *Hauntings: Psychoanalysis and Ghostly Transmissions*. Basingstoke, UK, Palgrave Macmillan.

Ginot, Efrat (2015). *The Neuropsychology of the Unconscious: Integrating Brain and Mind in Psychotherapy*. New York, Norton.

Grand, S. (2000). *The Reproduction of Evil: A Clinical and Cultural Perspective*. Hillsdale, NJ, Analytic Press.

Grand, S. (2009). *The Hero in the Mirror: From Fear to Fortitude*. New York, Routledge.

Grand, S. (2015). Circle of Witnessing: On Hope and Atrocity. *Contemporary Psychoanalysis*, 51(2), 262–275.

Hirsch, M. (2012). *The Generation of Post-memory: Writing and Visual Culture after the Holocaust*. New York, Columbia University Press.

Hoffman, Eva (2004). *After Such Knowledge: Memory, History and the Legacy of the Holocaust*. New York, Public Affairs.

January, B. (2007). *Genocide: Modern Crimes Against Humanity*. Minneapolis, MN, Twenty First Century Books.

Kiernan, B. (2003). Twentieth-century Genocides Underlying Ideological Themes from Armenia to East Timor. In Robert Gellately and Ben Kiernan (Eds.), *The Specter of Genocide: Mass Murder in Historical Perspective*. New York, Cambridge University Press.

Levine, P. (2010). *In an Unspoken Voice: How the Body Releases Trauma and Restores Goodness*. Berkeley, CA, North Atlantic Books.

Ogden, P., Minton, K., and Pain, C. (2006). *Trauma and the Body: A Sensorimotor Approach to Psychotherapy*. New York, Norton.

Salberg, J. (2015). The Texture of Traumatic Attachments: Presence and Ghostly Absence in Trans-generational Transmission. *Psychoanalytic Quarterly*, 84(1), 21–46.

Scaer, R. (2014). *The Body Bears the Burden: Trauma, Dissociation and Disease*. New York, London, Routledge.

United States Holocaust Memorial Museum. "Martin Niemöller: Biography Holocaust Encyclopedia. www.ushmm.org/wlc/en/article.php?ModuleId=10007391. Accessed on 11/1/15.

Chapter 9

War and Peace*

Eyal Rozmarin

> *Manche Schatten der Abgeschiedenen beschäftigen sich nur damit, die Fluten des Totenflusses zu belecken, weil er von uns herkommt und noch den salzigen Geschmack unserer Meere hat. Vor Ekel sträubt sich dann der Fluß, nimmt eine rückläufige Strömung und schwemmt die Toten ins Leben zurück. Sie aber sind glücklich, singen Danklieder und streicheln den Empörten.*
>
> Franz Kafka, Octavheft G (II,2)[1]

It seems to me hard to believe now, but I recall reading Tolstoy's War and Peace in the 5th or 6th grade. Reading was always one of my greatest pleasures, and my mother, although she kept hoping that I spend more time outside, "like the other kids," is herself a book lover, and so she would go to the public library once a week to replenish my pile of books. I suppose it was her idea that I would enjoy Tolstoy. How could I have had the notion that I should read him at that age myself? I remember the book, thick and heavy, bound in light blue canvas. The printed pages appear in my memory satin-like, smooth and vintage shiny ... but this recollection cannot be true. There could not have been such a fine book in our public library, a bare-bones municipal institution in the still somewhat socialist Israel of the 1970s. I delved into my borrowed *War and Peace* with great anticipation. It was a big book and I loved big books, they promised a long journey ahead. It turned out that this one would give me another, special pleasure. As I began to read I discovered that some of it was in French! Needless to say, *War and Peace* was written in Russian, but Tolstoy rendered some of the dialogue between his aristocratic characters in the language they would have spoken in the beginning of the 19th century. The translator to Hebrew, a renowned poet

* Reprinted with kind permission: This chapter first appeared as an article in Studies in Gender and Sexuality, Volume 12, Issue 3, 2011. Reprinted by permission of Taylor & Francis, LLC.

called Lea Goldberg who was herself from Russia, kept it that way. There was a Hebrew translation of the French lines in the form of footnotes, at the bottom of each page. The reading was, therefore, quite disjointed, especially since I insisted on first reading the French, using my limited knowledge of the English alphabet, before turning to the Hebrew translation to understand what the characters actually said. By the time I finished reading the book I had learned a few words in French. I registered them visually, but since I had only a faint idea how to pronounce them, I developed my own way of speaking French, quietly, to myself. It seems to me that this first encounter, with its undisturbed possibilities and hints of unknown plenty, is the root of French being for me, to this day, a special kind of phantasmagoric-linguistic Promised Land. Homi Bhabha (1994) writes about the sub-lingual, yet intensely meaningful chatter, originally described by Roland Barthes in retelling an afternoon hour in a café in Tangiers (1975, p. 49). It seems to me now that while reading *War and Peace* I experienced, and perhaps created, a similar kind of chatter, out of French sentences echoing in epic-poetic Hebrew a mysterious Russian universe. "Voila une belle mort" says Napoleon, looking at the dying prince Bolkonsky as the battle of Borodino draws to its bloody end ... All this unfolding one afternoon after another as I sit at my desk by a large, west-facing window, open to the front yard of our apartment building, to the street beyond, where the other kids were annoyingly, loudly playing, and to the blasting afternoon sun of the Eastern Mediterranean. I was hardly ever allowed to roll down the wooden shade. My mother wanted there to be in our apartment all the air and light there was to be had. As if there was always around us a foreign, stale darkness to be chased away. She would open the windows wide first thing in the morning, even on the coldest winter days. And so much of the visual in my childhood memories of home is in over-exposure. To this day, I sometimes find myself literally squinting as I try to remember. Still, as I read *War and Peace* it was somehow easy for me to imagine the colors and hues of the damp Russian landscape where it endlessly takes place.

Could it be that I somehow absorbed a sensual trace of Russia from my grandmother? She grew up in a small town called David Gorodok, not far from Pinsk, in White Russia, which is today the former Soviet republic of Belarus. Her stories were about being a pretty girl, the youngest of 10 children, 1 brother and 9 sisters, living a quotidian small-town life. She spoke with admiration about her father and beloved brother,

Naftali. I don't recall her ever mentioning her mother or sisters, except for the only other sister who wound up in Palestine, and therefore alive, as well. She told about receiving adoring attention from the Russian peasants, Cossacks she called them. Her eyes would light up when she uttered her name as it was spoken by them – Raisale. In Palestine she took up the Hebrew version of her diaspora name – Shoshana. Many European Jews, some proudly, some reluctantly, gave up their non-Hebrew first and often family names when they stepped off the boats in the Jaffa harbor. It was a way to pledge allegiance to the realization of the Zionist project and its repudiation of the Diaspora and its legacy of humiliation. She kept her last name until she married my grandfather. Listening to her I always tried to imagine what the characters and scenes she talked about might have looked and sounded like. There were a few photographs to anchor my imagination, although their value was compromised by their fading grayness. I did not know I should ask more when I could have, now it is too late, she passed away. I am left wondering. What was it like to be a young girl during the First World War and the wild years that followed, when from 1918 to 1921 the Red, White and Polish armies fought in the forests and plains for and against the future of the Bolshevik revolution. After the war had ended, Pinsk and its surroundings became a part of Poland, which is why everyone who came from this area knew both Russian and Polish. The times were difficult. Some Jews departed to British Palestine, some to join the despised Ost Juden of Germany, some to Western Europe and the Americas. If any of that had an immediate impact on her life, it had no place in her stories. She left her hometown for Palestine by herself in 1933, age 23, after training in a Zionist camp to be an agricultural worker. I never asked myself what made it possible for her parents to let their youngest daughter leave on her own towards such an unknown future. They must have thought that there, in Poland, it could only be worse. They must have realized that they would not be able protect her. They must have had great hopes and faith in their pretty, young girl. Did they discuss it with her? How come she was the one chosen? My mother recalls that my grandmother once told her that she was too pretty to be safe in that barely governed no man's land. She believed her parents feared her being coveted by a gentile whom it would be too dangerous to resist, and wind up being taken away from them. But was that not ultimately what they planned, and what happened to her? I wonder if this was the explanation they chose to give her, knowing that it would resonate and convince their pretty daughter better than others. Perhaps they thought that being the prettiest of them all she had the best chance to do well in the Promised Land?

In Palestine she worked in an orange grove, where she met a young, frail student from Vilna with the unusual name for an Eastern European Jew – Zecharia.[2] They soon married and became parents. They called their daughter Aviva.[3] When my mother was 3 years old her father died of tuberculosis. My grandmother was left a single mother. The year was 1940. Even if she had considered it, there was no way back home. War has broken in Europe. She told stories about raising my mother during those years, all on her own, but she never mentioned the obvious. It was probably around that time that she lost contact with her family forever. Germany invaded Poland in September of 1939, split it with the Soviet Union for close to 2 years, and after breaking its pact with the Soviets in June of 1941, took all of it, and further, most of western Russia. It is unknown to us whether my grandmother's family was executed in a nearby forest by the SS death squads that followed the German army in operation Barbarossa, as many were, or transferred to a nearby Ghetto, perhaps in Minsk, to await a more organized extermination. What we do know is that no one survived, except for a cousin, 16 at the time, who heeded the advice of Russian soldiers retreating through town, that she come aboard their train or be killed by the advancing Germans. But that cousin, who went on that train without looking back, and wound up in China before traveling back to the Russian front to join the partisans, arrived in Palestine only after the war, married to the leader of the partisans she joined in the forests. If my grandmother ever wondered about the fate of her family during the long years of the war, when news had begun to arrive of the mass killing and death camps, if there was a period of uncertainty and hope that was finally dashed after the war ended, it was never mentioned. The entire affair was summed up in one sentence that sometimes concluded a story about her old life: "הרגו את כולם הנאצים ימח שמם".[4] Did I absorb from my grandmother, together with the rhythms and shades of our ancestral Russia, the sense of history obliterated and unattended mourning that was her fate?

If I had, it all traveled deep into my unconscious, muffled by the needs of living and the nationalization of history that has been a dominant aspect of collective life in Israel. But as I age, and having left Israel more than two decades ago, some traces of my grandmother's past have begun to surface. They come behind memories of what she was like as an old woman, repeating her few stories to the young me who visited her loyally, although always in a state of angry disinterest. They hover in the background of the images I retained of the few pictures she brought with her from Russia and showed only rarely. And then a few years ago, well after her passing, the untold moment when she must have finally realized that everyone was dead began forming in my awareness. Since then, I cannot stop thinking about it, although "thinking" is not quite the right term to describe how this moment commands my attention. As they materialize in a transitional-melancholic space between knowledge, longing and imagination, these traces of things and people past carry with them a feeling of duty, as if demanding that I register something metaphysical. They drive my preoccupation with history, both personal and collective, and at the same time make this preoccupation a kind of desire for the future.

Sometimes a trace appears uncannily, in a flash. A while ago while on a visit to the Netherlands, a photographer friend took a few pictures of me in his studio. Showing me one of them he said: "this one, your mother is going to love, you look like a Rabbi!" My friend never met my mother, who in fact disapproves of my facial hair, which is what made him see me as a Rabbi. No one in my immediate or extended family ever grew a beard. Up until recently, beards were in Israel the provenance of orthodox Jews, an anathema to my secular, old Labor party family. I had never pictured myself a Rabbi before, nothing could be further from my world of associations. It seemed to me a perception of a well-meaning, contemporary Dutch man, thinking in old stereotypes. All the same I was taken aback, it felt strange. I keep being surprised by how much Jewishness is noted in Europe, noted and remarked upon in the most peculiar moments with an intensity that betrays the still largely undigested and unsettled place of the Jews in European history. But at the same time, as he said it, I saw it myself. Actually, I saw an image of my bearded great-grandfather, standing somber at the doorway of his house in the Shtetl. I could not recall this image ever having come to mind before, but there it was, sharp in its original out-of-focus black and white, held in my grandmother's soft hand. Bits of unclaimed memory rise unexpectedly, reverberating through time, carrying with them a past that, in my case, is destroyed and repressed and forgotten. A lifeline pulling together the present in which I now write, that moment of collision between image, stereotype and memory in the Netherlands, another moment in my grandmother's bedroom where she is showing me the photograph, the moment captured in the picture before the catastrophe that came upon us … a strange kind of haunting, cascading *Nachträglichkeit*. Haunting because beyond memory it has often the quality of witnessing, as if what comes up is not only past, as if it is still happening and I am being called to participate in it. Not surprisingly, as these commanding threads emerge I find myself concerned with the question of personal freedom. Are we all destined to either repress or express, in any case to compulsively participate in old stories that cast a spell too heavy to lift? Are we called to achieve an unachievable reconciliation between past and present? Is there the possibility of transcendence, or deliverance, or simply turning away from the departed whom, as Kafka lamented, insist on drifting back here?

I am asking these questions since what I can only begin to glimpse in myself I see more clearly with others. Under the anxieties and obsessions of the present there is often an unformulated fear that one is trapped acting out other lives, carrying ghostly burdens, paralyzed by ageless grievances. This quality of otherness and alienation echoes from beyond the familial. Other generations, other times and places, breaks and connections that extend across distant, often unknown terrains and epochs. As I begin to remember, and to suspect that as a child I remembered more, then forgot,[5] I realize how much I carry my grandmother and her history with me. Subtle sensations, as well as the kind of loneliness that descends when one's heritage has been obliterated. How one feels in her body after a long day of work, alone with her child, and as she prepares their evening meal, the taste of the food her mother once cooked for her. How one remembers in the absence of time and space for mourning. How one settles, as they sometimes literally did, on swampland and quicksand. Through the images and sensations emerging, and against the walls of repression that still tower, I wonder how much, and what kinds of imagination and remembrance are possible. And as a struggle for, and against, the possibility of remembering and imagining has forced itself into my life, demanding to become my destiny, I wonder how much choice I have to partake in, or abandon this struggle.

One aspect of this question has to do with one's particular position in the universe of relations between individuals and societies. History is registered both personally and collectively, memory and imagination transpire in both the singular and plural registers. Whether, and how, one's personal history can become intelligible depends on what kinds of stories it is possible for us to tell ourselves and each other. Our ability to give an account of ourselves (Butler, 2005) is a function of our particular time and location, affiliations and attachments. Despite all wishes to the contrary, there is no view from nowhere. Yet, what is the nature of any particular, personal moment, what does it strive to repress or express vis-à-vis the infinity of being and time? I find it telling that in formulating this question and in the quest to answer it, I am drawn to the work of a few German-speaking Jewish intellectuals who, writing during the few, doomed years between the first and second world wars, were themselves urgently concerned with the relations between society, history and the individual. I am referring, in particular, to Ernst Bloch, Franz Kafka and Walter Benjamin. These three thinkers investigated the endless spaces between reality, memory and imagination, between the tragic and the transcendental, between theory and fiction. Kafka's poetics of despair, Benjamin's effort to decipher the nature of historical consciousness, Bloch's encyclopedic exploration of the notion of Utopia, were all driven by a struggle to define some kind of truth that could be accessible to the individual despite the overwhelming enigma, impenetrability, or outright deceit, which the world and our life in it manifest. That this theme is as close as it gets to universal goes without saying. It is arguably the drive behind all philosophical thought. Yet these three approached it from a particular angle. The terrain they explored seems to me unmistakably reminiscent of an old, mythical Judaic landscape, a discursive reproduction of an endless out-of-Egypt desert to be lost in and discovered, an eternal expedition through an in-between present where identity can be shed and new essences can be revealed. Their sentiment crosses over from the pain of exile to the ambition of liberatory exodus.[6] They proceed by miracles that they plead and command into being. Their journey, both paradoxical and heuristic, strives to return to a promised future, and as in the original exodus story told in the Bible, it is full of hope facing the traitorousness of human nature and the reality of suffering. They create an echo chamber where ancient questions are recaptured and propelled ahead in a new language that is all the same traditional. They each offer their own idiomatic, idiosyncratic renderings of an infinite, collective *Nachträglichkeit* that echoes from antiquity all the way to the place where I now stand.

On the one end of the endless desert, Kafka's intricate despair. One of the many examples: a conversation between Kafka and Max Brod (recorded by Walter Benjamin writing on the occasion of the tenth anniversary of Kafka's death): "I remember," Brod writes, "a conversation with Kafka which began with present-day Europe and the decline of the human race. 'We are nihilistic thoughts, suicidal thoughts that come into God's head,' Kafka said. This reminded me at first of the Gnostic view of life: God as the evil demiurge, the world as his fall. 'Oh no,' said Kafka, 'our world is only a bad mood of God, a bad day of his.' 'Then there is hope outside this manifestation of the world that we know.' He smiled. 'Oh, plenty of hope, an infinite amount of hope – but not for us'" (Benjamin, 1955, p. 116).

Benjamin himself contemplated literature, art, theology, and the streets of European cities, most famously the characters and architecture of 19th-century Paris, in an effort to discern the elusive, fundamental presence of history in time, or in other words, the relations between the past and the present. As he travels across texts and landscapes, Benjamin draws a map of human consciousness as an infinite journey of forgetting and remembering, an ongoing Proustian moment of awakening that is always both eternal and impossibly too brief. He offers in this context some of his most opaque and enigmatic formulations, but he also quotes the grandfather in Kafka's "The Next Village": "Life is astonishingly short. As I look back over it life seems so foreshortened to me that I can hardly understand, for instance, how a young man can decide to ride over to the next village without being afraid that, quite apart from the accidents, even the span of a normal life that passes happily may be totally insufficient for such a ride" (1955, p. 135). When he famously writes that "There is no document of civilization which is not at the same time a document of barbarism" (1955, p. 256), Benjamin resonates with Kafka's view of life as an always too long a ride through a nihilistic, suicidal eternity. But he is also inspired by a perspective on time that he finds in the Judaic cannon, where, in his rendering, "every second of time was the strait gate through which the Messiah might enter" (1955, p. 264). Sober realism, yet the possibility of transcendence in every moment.[7] God may yet reveal himself, as he has, repeatedly, in the desert. The angel of history may untangle himself from the "single catastrophe which keeps piling wreckage upon wreckage..." (Benjamin, 1955, p. 257).

Bloch's ultimate design for our bleak existence is equally ambitious. He anchors it in a phenomenology based on the notion of a "not-yet-conscious." His project is the development of a subject-oriented version of Marxism by theorizing a drive inherent in all things and in history itself towards a perfect future – a hopeful essence that is already there yet needs to be brought up to consciousness, and made conscious, could change the course of history itself. Bloch opens *The spirit of Utopia*, with a stark, Cartesian-like statement: "I am by my self" (1964, p. 7). Yet, at the end of his journey he draws the outline of utopia. The son of an assimilated Jewish railway worker, a student of Simmel and an associate of Brecht and Lukacs, in the last page of *The spirit of Utopia* he finds his inspiration in Corinthians, and in the Zohar. The last sentence of the book echoes like a prayer: "only the unjust exist through their god, but the just – God exists through them, and into their hands is given the consecration of the Name, the very appointment of God, who moves and stirs in us..." (1964, p. 278).

I find myself surprised in realizing how much god and the messiah appear in Bloch, Kafka and Benjamin. Surprised, in a way, as I was when my Dutch friend saw in my face the likeness of a Rabbi. I find myself forced to re-cognize in the face of what appears to me as absolutely other, as Puget (2010) puts it, yet the otherness I am encountering is suspect. There is in this otherness something that feels forced, acquired, a form of forgetfulness or repression.... That I am surprised to find Jewish theology in the thought of Marxist scholars and in the poetry of alienation that came to define a certain European sensibility between the two world wars is an effect of the cultural revolution that raged through post-holocaust Zionism, by which I was educated. Where I learned to read and write, God was on the one hand a historical character one reads about in the Bible, and on the other a political asset in the haggling between religions and secular, right and left political parties. The messiah has been pulled from transcendence to mortal immanence. He, everyone was asked to agree, had already come in the form of the state of Israel. But what the ethos that formed my mind makes me see at first as a strange presence is in fact old and familiar. The heritage that animates the work of these three intellectual forefathers, barely disguised Rabbis, is becoming recognizable to me. It feels compelling and, moreover, urgent. As if through the fits and starts of my memory I rescued it from oblivion and in so doing I somehow became responsible.

It is from this place that I would like to engage Homi Bhabha's *The Location of Culture*. Bhabha's *The Location of Culture* is, among other things, an effort analogous to that of Benjamin, Bloch and Kafka, to find the place of subjectivity in the perpetual avalanche of culture and history. The question he investigates is this: what is the potential of subjective meaning and agency in a world where social forces govern the very coordinates of space, time and language. Bhabha suggests that subjective agency could be found in the gaps that open within, or on the margins of the discursive spaces and temporalities that structure our lived experience. He writes:

> The individuation of the agent occurs in a moment of displacement. It is a pulsational incident, the split-second movement when the process of the subject's designation – its fixity – opens up beside it, uncannily, *abseits*, a supplementary space of contingency. In this 'return' of the subject, thrown back across the distance of the signified, outside the sentence, the agent emerges as a form of retroactivity, *Nachträglichkeit*. It is not agency as itself (transcendent, transparent) or in itself (unitary, organic, autonomous). As a result of its own splitting in the time-lag of signification, the moment of the subject's individuation emerges as an effect of the intersubjective – as the return of the subject as agent.
>
> (1994, p. 265)

Nachträglichkeit – or as Bhabha paraphrases it, retroactivity – is where the prospect of our freedom lies; in moving sideways and against the flow of time, in remaking the past in the present, in what Bromberg (2000) called in a parallel context "standing in the spaces." Bhabha evokes the psychoanalytic notion of *Nachträglichkeit* in a framework where the relations between subjects, concepts and cultures are conceived in terms of difference and ambivalence. It serves his effort to emancipate subjectivity from the reifications characteristic of identity politics, be it the politics of majorities or minorities. It opens a perspective on a more subtly human world, where the sensual semiotics of signs transforms the harsh, oppressive nature of syntax, where Tangiers underlies and subverts Casablanca. There is, indeed, a remarkable range of freedom that transpires when, to use another distinction Bhabha makes, the desired mode of signification is translation rather than interpretation. We find ourselves in a domain where possibilities relate to, but are not overdetermined by the power of compulsive collective narratives. We make sense in a transitional space where meanings metamorphose as they move across discursive registers and cultural differences. Difference, translation, retroactivity are modes of signification that enable more subjective authorship in identity and experience. At its high noon, Bhabha's *The Location of Culture* offers a powerful outline for something quite unique: a positively postmodern strategy for living.

Yet, I find it lacking. His approach seems to me limited by a kind of realpolitik of subjectivity. It accepts the here and now of our present lives as the entire range of our potential existence. It is not directed towards something beyond this range, it has no notion of redemption or transcendence. What it attempts to find between the lines of the narratives given to us is a more subtly nuanced subject, and a greater freedom for this subject to construct his identity and experience within the parameters of the given. His time is the time of the now, but unlike Benjamin, he does not identify in its syncopes a prophetic future. His main concern is with individuation, with a triumphant return of a liberated subject. The trajectory of collective life in itself seems marginal to his project. The freedom he seeks is mostly a personal achievement. There is little concern in his thought for a more general kind of freedom, or justice. As if four centuries after Descartes' *Meditations*, Bhabha's essential thrust is to offer us a revision of the original cogito: I think against the grain, therefore I am, recaptured in my true, hybrid essence. There are both beauty and inspiration in this project, it is a deconstruction that leads to reconstruction, a humanistic kind of radical postmodernism. But resting, as it does, on what a Freudian might call a new type of ego ideal, it leaves me restless. It does not resonate with the conflicted yet utopian striving that has been stirring nameless in my unformulated experience (Stern, 1989) for a long time. It registers as too slow, too ambiguous, and too unambitious, in relation to how this striving has been coming up, urgent and explicit, in my recently more formulated experience of afterwardness.

It is striking how texts can be read differently at different periods of life, and across different emotional intersections. "Each 'now' is the now of a particular recognizability" writes Benjamin (1982, p. 463).[8] For a long time, whenever thinking of Kafka, what would have turned up in my mind was the image of Gregor Samsa turning into an insect in *The Metamorphosis*. Kafka and Gregor Samsa were in my internal landscape kin to Marcel Duchamp and Rose Selavy,[9] all characters in my Dadaesque high school drama. I was fascinated by the Dada movement, but as was true of how I was taught and read about it, without any awareness of its historical context. That it was originated by a group of WWI refugees in Switzerland, and spread across Europe once that war had ended, was something I knew, but simply as an anecdote. When, years later, I began to read Walter Benjamin, I read him as an inspired scholar of the contemplative life, as seen through his encounter with architecture, art and literature. It is impossible to read Benjamin without history staring one in the face, yet both Kafka and Benjamin registered for me for a long time as intriguing creatures of a foreign, inspiring culture, as did many years before Tolstoy's French-speaking characters. I did not recognize in myself traces of Prague or Berlin, of Jews a generation or so older than my grandparents who, by the time I was born, were far from their ancestral Europe, aging immigrants living under the bright sun of realized Zionism. These cities were personally irrelevant to me. Germany and Czechoslovakia appeared in my lexicon as the locations of Dachau and Theresienstadt. There was nothing there for me to identify with or imagine. This part of my heritage was erased by the violence that wiped out my grandparents' generation and its culture from its original location.

I visited Berlin for the first time only recently. I traveled to many places before, but always further west or south. I circled Germany but except for one necessary layover in Frankfurt, never stayed there. On this recent visit to Berlin, I was shocked to discover, while walking around, by chance, a little alley bearing my family name, just off the Unter den Linden. Only then, it came back to me as more than a fleeing curiosity, that my paternal grandmother's maiden name was Berliner. But even with a street in Berlin bearing my name, and a name suggesting that part of my family originated there, I felt nothing, except for a sense of foreboding. None of it coincided with the image of my grandmother's sunny apartment by the beach, with its smell of apples and sea breeze, or with the memories I have of my paternal grandfather's farm, with its chicken coop, orange grove and towering pine trees. The distance between my grandmother's apartment by the sea and my grandfather's farm just outside town was a ten minute drive on a road originally paved by the British. Ten minutes further down that road was, and still is, Tul Karem, already in the Palestinian territories. Pinsk, where she was from or Lvov, where he was born, surely Prague and Berlin, were very distant. Yet when, as a child, I read *War and Peace*, I knew something that I could know then, that I had to forget, and that now I can again remember.

Perhaps both my grandparents had to die, I had to become an American citizen, and years later travel to Berlin from New York, not from Israel, for something to change in the constellation. Perhaps it was this reconfiguration of distance and proximity, this re-mapping of the personal vis-à-vis location and time, that made me recall my experience of reading *War and Peace* as a child as I was preparing to write this essay. Perhaps it was also an uncanny reflection that I was unconscious of until this very moment, a reflection of my changing relations with my subjective and collective past in the hopeful trajectory captured in the book's title. It does feel as if a protracted war of worlds is drawing to an end, as if I can begin to imagine living in awareness and in some kind of peace with my ancestors and the ghosts of their legacy. Yet I remain uneasy, since this legacy implores, beyond remembrance and recognition, some kind of action that I cannot yet fully formulate. I do have a sense, all the same, that in writing these lines and in recollecting my past forward, some kind of action is already being formulated and practiced. Broadly defined, it is the kind of action that takes place between the individual and society.

What, then, might be the principles of such action? First, it seems to me crucial to recognize that theory, society and history are interdependent not only in the socio-historical-cultural register, such as, for example, we now have a theory that articulates a possible socio-historical relation between the Protestant Ethic and Capitalism. There is something obvious, yet largely dissociated about theory making. Any kind of theoretical linking necessarily involves the register of subjectivity, any idea of socio-historical forces and the relations between them requires a subject thinking in a particular place and time to become conscious of it, as, for example, the latter required Max Weber. Individuals, living their lives, aspirations and fears, are an irreplaceable link in the chain of meaning making. This necessary role of subjective process in constructing theories of the world gives the subject agency that extends beyond his self-consciousness and intelligibility. It gives him the power to remake the world in which he lives in the image of his newly formed consciousness. It is a back and forth not without constraints, since what goes into the subject to be contemplated and reconfigured depends on what goes on around him. It depends on where he is and, moreover, on where he comes from, on the conscious and unconscious of his subjective and collective history. But like the mother described by Bion (1959), facing the unformed and overwhelming that comes towards her from her child, the subject can resist the world's overwhelming demand, or he can take it in, and return something more manageable and constructive. This means, in my mind, that the subjective agency suggested by Bhabha, the agency made possible by reprocessing the world's cues, could be engaged not only on the margins, as a predominantly subjective event, but, even if in a minor key, front and center vis-à-vis the life of the collective. It is perhaps this kind of potent agency that Arendt evokes in *The Promise of Politics*, her evocation as well with clear theological resonance, when she writes: "In the last analysis: the human world is always a product of man's *amor mundi*" (Arendt, 2005, p. 203).

Which begs a question: if there is in subjective agency a capability towards more than the self, should we not regard this capability as a responsibility? So far as our remembrance and recognition of the past are actions in the present, do they not carry with them an ethical burden? Benjamin suggests this much repeatedly in contemplating the role of the historian. "In every era the attempt must be made anew to wrest tradition away from a conformism that is about to overpower it. [...] Only that historian will have the gift of fanning the spark of hope in the past who is firmly convinced that even the dead will not be safe from the enemy if he wins. And this enemy has not ceased to be victorious" (1955, p. 255). It seems to me that what Benjamin holds as an ideal for the historian could equally apply to every single individual. The destruction that Benjamin points to in how civilizations come to record themselves, the erasure of the traditions of the defeated by the victorious, have many counterparts in the lives of individuals. Such destruction and erasure, which we may call in psychoanalytic language repression or dissociation, are replicated in those particular intersections of self, history and culture that construct our subjective and communal existence. We may succumb to the repression, think and remember as we are told, or we may try to fan the spark of hope left to us by the defeated. This spark of hope that Kafka refused to fully deny, that Benjamin labored to wrest from the ashes, and that Bloch insisted is there all along to be made conscious, now echoes in my *Nachträglichkeit*. It was given to me by my grandmother who lived to be ninety. Perhaps also by my mother's insistence that there shall always be air and light enough to blind our ancestral demons. Now it is my responsibility to do something. This responsibility emerges between my most intimate memories and the kinship I feel with the poetic-theoretical efforts of Kafka, Bloch and Benjamin. It is held in a moment that is both retroactive and forward looking, in a place that is both personal and historical – it requires both translation and an archeology aiming to make possible an accurate record keeping.

What might the trajectory of thought or action vis-à-vis war and peace be? Here I will lean on the tallest tree. Contemplating the state of affairs between Christians and Jews in Europe after the holocaust, Emmanuel Levinas formulates his attitude to what he terms "insoluble problems." The principle he offers is this: "The presence of persons before a problem. [...] The presence of persons who, for once, do not fade away into words, get lost in technical questions, freeze up into institutions and structures" (1995, p. 87). Contemplating the notion of an insoluble problem, Levinas asks the reader to think "of Saint-Exupery's little prince, who asks the pilot stranded in the desert, who only knows how to draw a boa constrictor digesting the elephant, to draw a sheep. And I think" he adds, "what the little prince wants is that proverbial sheep who is as gentle as a lamb. But nothing could be more difficult. None of the sheep he draws pleases the little prince. They are either violent rams with big horns or too old. The little prince disdains the gentleness that only comes with extreme age. So the pilot draws a parallelogram, the box in which the sheep is sleeping, to the little prince's great satisfaction." Levinas concludes: "I do not know how to draw the solution to insoluble problems. It is still sleeping at the bottom of a box; but a box over which persons who have drawn close to each other keep watch. I have no idea other than the idea of the idea that one should have. The abstract drawing of a parallelogram – cradle of our hopes. I have the idea of a possibility in which the impossible may be sleeping" (1995, pp. 88–89).

Notes

1 Some shadows of the deceased are occupied only in licking the waves of the river of death, because it comes from us and still has the salty taste of our seas. The river then rears in disgust, the current flows backwards, washing the dead back into life. But they are happy, sing songs of thanks, and caress the angry waters (Author translation).

2 Zecharia means god remembers, or god remembered.

3 Aviva is the Hebrew feminine form of Spring. The Latin meaning of "viva" must also be present.

4 "The cursed Nazis killed everybody."

5 "The cut-out unconscious of a family line may sometimes rush, with an incredible concentration, into a mind and body too small to contain it" (Davoine and Gaudilliere, 2004, p. 149).

6 Lost in translation is the Hebrew meaning of the name Egypt, and therefore the full linguistic resonance of "the exodus from Egypt" in Hebrew. The Hebrew word for Egypt

is Mitzraim. The root of this word means "narrow" and in a different conjugation also "siege." To exit Mitzraim means in Hebrew to get out of "narrow straights."

7 As I write these lines I recall that once, when discussing with a patient the possibility that life can be dramatically improved in very small measures, a notion drawn directly from Benjamin's "weak messianism," this patient, who was educated as a mathematician, recalled with great satisfaction a mathematical proof that there is more infinity, or infinitely more, between any given two points, than from here to eternity.

8 "Each present day is determined by the images that are synchronic with it: each 'now' is the now of a particular recognizability. In it, truth is charged to the bursting point with time. [...] It is not that what is past casts its light on what is present, or what is present on what is past; rather, image is that wherein what has been comes together in a flash with the now to form a constellation. In other words: image is dialectics at a standstill. For while the relation of the present to the past is purely temporal, the relation of what-has-been to the now is dialectical: not temporal in nature but figural. Only dialectical images are genuinely historical – that is, not archaic – images. The image that is read – which is to say, that image in the now of its recognizability – bears to the highest degree the imprint of the perilous critical moment on which all reading is founded" (Benjamin, 1982, p. 463).

9 Rose Selavy was a pseudonym and alter ego of the French artist Marcel Duchamp. His/her image, Duchamp made up as a woman, or as we would say today in drag, first appeared in a 1921 Man Ray Photograph. The name is a reference to the French phrase "Eros, c'est la vie" (Eros, that's life), and "arroser la vie" (to toast life).

References

Arendt, H. (2005). *The Promise of Politics*. New York: Schocken Books.

Barthes, R. (1975). *The Pleasure of the Text*. Trans. R. Miller. New York: Hill.

Benjamin, W. (1955). Theses on the philosophy of history. In *Illuminations*. Trans. H. Zohn. New York: Schocken Books (1968).

Benjamin, W. (1955). Franz Kafka. In *Illuminations*. Trans. H. Zohn. New York: Schocken Books (1968).

Benjamin, W. (1982). *The Arcades Project*. Trans. H. Eiland & K. McLaughlin. Cambridge, MA: Harvard University Press (1999).

Bhabha, H. (1994). *The Location of Culture*. New York: Routledge.

Bion, W. (1959). Attacks on Linking. *International Journal of Psychoanalysis*, 40:308–15.

Bloch, E. (1963). *The Spirit of Utopia*. Trans. A. A. Nassar. Stanford, CA: Stanford University Press (2000).

Bromberg, P. (2000). Standing in the Spaces: The Multiplicity of Self and the Psychoanalytic Relationship. *Contemporary Psychoanalysis*, 32:509–535.

Butler, J. (2005). *Giving an Account of Oneself*. New York: Fordham University Press.

Davoine, F. and J.M. Gaudilliere (2004). *History Beyond Trauma*. Trans. S. Fairfield. New York: Other Press.

Harris, A. (2009). "You Must Remember This." *Psychoanalytic Dialogues*, 19:2–21.

Kafka, F. (1916–18). Octavheft G (II,2), unpublished works. www.kafka.org/index. php?ohg.

Levinas, E. (1995). *Alterity and Transcendence*. Trans. M.B. Smith. New York: Columbia University Press (1999).

Puget, J. (2010). The Subjectivity of Certainty and the Subjectivity of Uncertainty. *Psychoanalytic Dialogues*, 20:4–20.

Stern, D. (1989). *Unformulated Experience*. Hillsdale, NJ: The Analytic Press.

Tolstoy, L.N. (1869). *War and Peace*. Trans. (to Hebrew) L. Goldberg. Tel Aviv, Israel: Sifriat Poalim Publishing House (2002).

Chapter 10

The Colonized Mind

Gender, Trauma and Mentalization*

Sandra Silverman

My patient Ava tells me that when she was an adolescent she sometimes blindfolded herself. "I would imagine I was blind because then I wouldn't see anyone looking at me, staring, wondering if I was a boy or a girl." As I listen to Ava I am unnerved by the idea of blindness as comfort but what I find most striking is that she blindfolded herself when she was alone. She was not trying to avoid seeing others see her but to avoid seeing her self, her skin, her body and all of its parts. I have come to think of the blindfold as a shield protecting her from the intrusion of the outside world, from the penetration of other people's minds into her mind, from the demand to be what others want her to be, and from the feeling that what is coming in from the outside can destroy who she is on the inside, or perhaps more accurately, can destroy any chance she has of discovering who she is on the inside.

Not long into treatment Ava began to live in my mind, the boundary between us feeling thin and permeable. It was unclear whether Ava wanted me to help her to feel free to make changes to her body or whether she wanted me to help her to live in her body as it is, female. In this paper I explore what happens when a child's mind is not reflected back but is instead taken over by a parent or caretaker. I look at the intersection of body and mind and I describe a treatment that is, in one sense, about being transgender, in another about trauma, and in yet another about the interaction of gender and trauma and how it is lived in the mind as well as the body. This is not every trans person's story; it is the story of this patient, this analyst and this treatment.

In our first session Ava, who is 24, sits across from me wearing jeans, black oxford shoes, and a sheer white shirt through which I can easily see

* Reprinted with kind permission: This chapter first appeared as an article in the journal Psychoanalytic Dialogues: The International Journal of Relational Perspectives, Volume 25, Issue 1, 2015. Reprinted by permission of Taylor & Francis, LLC.

a black bra. She has long dark hair and an intense gaze. She exudes femininity and masculinity at once. She tells me she is beginning treatment as a last resort, one that she calls "desperate." She feels hopeless, alone and unable to imagine a future. Since she can remember she has felt that she was "born in the wrong body." She describes growing up feeling "deceived" because she was born a girl when she should have been born a boy. She tells me that she has she has fallen in love with many women but has never had a relationship. She attributes this to her feeling that she is male, "I don't want anyone to know." Her shame is palpable.

Ava makes it clear to me that what she does not want is to be transgender, a word that she utters with disgust. She fears that by coming to therapy that is what she will become, that it is her only option. I am aware of feeling that through our work we will come to understand the meaning of her feelings about her body and that hopefully she will be able to find comfort in the body that she is in. What I do not know and what Ava does not tell me until the second year of treatment is that her decision to begin therapy was a decision to seriously consider transitioning: "I knew when I came in here it was to talk about a transition but it was too terrifying for me to say it out loud to you or to myself." Ava was in treatment many times during childhood but it never helped, "They didn't want to talk about the gender stuff," she says. This is the first time that she is coming to therapy of her own volition.

Shortly after beginning treatment Ava tells me she had a dream. "I birthed a brain into the toilet. I took out the pieces and brought them to a lab. I handed them to a woman in a white coat, a scientist." I ask her what she means by "birthed" and she says, "Actually, I shit it out." In Ava's dream there is a brain broken in parts, a mind in pieces. Her dream tells of a mind that is toxic and riddled with "shit." Ava is trying to find her self in what is deemed repulsive, in what she longs to be rid of. Ava gives me, the scientist, her mind to hold and to repair (Bion, 1962; Fonagy & Target, 1996).

I have come to understand Ava's dream through the lens of mentalization, its development and its collapse. Mentalization, also referred to as reflective capacity (Bion, 1962; Fonagy & Target, 1996) describes the child's development of a sense of her own mind and of its separateness from the mind of an other. Mentalizing happens in the mind and the body (Harris, 2009). It is about being fully taken in, thought about and reflected on by a parent or caregiver. The parent who is able to hold the child's mind in mind (Coates, 1998) helps the child to develop a sense of herself as an individual with her own thoughts and feelings.

A parent carrying a history of unprocessed trauma will find it difficult to reflect on her child's mind, particularly when the child is experiencing states of fear or despair. These parents are likely to evacuate their traumatic experiences into their child's mind, to "write over" (Lyons-Ruth, 2006) the child's experience providing "little support for the child's elaboration of her own subjectivity and initiative" (Lyons-Ruth, 2006, p. 611). These are children whose minds are, in some instances, colonized rather than mentalized by the parent. These children often become comforters to their parents, acutely sensing their parent's needs, and taking on what Lyons-Ruth calls a tend/befriend role. There is then a confused sense of who is carrying whose trauma, hence one's needs, wishes and desires become difficult to decipher from those of an other.

Ava's dream illustrates this process. In her dream her mind is filled with toxic contents that come out of her body and go into the toilet. Ava's maternal grandmother was violent with her children. One story Ava's mother recounted was that her own mother, Ava's grandmother, pushed Ava's mother's head into the toilet when she was angry. And here, a generation later, we have a dream of a brain in the toilet. Whose brain is whose in this dream? Whose mind is whose? Ava's dream is, perhaps, indicative of her unconscious awareness that someone else's mind is lodged inside her own mind, of the intergenerational transmission of trauma. Williams (2004) writes about the developmental consequences of carrying a "foreign body" inside the mind, describing something similar to Ava's experience: "The individual who has incorporated an invasive object is likely to feel unstable, depleted of personal meaning and occupied or haunted by unidentifiable bodily perceptions" (p. 1345).

My project in this paper is to explore what happens when a mind is not mentalized but colonized. By colonized I am referring to the lodging of another's mind, another's evacuated fears and traumatic history, in the developing mind of a child. I have chosen to use the word colonize because the colonized are not just invaded but occupied. The colonizer seeks to own and control in the unconscious hope of preventing the colonized from developing an independent and separate identity. Mentalizing is about making space, about creating room for thought and reflection, about "thinking together in relationships" (Seligman, 2007, p. 11). It is about the reflective space between one's own mind and that of an other, between one's intent and one's impact, the creation of the space *between* being crucial. Colonization is about destroying space, about crowding an other's mind with the unprocessed contents of one's own mind, about restricting the freedom to think. To colonize is to invade, inhabit and alter. It does not feel as if Ava's mother just needed to get into her daughter's mind but that she wanted and needed Ava's mind as a *place*, a colony, to locate unbearable pieces of her own mind.

I am interested in what it means if colonization happens in one particular area, in this case, gender and sexuality. Do some children have a greater inherent receptivity to a particular colonizing parent? How does a child, and later an adult, resist the feeling of colonization? What are the mechanisms for survival? In my work with Ava I came to know her unboundaried experience with her mother and how a lack of mentalization left Ava in a flooded, frightened and incoherent state. Ava's attempts at expressing psychic pain were not recognized and she experienced both her body and her mind as sites of danger.

As Ava's use of the blindfold suggests, I have felt that Ava needed to blind herself to incompatible aspects of those around her, particularly her mother. I too have struggled with my sense of Ava's mother. This mother felt loving, warm, and attached. At the same time, this mother felt traumatized and traumatizing, penetrating and yet impenetrable. Her own unprocessed trauma which was, at least in part, a trauma of what it meant to be feminine, was projected into her daughter, creating a colony in her daughter's mind where the mother could store her unresolved experiences, particularly with regard to gender and sexuality. While projective identification, a term with many definitions, may be related to colonization it is not the same concept. Unlike colonization, projective identification is often described as a form of communication and as the wish to place something in the other person so that it can be processed and returned. In contrast, colonization is about the storage of unbearable and unprocessed psychic experience without any interest in it being transformed and then returned. Projective identification is certainly at work in the relationship between this mother and daughter but what I am discussing in this paper is not that aspect of their relationship but the ways in which the mother colonized her daughter's mind, disavowing her own trauma and depriving her child of her own psychic space (Faimberg, 2014).

Ava describes her mother as her ally. She tells me that she should have been more separate from her mother but she needed her too much. Early on Ava's mother becomes central to our work where her father barely exists. "He's irrelevant," Ava says, closing the subject. It feels to me as if a single mother raised Ava, as if her father was a periodic intruder on the intimacy of their relationship. I tell her as much and she agrees. She has nothing more to add about her father other than that he is a powerful and successful man. "I hate him," she says, "I always have." Over time bits of information come out about her father. He grew up wealthy, lived a wild and drug-addicted life in his twenties and was once psychiatrically hospitalized for months, the reasons for the hospitalization remaining unclear. He is now a high-powered businessman who is absorbed with his work. "He was jealous of my relationship with my mother," Ava tells me.

When Ava was an infant her father's sixteen-year-old nephew lived in the family home. He had a history of mental illness and expressed jealousy of the new baby and so Ava's parents had Ava sleep in their bed, between them. Her mother stacked dishes against the bedroom door so that if he opened the door the crash would awaken them. The nephew moved out of the house during Ava's first year and then visited periodically, often getting into violent fights with Ava's father. Ava remembers her mother taking her into the bathroom during one of those fights and then, after it was over, seeing broken glass strewn throughout the living room.

I am struck by how many words Ava has to describe her mother and how few for her father. Ava's mother is "beautiful," "loving" and "sexy." She grew up in a poor family, the oldest of five children, each of whom were born to different fathers. There was sexual and physical abuse in the mother's home but Ava only knows fragments of information that her mother dropped from time to time. "Her mother's boyfriends used to touch her," Ava tells me in one session. "Her father called her a little whore when she was in kindergarten," she tells me in another. Ava's mother dropped out of high school and began working as a waitress when she was sixteen. Her looks helped her to survive. "I opened my legs for many men," she told her preteen daughter. This mother's femininity was in keeping with the culturally accepted views of female sexuality, making it easy to overlook how much trauma was embedded in her expression of her gender and of her sexuality both of which she used to survive. As Saketopoulou writes, "gender in *both* its normative and non-normative iterations can become an expression of psychic pain" (2011, p. 193).

Ava's mother communicated her traumatic experiences to her daughter in a casual manner and without any explanation. This is one way that trauma is unconsciously passed from generation to generation. In this instance, it feels as if Ava's mind became a place for her mother to store her traumatic experiences, a colony, stirring up anxiety in Ava who said she "knew better than to ask any questions" when her mother mentioned her early sexual experiences. The mother's colonizing communication of sexual trauma was accompanied by something else, eroticism. Her mother's communications felt exciting and erotic while at the same time they were violent and scary. There was the sense of both danger and excitement as Ava became the carrier of her mother's history in what Harris calls "the haunting of gender" (2005, p. 199).

A picture begins to form of her parents, a glamorous couple dripping with sexuality. "They cleared the dance floor," Ava tells me after watching videos of a relative's wedding that she attended with her parents when she was a child. Sex is the lens through which identities are formed in this family and in all likelihood Ava was sexualized by her parents' gaze as well. The idea that her family has shaped her experience of her self is foreign to Ava. In her view she was born "a freak of nature" and that is why she has suffered. There is little room for reflection. One cannot help but think of Ava's use of the blindfold, this time metaphorically, to avoid seeing the impact her family history has had on development of her sense of self.

Integral to the development of mentalization is the development of a sense of personal history, of time (Seligman, 2007). Ava's family does not live "in time." Loss is disavowed; the past is not acknowledged; and generational differences are blurred. If the past is not granted meaning then losses, including the loss of what one may never have, in this case a biologically male body, cannot be mourned. Instead, Ava turned to fantasy and for much of her childhood she believed that eventually a penis would grow from her vagina. At night, when she was unable to sleep, Ava felt soothed by picturing herself in the future, as a man in a suit, walking through a park.

Accompanying the sense of timelessness is Ava's difficulty remembering what happened and when in her life. It's as if no one was there to reflect on her experiences, helping her to develop a sense of continuity or going on being (Winnicott, 1960). "How old are you when you still need your mother to take you to the bathroom?" Ava asks me in an early session. She describes being in the bathroom when her mother sees that she had stuffed toilet paper into her pants as a pretend penis. Reacting with alarm, her mother knelt down, looked Ava in the eye, and said, "You are a girl" while holding the toilet paper up. "That's when I knew what I wanted was bad," Ava said in session.

For this mother, gender was a site/sight of something that felt threatening and of something that could not be thought or seen. The blindfold might be considered a second-generation expression of the mother's fear of seeing. What did it mean to this mother for Ava to be a girl? What did it mean for her daughter to be a girl who wanted to be a boy? As the treatment unfolded what would emerge is the mother's feeling that boys could protect themselves while girls were in danger, that girls and women were sexually vulnerable but their sexuality was also an instrument of power. When Ava was in preschool she insisted that she wear the boy's uniform instead of the girl's. That school, unlike the elementary school she attended, was flexible and she wore the boy's uniform, including its clip-on tie every day: "My parents thought I looked adorable," she said. Much later in treatment Ava learned that her mother was hoping for a boy because "they are stronger, tougher and better able to survive." It seems possible that at times this mother, and perhaps the father as well, recognized Ava's boy self and treated her as a boy and at other times as a girl, depending upon the parents' needs or wishes.

Any capacity Ava's mother had to mentalize was not available to her in the moment in the bathroom. She was unable to hold together the pretend and the real (Fonagy & Target, 2000, p. 855). Something about her daughter pretending that she had a penis was threatening to this mother making her unable to engage in playful interaction, to be curious about her daughter's inner world while connecting it to the outer world. She was in a state of psychic equivalence (Fonagy & Target, 1996).

Early in treatment Ava tells me that she was afraid of seeing a therapist who "looked like a lesbian." She had not asked about my sexual orientation and I was unsure if she was aware that I am a lesbian. She recounts a story of a meeting with a college professor who was "obviously a lesbian" and remembers feeling that she could not get out of the room fast enough because the woman was so masculine. As I listen to her I realize I am feeling grateful that I decided to wear a skirt that day, not to mention the lipstick. I realize that I too am hiding, that when I am with this patient I am glad that I don't "look like a lesbian," and that this is reflective of the intense regulatory anxiety that this patient lives with and the ways in which this has stirred up my own anxieties about living in a culture that still attaches stigma to those who are not heterosexual. I feel anxiety clawing at my insides as I ask her if she is wondering about my sexual orientation. She tells me that she assumes I am straight and is relieved by that. Does she want to know? "No," she responds firmly.

What was I to do with her clear statement that she did not want a lesbian therapist followed by her statement that she did not want to know about me? This was one of many mixed messages I have received from Ava. I think again of the blindfold, of her capacity for deep in*sight* and her wish to be blind to what she sees around her. I knew that the disparagement Ava felt toward lesbians was reflective of her own self-hatred but I still felt its impact and feared the consequences of her "finding out" about me in a way similar to her fear of rejection if others found out about her boy self. This was another moment of enactment, of Ava's history of trauma and shame playing out between us.

Ava hides all pictures of herself as a child because she dressed as a boy, insisted that her hair be cut short and was often mistaken for a boy causing her mother visible shame. After the preschool where she was allowed to wear the boys' uniform her parents sent her to an elite all-girls school where she was forced to wear a uniform that made her look "like a boy in a dress." There was a contradiction in the way Ava's parents communicated with her. They sometimes allowed her to choose her clothes from the boys department and they let her attend a boys' baseball day camp registering her for camp as a boy and participating in this lie. On the other hand, they painted her room pink without her permission and expressed shame about her presentation saying things like, "don't sit like a dyke."

In school Ava was taunted by the children and humiliated by the teachers. She tells me stories of the other girls calling her names, of their exclusion of her when, in fifth grade, they found a book about the developing female body. She recounts stories of girls blocking the doorway and calling her "faggot," as if even they sensed something about her gender as well as her sexuality. I wonder aloud where her parents were when this happened and why the school allowed it. She is conflicted about her parents, protecting them at first, claiming there was nothing they could have done, and then wondering, tearfully, why they didn't help her. She can tolerate her conflicted feelings for only a few moments.

At fifteen Ava grew her hair long and transferred to a new high school where she was not only accepted but was envied for her attractiveness. She was in love with her best friend but never let her know. The most popular boy in the school wanted to date her. "It was all an act," she says when she describes the change in her presentation. "It still is." I ask what makes her so certain that being a man would not be an act. "What's not an act? I just know that it would feel more real."

Three months into treatment Ava arrives in my office carrying an old shoebox filled with the pictures she doesn't want anyone to see. She hands me the first photo. Two little boys stand in front of an attractive woman. The boys are wearing shorts and T-shirts. She tells me the picture is of her mother and her cousin John. I ask who the other child is and she says, "That's me." In picture after picture Ava is a little boy, her stance, her expression, her short hair, all say "boy." I feel disoriented and unable to think. The "boy" in the pictures is in complete contrast to the woman sitting in front of me. Ava cries and tells me she fears something is terribly wrong with her. "I knew I was a girl but I felt like I was a boy."

Ava's mother was "thrilled" that she left "that boy stuff" behind. "I don't know what it would do to my parents if I told them how I really feel," she says. Ava is surprised at what she "blossomed into," how she went from an awkward girl who looked like a boy to such a beautiful woman. She enjoys the power her looks grant her and she uses that power to gain attention and to intimidate. She fears giving it up. Strangely, her feminine appearance would be another loss. Again, it feels as if her identity happens *to* her, as if she has had no role in shaping who she is in the world. Her parents, after years of shame, are proud of their attractive daughter, a daughter who has followed in her mother's footsteps. According to Ava no one ever talked about "the boy stuff" when it was happening and no one talked about her change to a more feminine presentation. It is as if something true or real or dangerous in this family has now been covered by something more palatable, acceptable and appealing.

Ava is clear that her attraction is to women. In spite of this clarity and her presentation of sexual confidence, her sexuality causes her considerable anxiety. Ava prefers to think of herself as heterosexual and male, but in the wrong body. At various points during our work together I wonder how homophobia impacts her belief that she is supposed to be male. I have wondered if Ava feels she is "sick" not only because of her feeling that she should be male but because of her desire for others who are female. I ask questions with these thoughts in mind. She tells me I am on a campaign to get her to like the idea of being gay. "You don't get it. You don't understand how it has felt to be called gay, to be bullied for it, when that is not really what I am."

Ava returns from a trip to Italy with her mother and her aunt. She tells me that at one point a handsome man around Ava's age gave them directions. When he walked away her mother talked about how sexy he was, making it clear she was attracted to him. Ava looks both embarrassed and curious when she says, "I was jealous. I wanted her to feel that way about me." Our exploration of how sexuality was lived in Ava's home begins to deepen. What did it mean to hold her mother's attention? What was it like when her father was home? She describes one of two dynamics: "He was jealous of me or my mother ignored me for him."

Ava continues to tell me that she cannot bear the thought of transition nor can she bear the thought of living her life as a woman. I feel stuck with her in an intractable place of pain. She cannot imagine a body that is a livable option unless it is what she cannot have, a biologically male body. She sees her body in a purely physical way, as concrete and static. While this may help her to feel she is not at fault for her experience of her body, that she was just "born this way," it leaves her at the mercy of her biology. We come to know our bodies largely through a psychic representation that is constructed over time (Saloman, 2010; Schilder, 1950). Our body image is multiple and flexible. It develops out of our relationships with other people. Not only is it true for those who are transgender but for all of us that the body image we carry in our minds is rarely identical to how our bodies are perceived from the outside. When Ava tells me that she doesn't feel "real" or "complete" and I try to explore those feelings she insists that it is because she is supposed to be a man, that is what would make her feel "real." Helping Ava to reflect on her experience of her body, to mentalize her body, while recognizing that there are biological limitations to it, feels essential to helping her move forward and make crucial decisions about her life.

The relational aspect of Ava's bodily experience is apparent when she tells me that she has felt "deceived" because she was born a girl. "Deceived by whom?" I ask. Ava looks surprised by my question. "By nature," she tells me, "by luck, by fate, by God, even though I no longer believe." As treatment progresses her dreams tell us more about "deception." She dreams of secret places in her parents' home and hidden compartments under her parents' bed where mysterious blueprints are stored. She makes statements that come from a part of her that she seems only partially aware of: "My parents will never tell me what I need to know." I tell her that she is implying that they know something and have kept it from her. "I feel that way," she says. When I link this more directly to her feeling of deception about her body she becomes anxious and her mind goes blank.

The feeling I've had from early in our work is that on one level a transition was unthinkable and on another a transition had to happen. It's not unusual for Ava to tell me that "it's sick to want to be a man," that she has to find a way to feel comfortable as a woman and then, in the following session, that she has to transition because she is "in the wrong body and cannot live this way any longer." She has begun to talk about articles and blogs she has been reading about those who are transgender. After describing what she has read she tells me she cannot bear to think about transitioning but it is also clear to me that she cannot bear *not* to think about it. Reflecting on how unsettled I feel when I think about Ava transitioning, I begin to question why I have needed to believe that she can remain female, that these issues are largely psychic and that it is a matter of working them through. I fear that I am thinking about Ava with the same bias that the psychoanalytic world has historically thought about those of us who are gay or lesbian (Mitchell, 1981). I do not want to be so grandiose as to assume that I know what is best for Ava. I realize that the irreversibility of a transition makes me anxious. I fear that Ava will move too quickly and regret her decision. I am concerned that she believes she can escape into another life, another identity. At the same time I feel that just as we must explore what it means to her to live in her female body, we must also explore what it would mean to her to transition.

When I try to explore Ava's feelings about a transition she is adamant. In her view, there are masculine men and feminine women and nothing in between. Those who transition, particularly from female to male, are "sick," "gross" and "disturbed." "They all look like freaks," she says. She tells me that she has slept with many women, usually straight or bisexual women who reject her for men, but she continues to be uncomfortable around lesbians. In spite of this, she spends a considerable amount of time in a bar in her neighborhood that caters to gay men and lesbians. She tries to feel a part of things and flirts with the women there. She describes sex as a site of anxiety and confusion. She is confused by the intense desire she elicits in others while her own desire is most powerful for those she cannot have. When she does have sex she is disappointed that she cannot allow others to touch her genitals, leaving her envious of the other's pleasure and unable to experience pleasure of her own. She tells me that if she were in "the right body" she would be able to have sex without anxiety. We talk about the possibility of changing her female presentation to one that is a bit more masculine, truer to who she is. She is adamantly opposed: "I'm not going to be that kind of woman." I suggest that she get to know some people who are transgender. With a friend, she attends an event for the transgender community but returns home feeling so sick with fear and disgust that she throws up.

There seems to be no viable body for her. She speaks of suicidal thoughts saying that one of the reasons she won't kill herself is because, "if this could happen to me in this life, what could happen in the next life?" She fears that if there is a heaven and a hell she would go to hell, that she is bad, sick and dangerous. It's unclear where these thoughts originate. They are, perhaps, indications of the colonization of her mind, of her mother's unthinkable thoughts and experiences having been lodged in her daughter's mind.

We return to a frequent topic: her hair. Ava wants to cut her hair but cannot imagine doing so. She fears what she will look like, how others will react, and she fears giving up the positive attention and envy that others feel toward her because of her hair. Most of all, she fears her mother's disapproval. She tells her mother that she is thinking of cutting her hair and wants her "blessing." I try to explore why she needs her mother's blessing to make this change and she tells me that she fears upsetting or hurting her. "She is my lifeline." She receives a phone message that she plays for me in session. Her mother is troubled. She sounds sad when she says, "you're going back to that?" Ava tells me she feels she is doing something bad. We talk about how difficult it is to make her own choices without feeling she will hurt someone else. During the session another call comes in from her mother. She doesn't answer but plays the message and we listen together. Her mother tells her that she does not need her blessing, that if this is what she wants then she should do it and then her mother sounds tearful and hangs up. Ava begins to cry. She tells me that it is rare for her mother to cry, that she must have hurt her and that she cannot go forward with her decision to cut her hair short. It is a moment when she is aware of the conflict between her wishes and those of her mother and of her fear that she will lose her mother if she pursues her own wants and needs. I tell her that what I heard in the message was not just her mother's pain but her mother's love for her, that their relationship will survive her decision to cut her hair. There is nothing permanent about cutting her hair. It will give her, and us, an opportunity to see what it feels like for her to live differently in the world, still as a woman but hopefully a woman that feels more like who she is on the inside. Her response: I feel like a man on the inside.

Once her hair is cut short she is initially relieved and says she is beginning to feel more like herself. After a week she becomes self-conscious. She is upset that she looks "too much like a lesbian." I hear disgust in her voice when she tells me this. She is now in a relationship with a woman whom she describes as feminine, sexy and smart, the kind of woman men would want, making Ava feel good that this woman has chosen her over men. Sex, however, is a challenge. "It doesn't feel right, two women's bodies, two vaginas." She tries to joke about this but I can feel that it is serious. She tells me that she cannot have sex in this body because it is her mother's body. "I tried to be my mother and I succeeded but it isn't me," she says. Her tone is more confident than usual. Her wish to transition begins to take root. She finds one transman that she is willing to talk with about transitioning.

Suddenly, everything is moving quickly. I wonder aloud how Ava has moved to seriously considering transitioning when prior to this it was hard to get her to think about what it might mean to her. She tells me that when she cut her hair several months earlier she knew inside that this was a first step, that although I saw it as a move toward a more expansive sense of herself as female she saw it as the beginning of seriously considering a transition. I want more time to talk about what it feels like to be a woman who is not her mother. Ava wants to talk about transitioning.

Although I did not realize it at the time, I believe that throughout the early period in our work, the part of Ava that was seeking a way to feel comfortable to begin the process of transition was *listening in* to our sessions. I am thinking of Davies' description of her work on multiple self-states, that there are "other aspects of self that were at least potentially available, seated around the sidelines" (2004, p. 758) of our sessions, and I am thinking of Fischer's description of doubling, of holding two realities at once, in this instance those two realities are the wish to transition and the wish to remain in a female body. As Harris (2005) writes: "it is precisely this doubleness that creates the conditions of reorganization and movement" (p. 93). Indicative of the beginnings of internal reorganization, of Ava gaining greater access to self-states that were previously out of reach, was a dream Ava brought in: "I was standing on the beach with my parents and my girlfriend. A wave rose out of the water and wouldn't break. The earth was going to come off its axis. Everyone was going to die." Ava said she knew the dream was about transitioning. This dream spoke of her fear of what it might mean to unearth her feelings about her self, her parents and her history, not just transitioning from female to male but from colonized to mentalized, from someone who was crowded in by the needs and desires of others to someone who could know and pursue her own needs and desires. The dream reflected her fears of who might be hurt or destroyed in the process.

Ava believes the most important part of being male is having a penis, something she can never have as "bottom" surgery is far from adequate. She is in a perpetual state of longing for what she cannot have and of self-loathing for what she does have. She hates her vagina and says she would rather have nothing between her legs, "like Barbie." For Ava, gender and sexual desire are inseparable and so getting pleasure from her female body is experienced as a defeat. "I don't want to feel like a lesbian or like a woman who has desire for other women because that's not who I am." She tells me that to experience pleasure in the body she has would feel like a betrayal. "It would be like those women who have orgasms when they get raped."

Ava tells me that if she gets pleasure from her body *as a woman* then she is not a man and cannot transition. She remembers having had sex with a woman in college and having an orgasm. She recalls feeling disgust soon afterward. There is the part of Ava that cannot bear to experience sexual pleasure in the body she has and there is another part that despairs about this and longs to feel sexual pleasure with her girlfriend. "I want that so badly but it feels impossible," she tells me. I ask her what it means to her that she is in a female body and has desire for others in a female body. Her anxiety skyrockets. "That can't be. Then who am I? This is so confusing." She tries to close the subject.

I tell her that her confusion is not something bad but instead a sign of movement. Allowing the experience of uncertainty will help open more possibilities, increasing the likelihood that she will find access to the different parts of her self, different self states that have been dissociated because they felt threatening. For Ava, strictly defined gender categories help her to feel as if she has a sturdy sense of self but, as Ava has said, it's all an act. These separate and highly gendered categories are reflective of separate self states including the self that wants to be male, the self that is disgusted by her sense of herself as male, and the self that does not want to give up the power of being a beautiful woman. Ava steps into and out of these separate states without any communication between them (Bromberg, 1998; Davies, 2004).

"Does your body feel unsafe?" I ask her. "Only in the sense that someone can get in," is her response. It seems clear that someone did "get in"; what is less clear is whether they violated her physically as well as psychically. I am thinking of Ava's mother, of the intrusion of her sexuality into Ava's mind, of her mother's words to her young daughter: "I've opened my legs for many men." I wonder what these words communicate about gender and trauma, about the power of men and the submission of women. What Ava wants is to have an impact on an other, to have what Elise (2008) describes as a healthy part of male as well as female psychology: "Healthy exhibitionistic expression of phallic intention takes the form of wanting to make a positive impression on another person and includes the bodily component of wanting to 'press in'—to penetrate" (p. 79).

In my work with Ava I have often felt a flood of feeling, perhaps similar to what Ava has felt with her mother. It feels to me as if what Ava cannot bear is given over. I have had the image of an IV, delivering her feelings into my body. The image is notable because of her fear of having her blood drawn. Ava cannot bear the thought of a needle inside her vein. When, in the second year of treatment, she has a blood test she responds by covering her face with her hand, crying, sweating and repeatedly saying, "please stop" even after the test is over. Ava and I begin to talk about the possibility of trauma in her history. She is newly able to recognize that her fear of a needle staying in her vein may be linked to sexual terror. She tells me she cannot remember anything but feels that "something must have happened." In one session she wonders aloud, "How come no one ever did anything to help me?" She is referring to everyone knowing and seeing that she felt like a boy but refusing to talk about it. Her words, however, could refer to other types of trauma as well.

Ava and I have talked about the possibility of abuse, of some type of sexual violation, but it has felt to me more likely that the trauma was at the level of colonization, a way in which this mother took up residence in her daughter's mind. Ava's sense of her body, of its boundaries, her use of the blindfold, all relate to a feeling that one's mind is not one's own, nor is one's body. My sense is that Ava frequently had the feeling of intrusion or invasion of her body and mind and that this is part of the reason why she frequently feels her mind is crowded as well as why she often loses her train of thought, dissociating in the midst of talking about what she feels. The blindfold is an attempt, albeit a failed one, to create a boundary, to keep things from entering so that she can discover and experience her mind and her body as her own.

Early in our work I am aware of feeling drawn in. She is half my age and yet a frequent feeling for me is that we are peers in some way. Later in the treatment she would describe her relationship with her mother saying, "I feel like her twin. I always have." I feel a strange mix of maternal, protective feelings and a more mutual, adult engagement during our sessions. There are moments when I feel a seduction from her but then I wonder whether that is really what is happening. I wonder whether it is *wrong* (a word Ava has used to describe her own feelings) that everything feels so intense, that there is some sort of sexual element in the room that I can't quite pin down. Later in treatment she describes her shame regarding the feeling that she is male: "I feel like I am as sick as a pedophile," Ava says to me through tears. I am stunned by her use of the word pedophile. What would become clear is how "sick" and "wrong" Ava feels for wanting to be a man. Her inability to rid herself of her feeling that she is male feels to her like a sign of illness and depravity, similar to a pedophile who cannot contain his or her sexual desire for children. Her use of the word pedophile indicates that Ava's feelings about her gender are related to her feelings about her sexuality and that both her gender and her sexuality are bound together in a sick and shameful package.

Ava has begun having conversations with her parents and they have said they will support her if she has to transition. One day Ava has lunch with her mother and tries to express the pain she has felt. Her mother tells her that she tried to "shame" Ava out of her wish to be a boy. Ava is horrified. Her mother tells her that she wants to help her now: "Let's get this done and move on," she says, as if it is now a group project. There is a sudden and strange turnaround. Her mother is more than on board. I wonder if there is something hidden, something that no one wants known. I think of the "deceived" feeling Ava described when she told me about feeling like a boy. Ava is relieved by her mother's support but also fears that she is disappointing her.

At around this same time Ava begins to wonder about my life. She wants to know my sexual orientation. After considerable exploration I tell her that I am a lesbian. She looks shocked. Her eyes fill with tears. "I don't know why I'm crying," she says, and then, "I wish I was a lesbian." She is stunned by her feelings. It is as if a dissociated self just emerged (Davies, 1998). We talk about the wish that her journey could end here, that she wouldn't need to transition to feel she could live in her body. She tells me in a subsequent session that she was also crying because she felt for me, for the difficult road that I too must have traveled. "I feel closer to you now," she says.

Ava begins considering going on hormones. She considers this some-times defiantly, sometimes with anxiety, and sometimes with longing. She makes the decision to start with hormones because her breasts are very small and she feels she can wait on surgery. I let Ava know that I am uneasy with her plan to start hormones. I wonder if she is willing to wait longer. "No, I have to get on with my life, I have to try this," she says. I want to leave her the space to make her own decision, not to push my needs into her mind, not to colonize her. I tell her that I understand that the hormones are her decision, but that I am going to continue to explore her feelings about her body, her hatred of it and that it is my hope that regardless of whether she transitions or not she can have positive feelings about her self and her body.

Several days before Ava is to start hormones she brings me a photo album her mother made for her when she turned 21. It has pictures of her from birth until her twenty-first birthday. We look at it together and then she requests that I keep it in my office until after the weekend. She is to see the doctor on Monday and possibly get her first injection. After she leaves my office I look through the book again. There are pictures of her looking like a boy and then gradually looking more like a young woman. I feel incredible pain. She looks happy and vibrant in many of the pic-tures, sad and alone in others. I can see and feel her struggle. Over the weekend I feel sad and mournful. I well with tears at one point. I wonder if the transition will achieve what Ava hopes and I wonder whether I have done everything I can to help her come to this decision.

At our Monday session, just prior to her doctor's appointment, Ava tells me that she feels terribly depressed. Her mother spent much of the weekend insisting that Ava had a happy childhood, leaving Ava feeling alone and unrecognized. This feels like a colonizing moment indicative of a history in which there was only one reality, a reality that Ava was coerced into believing. "I am going on hormones because I feel I have no other choice. I can't live this way anymore," she tells me. I ask her if she feels we should try harder to help her live comfortably as a woman and she responds with a definitive no. "I don't want to transition but feel I have to. What kind of life is this?" An hour later I get an email from her, "I just got my first shot and can't stop grinning from ear to ear! Just wanted you to know!" When I read the email I can feel the contradiction, the doubling in the way that Ava lives, the different selves, out of view of one another.

After Ava begins testosterone her body shifts, her shoulders become broader, her hips disappear and her voice deepens. She begins to struggle with the feeling that she is again a pre-adolescent who people cannot figure out, *is that a boy or a girl.* When I suggest changing pronouns she refuses. "Not until I pass." I continue to push for exploration of what is happening, for what this change means to her, for what it will mean to be a transgender man. She tells me she just wants to be further along in the process, that she wants her inner sense of herself to match her outer self.

Ava has always been confused by the reaction she gets from others. She is aware that she elicits an intense response, one that is frequently sexual. In our third year of work I tell her what it felt like to sit with her in the early months, explaining that I felt an intensity from her that seemed to contain both an invitation and a challenge. I tell her that it also had a sexual feeling. She does not seem surprised. "That's how I feel all the time," she says. I tell her that her mother probably gave something off too, something similar to what I felt from Ava, a charisma laced with sexuality. "My mother?" she says: "My mother has been flirting with me since I was really little." What Ava describes in her family home is an overflow of sexuality, particularly from her mother but from her father too. There is what Ruth Stein (2008) would describe as "excess," that which is "uncontainable ... by the adult-child pair, or by culture and society." Something in Ava's history has overwhelmed her and made her sexuality as well as her body, in any form, difficult for her to bear.

Two months after Ava begins hormones I experience a countertransferential shift. I begin to feel that I am complicit in the violation of her body. I wonder if I have been irresponsible by not questioning more intently her decision to begin testosterone. I feel puzzled by the intensity of this shift in my feelings and I come to realize that this is about a history of trauma being enacted between us, trauma that has become more accessible to both of us. It is about assaults or violations of Ava's mind and body as well as violations of her mother's body that have been unconsciously transmitted to her and are now a part of our work together.

What is notable is that as the transition has progressed, as "she" has become "he," it has become more possible to explore the question of abuse or violation. Something has been freed, opened, making it possible to explore aspects of self that were inaccessible prior to the transition. Suchet notes something similar in her work with a transitioning patient when she writes that she has come to recognize that "something fundamental cannot shift until he alters his body" (2011, p. 182). A more male body has provided Ava a greater sense of safety. There is less rigidity and the beginning of more fluidity, of a more softly assembled gender (Harris, 2005).

Six months after Ava began hormones and one month before she changed her name and began using a male pronoun, Ava continues to struggle with feelings of sexual desire. She is now living with her girl-friend who has been supportive of her transition. At times Ava experiences her girlfriend's touch as "a violation," even when it is arousing. Ava arrives for a session in a distressed and confused state, having been at her parent's home the night before while her mother was dressing to go out to dinner with the family. She describes how her mother walked around in a "see-through bra," playfully holding a towel in front of her. I wonder aloud what that was like for Ava, whether she felt aroused by her mother. She looks down and says, "Yes." I ask her if she remembers feeling arousal with her mother when she was a child. "Yes," she answers and then tells me that she remembers being in her mother's bed, laying on top of her, her head on her mother's chest, able to feel her mother's breasts and then experiencing intolerable anxiety, along with arousal.

"How old were you?"

"It was my whole life," she says in a soft voice. "Until just a few years ago."

I feel stunned. Ava looks at the floor and shakes her head.

"How did it happen?" I ask. "Did you crawl over? Did she ask you?"

"She asked me."

There is a heaviness in the room, a mixture of sadness and relief, of horror and shame.

In our next session we revisit the powerful material from the day before. Now the story is different. When I try to explore her mother's seductiveness, its impact on her, she minimizes it. She tells me she "didn't exactly" lie on top of her mother, just from her torso up. She wonders whether it was really her mother who always initiated it. There are parts of the session that she does not remember at all. I feel as if I have made up the disturbing details. I think of her comment that she feels "like a pedophile" and I understand how she can feel perverse and distorted inside. I tell her that I feel uncomfortable, as if I have made up something that I experienced. She tells me she has often felt that way. What is different about this statement is Ava's recognition of how she feels, her ability to think about the confusion and distortion in her family and in her life.

After Ava legally changed her name to David and announced to her co-workers that she was now going by a male name and a male pronoun, she, now he, began to feel a sense of recognition that had always been elusive. It was at this time that David had a dream that a man had damaged his back. "There was a slash down my back from being whipped. I couldn't see it but I knew what it looked like. I needed to get to you to show you the damage." The blindfold was beginning to come off. David had begun to allow more to come into view since beginning to transition than he ever had allowed himself to look at before. Feeling more secure in his body gave him more access to his mind.

Nearly nine months after starting hormones David describes a dream in which he returned to his childhood home to babysit for his child self. "She was sitting on the couch playing with her cars. She had no idea that I was her but grown up. She looked so happy. I knelt down beside her. I started to cry and she said, 'Don't cry. I only cry when my mama cries.' I was so sad for her because she didn't know what was ahead. I wanted to get her out of there but I couldn't find my keys."

As this dream indicates, David is mourning all that has been lost. When the little girl in the dream says, "Don't cry. I only cry when my mama cries," one can hear the colonization of her mind, the redirection of the child's wants and needs to comply with the mother rather than with what Ava, now David, may have felt. In the dream David cries but his child self does not understand why he would express a feeling of his own, a feeling that is not connected to the mother's feelings. Again, there is the question of trauma and gender and how they interact. This dream speaks to the possibility of something terrible that lay ahead for David's child self, the trauma of feeling unrecognized (Benjamin, 1988), of living in a body that feels alien, and the trauma of psychic or perhaps physical violation. There is something that David cannot find the key to and that, quite possibly, is about his own history of trauma.

Shortly after starting hormones, but while still going by a female pronoun, Ava had the following dream. "I was with my mother. These guys started beating me up. My mother couldn't help me because she was holding something and she couldn't put it down." This dream reflects the ways in which what the patient's mother held in her mind kept her from being able to hold or help her child. In my work with Ava and now David I have struggled to let go of what I was holding, my wish that Ava would not have to transition, my investment in the belief that we could resolve her feelings about her body through analytic work and my fear that life as a transman would leave this patient feeling more dissatisfied rather than less. I believe that Ava, and later David, felt my struggle as well as the subtle changes, the micro shifts, in the ways I began to hold in my mind the potential selves that were emerging in our work together. As Davies (2003) describes in her writing on emergent selves, "it is who the patient discovers residing in his analyst's mind, as well as the transformation of that who—the multiple and emergent who's—that determine the breadth and scope of therapeutic potential" (p. 25). I believe Ava/David sensed these shifts and experienced them as mentalizing rather than colonizing moments, openings to different selves that were previously buried in shame.

As David begins to feel more comfort and safety in his body he is able to entertain thoughts that would not have been thinkable before the transition including thoughts and feelings about his father. He is able to talk more deeply about his experiences with his mother, about feelings of violation and conflicting feelings of love and anger. He has also begun to think of his body in a different and more playful way. The vagina that he once hated now has a new name that he invented, one that encompasses both words, penis and vagina, and that he and his girlfriend refer to in a playful way. His sense of sexual freedom and exploration has expanded and his genitals are no longer off limits during sex but are now part of what brings him pleasure with his girlfriend. This is not to say that everything has been resolved. The struggle continues and there are times when

David is overwhelmed with feelings of inadequacy because he is a trans-man and will never be a biological man. Recently, he has been haunted by what he calls "Ava dreams." He is negotiating loss and integration, building bridges between the different parts of himself. Mourning continues to be central to our work and it is unclear what kind of challenges lay ahead in regard to his trans identity.

I will never know what would have happened if David did not transition, if he still would have found the freedom to reflect on the thoughts and feelings he was able to access after beginning the transition. What I do know and what has been meaningful is experiencing together what this patient has for so long experienced alone and that is the feeling of shame, isolation and incoherence. In this way David can mourn what has been lost and make room for what can be found. Our work continues and I feel honored to be a part of this journey.

References

Benjamin, J. (1988). *The bonds of love: Psychoanalysis, feminism and the problem of domination.* New York, NY: Pantheon.

Bion, W.R. (1962). A Theory of Thinking. *Int. J. Psycho-Anal.*, 43:306–310.

Bromberg, P. (1998). *Standing in the spaces.* Hillsdale, NJ: The Analytic Press.

Coates, S.W. (1998). Having a Mind of One's Own and Holding the Other in Mind: Commentary on Paper by Peter Fonagy and Mary Target. *Psychoanal. Dial.*, 8:115–148.

Davies, J.M. (1998). Multiple Perspectives on Multiplicity. *Psychoanal. Dial.*, 8:195–206.

Davies, J.M. (2003). Falling in Love with Love. *Psychoanal. Dial.*, 13:1–27.

Davies, J.M. (2004). Whose Bad Objects Are We Anyway?. *Psychoanal. Dial.*, 14:711–732.

Elise, D. (2008). Sex and Shame: The Inhibition of Female Desires. *J. Amer. Psychoanal. Assn.*, 56:73–98.

Faimberg, H. (1988). The Telescoping of Generations:—Genealogy of Certain Identifications. *Contemp. Psychoanal.*, 24:99–117.

Faimberg, H. (2014). The Right to Our Own History: Paradoxical Transference and the "Friendly Foreigner": Commentary on Orna Guralnick Paper. *Psychoanalytic Dialogues*, 24:154–162.

Fonagy, P. & Target, M. (1996). Playing with Reality: I. Theory of Mind and the Normal Development of Psychic Reality. *Int. J. Psycho-Anal.*, 77:217–234.

Fonagy, P. & Target, M. (2000). Playing with Reality. *Int. J. Psycho-Anal.*, 81:853–873.

Harris, A. (2005). *Gender as soft assembly.* Hillsdale, NJ: The Analytic Press.

Harris, A. (2009). "You Must Remember This." *Psychoanal. Dial.*, 19:2–2.

Lyons-Ruth, K. (2006). The Interface between Attachment and Intersubjectivity: Perspective from the Longitudinal Study of Disorganized Attachment. *Psychoanl. Inq.*, 26:596–616.

Mitchell, S.A. (1981). The Psychoanalytic Treatment of Homosexuality: Some Technical Considerations. *Int. Rev. Psycho-Anal.*, 8:63–80.

Saketopoulou, A. (2011). Minding the Gap: Intersections between Gender, Race and Class in Work with Gender Variant Children. *Psychoanal. Dial.*, 21:2, 192–209.

Salamon, G. (2010). *Assuming a body: Transgender and rhetorics of materiality.* New York, NY: Columbia University Press.

Salamon, G. & Corbett, K. (2011). Speaking of the Body/Mind Juncture: An Interview with Gayle Saloman. *Assuming a body: Transgender and rhetorics of materiality* (New York, NY: Columbia University Press, 2010). *Psychoanal. Dial.*, 21:221–229.

Schilder, P. (1950). *The image and appearance of the human body: Studies in the constructive energies of the psyche.* New York, NY: International Universities Press.

Seligman, S. (2007). Mentalization and Metaphor, Acknowledgment and Grief: Forms of Transformation in the Reflective Space. *Psychoanal. Dial.*, 17:321–344.

Stein, R. (2005). Why Perversions? *Int. J. Psycho-Anal.*, 86:775–779.

Stein, R. (2008). The Otherness of Sexuality: Excess. *J. Amer Psychoanal. Assn.*, 56:43–71.

Suchet, M. (2011). Crossing Over. *Psychoanal. Dial.*, 21:2, 172–191.

Williams, P. (2004). Incorporation of an Invasive Object. *Int. J. Psycho-Anal.*, 85:1333–1348.

Winnicott, D.W. (1960). The Theory of the Parent-Child Relationship. *International Journal of Psycho-Analysis*, 41, 585–595.

Chapter 11

My Attachment Disorder with Truth

David M. Goodman

I have an attachment disorder with truth. It's a disorganized one. Not especially pretty either.

My mother grew up in an Orthodox Jewish family, deeply observant and tethered closely to Ukrainian and Lithuanian immigrant life in Chicago. My Bubbie, at a towering 4′8″, was a young widower who raised my mom and aunt on her own. She spent the majority of her adult life standing on a cement floor in a windowless basement ironing clothes. Making it by with little English-speaking ability—Yiddish being her native tongue—my Bubbie was devoutly connected to the synagogue and to a simple and beautiful Jewish faith. I don't know where exactly she came from, whom she came with, or who she may have had to leave behind. I don't know why they came, nor where she derived her kindness and faith.

My father grew up in a "secular" Jewish family in Los Angeles. My grandfather was a staunch atheist who identified with his Jewish roots, but was immediately willing to tell anyone that there is no God and that we are born from dust, return to dust, and that all is "oblivion." As a radio announcer in WWII, he was profoundly concerned about the Jewish people and felt himself to be deeply connected to Jewish identity. My dad understood little regarding Jewish ritual or religious beliefs more generally, but knew he was Jewish and that this was the source of some fundamental position in the world that was unique and important. A "cultural" Jew, some like to call this. Where my father's ancestors came from, why they came, the origins of their secular tradition, my paternal grandfather's certainty about death's finality: these are missing links in my history.

But certainly, a strong Jewish identity was the hallmark of both families, and what I don't know about their history, I can guess: anti-Semitism had probably cast its shadow over my forebears. Loyalty to the "tribe" was deemed essential. Then, when my mother and father met in their late 20s and early 30s, the unspeakable happened. They found Jesus. My parents were suddenly alive in a small community of individuals who understood that Jesus was the Messiah. A very important point, however, was that they hadn't converted. No. They were still fully Jewish—that could and would never change. They were not Christians. They were Messianic Jews. Jewish law, rituals, and identity remained intact. Jesus was the fulfillment of the most precious parts of the Jewish tradition, the "Old" Testament finding its resolution and continuation in the "New" Testament. The Messiah that the Jews were waiting for had actually come in the historical figure of Yeshua and salvation was available through him. Jesus was Jewish and didn't see himself overturning Judaism to instate the Christian world. Rather, Jesus came to fulfill Judaism. My parents held that Christians that forget about the Jewish core of Jesus's teachings and calling are misguided in what they hold to be true (e.g., supersessionists). And, Jews that cannot see that Jesus is the Messiah, even though they are the "chosen" and "elect," are particularly "blind."

Both sides of the family—Orthodox and secular—saw this as ana-thema to Jewish identity. My parents were "converts," "religious zealots for the wrong side." They were an embarrassment. None of this made sense to others and it was profoundly hurtful to the family. Now, I can attempt to think of all of this through a trans-generational lens, through the mysteries of my unknown history. Did their families feel they were going over to the "enemy," affiliating them-selves with that Otherness that had once been their persecutor? Or did this evoke another radical break in familial links that had been previously broken by forced emigra-tion? The religious choice of my parents: Was it rupturing the group loyalty and insularity that allowed my ancestors to survive? Was it a frightening identification with the "Cross-bearers" who were the very source of much of their persecution? Or might it have been something even more particular to the Lithuanian strand of "Litvak" Judaism that attempted to protect the Jewish faith from the shifting landscape of Eastern European Judaism that had been taken by a more pietistic, emo-tional, mystical, and (dare I say) charismatic Hasidic Judaism that spread throughout the region in the eighteenth and nineteenth centuries? Perhaps it wasn't a coincidence that the version of Christian worship and doctrine that attracted my parents most *was* a Pentecostal and charismatic form—

yet another step removed from the Litvak faith of their Lithuanian for-bearers—causing even more distance and distrust. I cannot answer these questions. What I know is this: an Orthodox Jew and a secular Jew became passionate believers in a faith tradition that cut them off from their families and entrenched them in a type of identity that required con-stant protection and management. And, in their communities of friends and neighbors, there was confusion and varied responses. My parents were no longer Jewish in the eyes of most Jews. They were not Christian in the eyes of most Christians. In their own eyes, however, the confusion of others, the rejection of others, and the dislocation from clean and clear meaning for others was a sign of a special place—a location that few stood in but that Jesus had inhabited. A position from which they could uniquely speak to both Christian and Jewish brothers and sisters. They carried the mantle of God's vision at an intersection of identity that would provide a purer and truer inspiration of God's truth in the world. The heavier the mantle, the truer the truth became. It meant they were on the "straight and narrow" and doing God's work to forge a path that the world had covered over. Truth was likely to be most true when they were having to protect it from a defended position. It was a sign that it has been uniquely given to them. It was a part of their blood, their calling, and required a very specific set of beliefs and style of living to maintain. Again, I find myself wondering: Did my parents have an inherited, incho-ate, religious mission to speak to *both* Christians and Jews? Through this truth, could they bring Jews and Christians into a sacred we-ness? I wonder. As two committed Jews, my parents' marriage became an earnest attempt to marry two historically alienated faiths. Perhaps, in some way, they were trying to breach the barrier of Otherness that had haunted their forebears. I can only speculate here about the spiritual enactments of their trans-generational unconscious. Sadly, their lives seemed to reconstitute loss and alienation even as they tried to live in the truest of truths.

This was the world into which I was "thrown." I grew up in the San Fernando Valley, one of the enormous basins that are part of Los Angeles County. Twice weekly, I attended a charismatic, Foursquare Christian church where the inerrancy and infallibility of Scripture, capacity to speak in tongues, recognition of the Holy Spirit's "gifts," ability to be "on fire" for God, and submission to the passionate preaching of our Pastor were the warp and woof of daily life. "For God so loved the world that he gave his only begotten son so that whosoever believes in him should not perish but have eternal life" (John 3:16) was the nuclear core from which all things emanated. It was a vital and expansive community with thousands of members that were "all in." From a young age, I was a leader in this community—a "servant leader" in junior high and a member of the outreach teams in high school. I was slain in the spirit at a Benny Hinn (televangelist) gathering. I went on at least a dozen mission trips to Mexico. I attended a Presbyterian elementary school, a Baptist High School, a Wesleyan university, and an evangelical seminary.

Simultaneous to all of this, I was an active member of a synagogue. I had a Bar Mitzvah when I was 13. I learned just enough Hebrew to chant and read, gave a compelling talk on Moses's leadership style, and picked up some pretty essential dance moves while moving around in a circle. At Passover, I had the reputation of being a fierce competitor that always found the hidden *afikoman*; the undefeated champion for six years. Then, when I was 10 (year 7), Reuben cheated. I'm sure of it. How could he have known it was in that curtain at the far side of the room if he hadn't watched it get placed there? But, that's beside the point. My mother took tremendous pride and joy in celebrating all of the Jewish holidays and keeping the narratives of Esther, David, Ruth, Solomon, Isaiah, Elijah, Moses, and the Maccabees at the forefront of our religious life. I would go on kibbutz as my mom toured and sang with a group of Jews called "Jews for Jesus."

We celebrated Yom Kippur and Easter. Hanukah and Christmas. Purim and Ash Wednesday. I grew up having many friends asking me the question: Are you half Jewish and half Christian? *Sure* (facetiously). I believe that Jesus is the Messiah half the time and the other half of the time I'm still waiting for the Messiah to come in the first place. I became adept at answering such questions. And, my father's voice was always strong in my mind, reminding me that we had the corner on truth. We lived in the fullness of belief—the inspiration of the Holy Spirit along-side of our chosen status. We were God's ambassadors of truth and sal-vation. Others resist this because of sin and Satan's desire to keep people from the truth. Some of the (not so subtle) subtext in this was that we were living in truth and others weren't. Our interpretation of Scripture, our read on God's purpose, and our hold on God's living truth was in our possession and couldn't and needn't be questioned. It was a hermetically sealed version of truth that was assured and that could stand up against worldly ideas, rationality, logical argument, and any other faith traditions. We didn't have to justify it because it was given and more fundamental than all of these other things. End of story.

Our family was heavily involved in hosting Bible studies, evangelizing, and helping to bring the Good News of salvation to the world. My dad would get into fierce debates with people about complex theological questions. Waitresses at restaurants wouldn't even know what hit them. We sought to spread our uniquely revealed truth to others. If you believe that others will go to hell or live in lifeless traps under Satan's grasp, then the most loving thing one could do (the only thing one *should* do) was to attempt to bring salvific truth to their lives. I remember rejoicing in the moments when I was able to share with friends or strangers about Jesus's love and the possibilities of heaven and redemption.

In the summer before I started 9th grade, I had been away at an evangelical Christian camp for nearly a month and when I returned the hull of assurance was breached, though I wouldn't know it for some time. My mom wasn't there to pick me up at church. I had to call from a payphone at the Dominos pizza shop across the street and I received a warm but cryptic, "Your dad is on his way." When I got home, the seriousness in the house was palpable. They sat me down. "Mom has a grapefruit sized tumor in her abdomen and they will need to perform surgery on Tuesday." "It's not clear what might be happening." Many assurances came about God's care for His children and the power of prayer: "in the presence of faith, God's healing love would abound." Even at 14 years old, the assurances started feeling thin and stale. I had been held by reassuring, totalizing certainties, and now, these certainties were challenged by death. They didn't seem to close the distance of this new found terror. I experienced this as my fault—my faith couldn't reach far enough. God wanted to assure me, but my fear and sin kept me from knowing His comforts and will.

Two years later she would die at the age of 46. Chemotherapy, alternative treatments, surgeries, prayer groups, pastoral visits—skin and bones and nausea. I witnessed a beautiful, creative, playful, and vivacious woman emaciate and her spirit fill with desperation and fear. My father just couldn't do it. He wasn't there. As a 14-year-old, 15-year-old, and 16-year-old, I sat in the hallway outside of my mother's bedroom responding to her ever-growing and overwhelming needs. Cooking, cleaning, laundering, medicating, and carrying her body to the bathroom.

Suffering and screams that adolescent boys should not be responsible to see and respond to alone. All the while, trite assurances and faith claims were speeding through our home in high volume along with the tin foil covered lasagnas that were being dropped off by loving members of our church.

When my mom passed away, the dinners stopped. The phone calls ended. "There must have been sin in our home." "There wasn't enough faith." "God wanted to intervene, but we didn't create the space and respond to His generous and loving hand." I couldn't find my way back to church. The rumors circulating and the hurtful explanations were utterly abhorrent. The suffering was too much for many of our friends and members of our fellowship. It was abject.

Not only did the dinners stop and the silence grow, but my father exited the scene entirely. He quickly found another woman, got married, and left me, at 16, to fend for myself. I didn't want to end up in a foster home in the custody of Department of Child and Family Services so I stayed off grid. I worked four jobs, finished high school, lived alone with the family dog, and scraped together what I could to make it. I had keys to many friends' homes and bounced around to different dinner tables any given night. I kept moving forward. I maintained my equilibrium. I still hadn't lost faith. I held it firmly and despite everything, but it had been compromised and I didn't know it yet. Life had become too fragile to begin asking the questions that would cause the edifice to crumble entirely. So, during that time, I was able to spout the assurances of a God that I grew up knowing and whose attributes were clear and knowable. God was in control and had a purpose. And, this purpose was full of goodness and a truth that I could not see in my finitude. "'For I know the plans I have for you,' declares the Lord, 'plans to prosper you and not to harm you, plans to give you hope and a future'" (Jeremiah 29:11 New International Version).

I honestly don't know what kept me going. I am loath to describe it as a type of resilience. The cost of it later in life—the pains I still suffer—makes me uncomfortable to use terms of this sort. People ask me what sustained me and drove me forward without devolving into drugs, alcohol, depression, or anything else of the sort. I don't know the answer: perhaps it was my wish to please God, the invitation and love of particular families who fed me, the profound moral desire to remain "good" despite circumstance, an anger that stoked a fire in me, a hatred for my father that made me want to succeed and dis-identify via that success, or the loving voice of my mom and her hopes for my life. Or, might it have been a fear that I can never describe—a fear of the entire world being taken away if I didn't step up and surge forth. Whatever the combination, I lived as a 45-year-old adult at 16 years old. I survived and succeeded—but it gnarled me. I'm still untangling.

Entering college was an exciting relief for me. It wasn't a time of experimentation and stupidity. There was a dining hall where meals were made for me and a dormitory where the electrical bills and roof repairs weren't my responsibility. In an odd way, I felt taken care of. My 18-year-old mind wasn't colonized with the overwhelm of adult logistics as it had been for the four years previous to this. I didn't have to scrap and hope that things were going to be okay. It gave me the opportunity to breathe again—and to think. During my freshman year, I took a writing seminar that focused on the work of C.S. Lewis. A Cambridge don and Anglican theologian, his work was incredibly smart and represented Christianity in terms that intrigued me and that took a different angle than what I grew up with. It was cogent, incisive, and rationally argued. His radio talks and book, *Mere Christianity*, were an apology for the Christian faith. I started eating this up. I started asking questions.

When the life of my mind entered full stride, I started taking as many theology and philosophy courses as I could alongside of my psychology major. Now, as a reminder, I was at an evangelical, Wesleyan university, so the courses remained in orbit of an orthodox frame that didn't question the fundamentals. Then, it happened. Perhaps it was the combination of a safe enough space where food and domicile were present. Perhaps it was a couple years of time lapsed after the dark terror of my mother's dying. Perhaps it was the developmental possibility that had been latent and was now being nourished. I split open. I was introduced to Nietzsche, Freud, Feuerbach, Marx, and Foucault. These philosophers of "suspicion," as they are often called, were taught to us in order to prepare us to debunk and protect from such atheistic arguments. We were being trained to be smart apologists for the Christian faith and these were enemies of the faith; "popular" philosophers that we were likely to encounter in the "world." However, working through these texts had the opposite effect on me. Their arguments were incredibly compelling and seemed irrefutable. I went into class hoping the professors would give us equipment to overcome these brutal exposés of the Christian faith tradition (and belief in God more generally). On the contrary, their counter arguments seemed to me like they were using a fly swatter to deter a raging bull. They fell woefully short. I even set up times with professors to ask the harder questions. They were gracious and curious with me, but their encouragement did not touch my growing cynicism.

I spent nearly two years walking around with tears in my eyes. The hull had indeed been breached. It wasn't merely a crisis of faith or a loss of faith. I had been *deceived* by truth. It wasn't just a particular perspective that was called into question. It was my attachment to the world, to people, to purpose, to will, to love, to life. Without the ground of *the* assured truth to stand on, I lost my footing. And, any new "ground" was suspect and equally false and deceptive. There was an infinite regress of questions for every reality—that's part of what Foucault can do to you! The flood of despair brought with it the meaninglessness of my mother's death, my father's abandonment, and the absurdities of suffering and knowledge. I became rageful. I thought it was about being deceived by an ideology that I was raised with that didn't cut the mustard. It was far more than that. I was rageful because I grew up in what felt like a safe and secure home. And, I had become homeless—the loss of my family, my mom and dad, and the things that bound my psyche. The loss of my ability to orient to this world and to make sense of what I was experiencing. Losing *this* God was the dismantling of realities across every level of thinking, feeling, and connecting.

The attachment disorder was in full view. Though, to be clear, these traumas had not created the attachment disorder, but brought this long-standing way of being into focus and into the light. Ironically, growing up with an assured and unassailable attachment to a type of truth, I had been living in a profoundly insecure attachment. Truth needed to be inspired, impenetrable, unquestionable, and perfectly known to be real. There was no space for ambiguity and the unknown. From a trans-generational perspective, I understand now that my parents may have been carrying *their* forebears' losses, anxieties, abandonments, and insecure attachments. For my parents, absolute truth may have seemed like an antidote. But, secure attachment doesn't look like this. It *isn't* lived in a fixed, predictable, and stable manner. Like any true attachment to dynamic, dimensional, and changing beings, it is somewhat unsafe and untamable. Secure attachment does not revolve around control, mastery, and ownership. It ceases to be secure once these needs are in play. But, I didn't know this. It felt as though all was truly and irrevocably lost.

At the recommendation of one of my favorite faculty members, I attended a Mennonite Church in Pasadena. I had a picture in my mind of individuals in bonnets and horse-drawn carriages, but it was nothing of the sort. I remember walking into the church—already suspicious about the entire thing—and being taken off-guard by the sermon. The pastor was speaking about the resurrection of Christ being most intimately known and lived in shared meals with others. He described Mandela's first action upon his release from prison: inviting his captors to a meal together; the breaking of bread as the initial possibility of redemption and restoration. This gritty and carnal interpretation threw me off balance and kept me interested. It was enough to earn a return visit the following Sunday. I would spend the next four years in this community. And, it was during this time that I was exposed to brilliant, highly educated, and successful individuals constantly doing the hard work of forgiveness, taking care of one another's families in the midst of sickness, and attending to the needs of our world in a manner that I had not previously witnessed. The Gospel, in this community, wasn't fundamentally a series of propositions or a set of truth claims. It was a lived ethic of God's love and responsiveness to injustice—environmental, racial, economic, and international. It was an imperfect embodiment of the Sermon on the Mount where the poor and the weak were held up as the focal point of God's heart in the world.

I recall walking into church one Sunday with Nietzsche's *Beyond Good and Evil* under my arm (oppositional-defiant trait perhaps?) and, at one point before the service started a leader in the congregation sidled up to me and whispered "that book messed me up for a good 6 months" with a smile on his face and a playful look in his eyes. Over time, I went on to share my struggle, the jettisoning of my faith, my anger, and my confusion with members of the community. There was no fear or judgment in their responses. They were sincerely interested and receptive and even felt so intrigued by my Messianic background that they invited me to give a short talk on the subject. Over time, they nourished a type of space for something that I hadn't anticipated—an interest in Jewish theology and philosophy. Yes, it was in a Protestant Christian church that I found myself focusing back on my Jewish roots. Not with a Messianic bent, but with an eye to what was salvageable about God, faith, truth, home, community, and suffering.

At that time, I was studying at an evangelical seminary (yes, complicated right!) where I was to earn my doctorate in Clinical Psychology and a Masters in Theology. I used this time as an opportunity to dive deeply into the works of Abraham Joshua Heschel and Martin Buber. I was still largely homeless in mind and spirit, but my intrigue with Jewish thought was flowering and some of the darkness began giving way to curiosity. There was something about Jewish philosophy that dislodged me from hypercritical and perpetually deconstructive protections. Critical theory, though largely a type of dis-attachment with truth, had become for me another site for insecure attachment. I didn't want to be deceived into another truth tradition that might fail, so I hung onto critical philosophies as a tool to dismantle truth to such a degree that it became the central organizer of my truth! I even maintained a type of righteous indignation toward people holding truth about nearly anything. I learned to decimate their core beliefs with a few swings of the Foucauldian or Freudian axe. The attachment disorder wasn't merely connected to my previous belief system, it was something more elemental to how I related to truth and protected myself from ambiguities and precarity.

I was fortunate to have a doctoral advisor, Al Dueck, who treasured the deeper aquifers of living tradition and believed that modern society often lives in the shambles of a thin and morally anemic body politic. This was a man that opened his swimming pool to the entire neighborhood in the summer time and fed students, neighbors, and strangers soup and bread in his home several evenings a week. During one evening together, Al asked me why I wasn't drawing from my Jewish heritage and interest in Jewish philosophy while writing my dissertation (by the way, this was in an APA accredited and largely mainstream Clinical Psychology program). He had gotten a whiff of my existential and transitional angst and was taking it seriously and without regard for disciplinary boundaries and normal pathways. He had recently discovered the work of the Jewish philosopher, Emmanuel Levinas, and wondered whether I might be interested in working with Levinas's ethical phenomenology in my doctoral research. Knowing little about Levinas's work and being quite nervous about his notoriously dense and elliptical prose, I wasn't sure how far down this path I was willing to wander. But, after drowning for long enough in the quagmire of his writings, something began to change—a change for which I will be forever indebted.

Without going hog wild into the world of Levinas and some of the Jewish tradition that he represents, let me attempt to share his import into my journey and why he served as a formative influence on several fronts.

First, Levinas *knew* suffering. And, his philosophy contends with this "knowing" by never letting it disappear behind protections and assurances. His work is a challenge to Western philosophical traditions and disciplines that abstract experience and define realities that reduce our exposure to one another. He is known as one of the great philosophers of the "Other"—ever concerned that we remain exposed, vigilant, and proximal to the experience of one another; never losing to category, theory, or egoism the face of the Other, in all of its nakedness and all its address. Levinas lost the majority of his family in the Holocaust at the hands of Nazi collaborators in Lithuania, his home country. He witnessed "advanced" Western philosophical and technological systems reduce bodies into bars of soap. This remained a "tumor" in his memory and work (as he described it)—much as Eastern European anti-Semitism may have been a forgotten "tumor" in my Bubbie's history.

In one of his most powerful essays titled *Useless Suffering*, Levinas denounces as violent all explanatory systems that make sense and usefulness out of suffering. He was highly critical of theodicies, ever around us, that explain and justify how there can be immense suffering in a world where there is a loving and sovereign God. Levinas makes clear how these theodicies promote a type of relationship with the Other that is mediated by categories and propositions; and how in this we achieve a type of distance and non-proximal relationships that are forgetful of ethical address.

As I worked with Levinas's thought, I started seeing theodicies everywhere. And, these were not just theological and religious in nature. They also took the shape of cognitive, scientific, neoliberal, and socioeconomic explanations of what causes suffering. I found in my clinical placements and training as much temptation to utilize easy, quick, and shorthand versions of truth as I had in the church community in which I grew up. *Neurotransmitters. Sin. Irrational beliefs. Lack of faith. Maladaptive learning. Willful disobedience. Self-regulation issues.* Language and words often are pulled into guild-bound axioms and don't always facilitate an openness and exposure to the particulars and wonder in front of us. Ultimately, theodicies (or whatever name we want to give them in their secular forms) are reductions of the Other. Levinas argued, throughout his entire corpus, for the irreducibility of the Other. And, this is not because the Other is bigger and greater than we can conceptualize and that we are supposed to be true to that reality. No. It is because reduction is a type of foreclosure that is violent and that cuts off the voice of the unrepresented. He did not view language as inherently reductive. Certainly not. Actually, he put enormous weight on language, reminding us that language isn't merely a signifier for "reality." It is the medium of expression that exceeds itself—the attempt of the Other to bring the nakedness of need and the exposedness of request. And, the responsibility to listen to language in this manner provides the possibility of language performing on the ethical plane to which it belongs.

Second, part of my attachment disorder with truth was that "truth" was first and foremost an assent to particular propositional claims and affirmations. If I believed that Jesus was the Messiah, then salvation was available to me. Or, if I believed that the Bible was an inerrant document that conveyed God's truth to us, then by knowing it and abiding by its pages, I would know God's will and hope for my life. The goal was always to have a direct line to true knowledge and there was always a pressure and anxiety about whether this was being achieved. However, Levinas, coming from the long line of Talmudic scholars and as a student of Midrash, would have a different take on all of this. "Knowing" is never merely a correspondence to truth as it "really" is. Knowing is an invitation. It is two persons, or a community, addressing livedness together and inviting God to pass between them. Midrash involves two people studying the same text and bringing their studied interpretations to bear on it with one another. Neither has the corner on truth. Both struggle with one another's interpretation and, in so doing, invite the Divine. It's messy, but we invite something that transcends and calls us to a revelation beyond ourselves. Levinas contended that conversation is a marvel and a miracle. And, in his thought, each person's eyes are understood to be revelation of truth that would otherwise not be invited into this world.

In this simple yet impossibly radical shift, I found myself struggling to relate to truth as the hard and wild work of invitation, listening, and exposed learning rather than the seeking of assured definition and clarity. Donna Orange reminds us that this fallibility gives rise to a freedom for more profound attention and generosity. Yet, I wonder whether the institutions that we have that address suffering and identity are moving closer or farther from this recognition of fallibility and this exposed and dialogical invitation? With the rise of neuroscience, our reliance on numeric and aggregate claims in research, the metric of therapeutic success being defined by accountants and expediencies, the attraction to STEM disciplines along with a distancing from the humanities, and the disregard for philosophical and theological foundations within our theoretical and clinical approaches, I fear that psychology remains bewitched by a version of scientism and need for legitimization that calls it in the opposite direction. The allure of assured truth and foundational knowledge is not foreign to me and I see it hard at work in the clinical community. Entrenched, militant, and highly defended belief systems also quickly tickle my "spidey sense," be they religious, secular, scientific, or political. My attachment disorder with truth is not merely my own—our institutions reflect some of these attributes as well. Perhaps I am a bit sensitized to its presence.

How do we hear one another and create a context that *invites* truth? One of Levinas's core goals was to upset the Greek heritage in Western thought wherein "love of wisdom" was made central. Instead, he proposed that the "wisdom of love" is an entirely different starting point, one that is crucial to being able to remain vigilant and awake to the Other. That is, the ways that we treat the "widows, orphans, and strangers" in our society is the very center of our identity from which all else emerges. Ethics—that is, visceral and responsive moral attention to the suffering of the Other—is the beginning of truth's formation. Perhaps we don't start with assured truth and then attempt to live it out, as I had grown up believing. Maybe in struggling to live justly by orienting my life to the subtle cries of the Other's need, toward the outside of myself, and against the stream of a society that calls for fulfillment and individual gains, the possibility exists that a community of people inviting truth together can take form. But, without this justice, truth is merely a type of complacency and flows with the tides of the sociopolitical currents. For Levinas, love is the prerequisite of truth. And, to be clear, Levinas disliked the term love in his early work because of its frequent bastardization and co-opting. He ultimately understood love to be inexhaustible work of ethical attunement and moral attention.

Levinas's voice was my entry point into a conversation that remains very alive to me and lives as the heartbeat of my current work to create such conversations for others. It is important to add here that all of this exploration wasn't merely a sidebar in life. There was and is a fire ablaze under me and my sense of purpose and vocation in the world is attached to this working through. Though I did not have a clear sense of what form or shape it might take, I knew that the presence of cheap and thin explanations for suffering and identity that can abound in our society, in our communities, and in our disciplines was to be the focus of my work and my energies professionally. All of my Levinas studies were being done concurrent to my neuropsychological placements, in-patient rotations, Cognitive-Behavioral workshops, Object Relations Seminars, and long hours in community mental health centers. I was living in several worlds at once—psychology, philosophy, and theology. And, I hungered to see these disciplines intersect and interface as a means of enriching our responsiveness to suffering. I wanted to see these institutions upset each other's easy truths and deepen their fidelity to experience and moral awareness. Despite my disillusionment, or perhaps because of it, I carried a deep concern about the condition of our society, the languages that we employ in our professions, the misshapen identities out of which we live, and our anesthetized responsiveness to one another.

In losing my "home"—my God, my family, my way of knowing and orienting to the world—I have lived restlessly in several homes. Whether this references the bouncing around to various dinner tables when I was 16 years old, my Messianic Jewish heritage wherein I was neither Jewish nor Christian and simultaneously both, or my wanderings in the disciplines of psychology, philosophy, and theology, I have lived as a bit of a misfit and in a type of dispossession that makes it difficult to rest easy in any particular frame. Perhaps this has linked me to the suffering and to the dispossessed—to those homeless children who have seen what no child should witness. Levinas did not provide me a new home where I could once again feel the assurance of a type of truth or access to a truer orientation to life. His philosophy was one that spoke to my "homelessness of consciousness" (Levinas, 1989, p. 238) and connected me to a type of truth that is emergent from relationship, from our vulnerabilities, from shared meaning, from complex conversation with conflict, and from the frightening and beautiful ineffability of myself and Others.

This path feels like my inheritance. If my ancestral ghosts are speaking through me, I don't really know what they are saying, and it grieves me that I may never know. My Bubbie is gone, my mother is dead. I cannot ask them questions and I cannot locate myself in their transgenerational history. Their absent stories are another layer of loss, another kind of homelessness for me. I can only create from the place that I find myself now. It is my hope that my deluxe attachment disorder provides an invitation for enduring conversations and a form of hospitality in our struggle for truth in love. One hope that drives my passion is that the tides of scientific commodification, ungenerous medicalization, and the sleepfulness of our consciousness can be re-channeled into more abundant possibilities.

I end with three statements that represent something of the heart of this piece. The first is a Jewish proverb that is one of Levinas's favorite sayings: "The Other's material needs are my spiritual needs" (as quoted in Levinas and Kearney, 1986, p. 24). The second, a well-known excerpt from St. Paul:

> If I speak in the tongues of men or of angels, but do not have love, I am only a resounding gong or a clanging cymbal. If I have the gift of prophecy and can fathom all mysteries and all knowledge, and if I have a faith that can move mountains, but do not have love, I am nothing. If I give all I possess to the poor and give over my body to hardship that I may boast, but do not have love, I gain nothing.
>
> (I Corinthians 13:1–3 New International Version)

And, the third, wisest of them all, are the three simple words that my Bubbie would sigh when she received tragic news or was in a difficult situation. She would simply say: "Such is life." I've come to see this statement as one of the most theologically robust, philosophically rich, and psychologically sophisticated wisdoms that I can aspire to know and to live.

References

Levinas, E. (1989). *The Levinas reader.* (S. Hand, Ed. & Trans.). Cambridge, MA: Blackwell Publishers.

Levinas, E. (1998). *Entre nous: On thinking-of-the-other* (M. B. Smith & B. Harshav, Trans.). New York: Columbia University Press. (Original work published in 1991).

Levinas, E., & Kearney, R. (1986). Dialogue with Emmanuel Levinas. In R. Cohen's (Ed.) *Face to face with Levinas.* Albany, NY: State University of New York Press.

Index